SECOND EDITION

The Politics of the Federal Bureaucracy

ALAN A. ALTSHULER
Massachusetts Institute of Technology

NORMAN C. THOMAS
University of Cincinnati

HARPER & ROW, Publishers
New York   Hagerstown   San Francisco   London

Sponsoring Editor: Dale Tharp
Project Editor: Holly Detgen
Designer: Frances Torbert Tilley
Production Supervisor: Will C. Jomarrón
Compositor: The Maryland Linotype Composition Company, Inc.
Printer and Binder: The Murray Printing Company

THE POLITICS OF THE FEDERAL BUREAUCRACY, *Second Edition*

Library of Congress Cataloging in Publication Data
Altshuler, Alan A   Date-   Comp.
    The politics of the Federal bureaucracy.
    Includes bibliographical references.
    1. Public administration—Addresses, essays, lectures. 2. United States—Politics and government—20th century—Addresses, essays, lectures. I. Thomas, Norman C. II. Title.
JF1351.A37 1977   353   76-26133
ISBN 0-06-040246-6

Contents

v

RATIONALIZATION OF THE BUREAUCRACY 242

SECURING A RESPONSIBLE BUREAUCRACY 329

Preface

In revising *The Politics of the Federal Bureaucracy* we have sought to retain the central concern of the first edition—the problem of how American society reconciles its dependence on a large-scale public bureaucracy with the ideals and processes of mass democracy—while accommodating the substantial developments in the study and practice of public administration that have occurred in the past decade. We have also attempted in the present edition to organize the selections so that they may serve as a general introduction to the field of public administration.

Our focus is on the federal bureaucracy because we believe that most major administrative innovations either occur at the national level or are initiated with federal stimulus and because of the central role of the national government in the federal system. We are not unmindful, however, of the importance of local and state bureaucracies—indeed, several selections treat them in some detail.

During the years since the preparation of the first edition, American public administration has come through a period of severe "turbulence."[1] Important developments have occurred in the operation of our public bureaucracies in consequence of the events of those troubled times and of long-term forces and patterns in public administration.

The continuing difficulty of reconciling bureaucracy with democracy is reflected in expanded concern over the costs of the professionalism and expertise that are the foundations of bureaucratic usefulness and power. As the economy and society become increasingly dependent on technology and the expertise of professionals, the average person is correspondingly disadvantaged in his or her efforts to understand and cope with the complex organizational structures that are encountered in everyday life. One of the primary responses to growing bureaucratic complexity has been a demand for expanded participation by citizens in the processes of administrative decision making. Participatory democracy has been undertaken experimentally at the local level through such devices as community action agencies of the Office of Economic Opportunity and the Model Cities Program and at all levels of government through various forms of advisory councils.

[1] See Dwight Waldo, ed., *Public Administration in a Time of Turbulence* (New York: Intext, 1971).

A related development has been the attempt to involve the members of bureaucratic organizations at all levels in their agencies' internal decisions. This is an outgrowth of the human relations approach to organizational leadership but it is more explicit in its objective of humanizing bureaucracies, increasing their internal flexibility, and thereby rendering them more sensitive to the needs of the individuals who work in them.

Along somewhat similar lines there has been a major attempt through "affirmative action" programs to open up bureaucratic career opportunities to members of groups, principally women and racial minorities, who were previously disadvantaged by social prejudices. Concern for minorities has also involved an effort to make public agencies more explicitly conscious of and responsive to the needs of their female and minority clientele.

In spite of the pressures for a more humane and broadly based public administration, efforts to increase bureaucratic efficiency have continued to occupy substantial attention in recent years. The major developments in this area have been the rise and decline of the Program, Planning, and Budgeting System (PPBS) in the federal government and the use of quantitative analytical techniques to evaluate the performance of governmental programs. PPBS was an attempt to incorporate the control and managerial aspects of conventional budgeting with long-range planning through cost-benefit analysis. Although PPBS did not fulfill the initial enthusiastic claims that accompanied its inception, it left a legacy of concern for disciplined analysis of the consequences, unintended as well as deliberate, of governmental programs. The program-evaluation aspects of PPBS appear to have survived as a permanent feature of public administration.

No review of major developments in the federal bureaucracy in recent years would be complete without consideration of the Nixon presidency. By far the most notable event was the Watergate scandal. The causes and consequences of that unfortunate affair are far too complex to delineate here, but it must be noted that Watergate raised anew fundamental questions of ethics and morality in the public service. Much less visible than Watergate, but of major significance, were the efforts of the Nixon administration to strengthen presidential control over the federal bureaucracy and to transform the administrative aspects of the federal system through revenue sharing. Indeed, the verdict of history may well be that the most important consequence of the Nixon presidency for American politics was that it revolutionized the administration of domestic programs.

In revising this book to serve more specifically as an introduction to public administration, we have retained the intention of the first edition to be more analytical than normative and we have avoided adopting an explicit methodology. We have tried to demonstrate how bureaucracy functions as a major subsystem of America's pluralistic political system. It is our belief that public administration cannot be fully understood apart from its political context. We also hold that the essence of the bureaucracy's political function lies in the act of decision. Hence we have placed considerable emphasis on decision making and bureaucratic politics. We have included selections by authors who are descriptive and analytical, empirical and normative, liberal and conservative. We have not sought to grind specific axes, except that our own conceptions of scholarly and analytic excellence are reflected throughout these pages.

In the introductory comments to each section, we shall amplify and expand many of the points made above. The selections in each section are intended to be representative of the problems, concepts, and viewpoints at issue. We have suggested additional readings for those who are inclined to pursue various topics further. We hope that this edition will prove to be as useful and as well received as its predecessor.

Norman C. Thomas
Alan A. Altshuler

Preface
to the First Edition

I have approached the federal bureaucracy in this reader as a major subsystem of the American political system, one which deserves the closest attention of political scientists both as a fascinating political system in its own right—fully as interesting in this respect as the legislative, judicial, and party systems—and as an actor of fundamental and rapidly growing importance in the American political drama taken as a whole. The selections are predominantly descriptive and analytical rather than normative. At the same time, they have been chosen for the provocative light that they shed on *important* political relationships, and importance, needless to say, can ultimately be measured only in terms of values.[1]

Most students will be wondering as they approach this volume: Why study American public administration? Why consider *it* important? The most fundamental—though certainly not the only answer, it seems to me, is that the bureaucratization of society and government over the past century has radically transformed the nature of American democracy. The countless small private associations that aroused de Tocqueville's wonder have largely been replaced—if we confine our attention to those of political significance—by regional and national organizations of the sort that led Michels to formulate his "iron law of oligarchy." The capitalism of small enterprises struggling constantly for survival against severe competitive threats has been superseded by one of giant corporations able to control their competitive environments in very significant degree, and thus to provide most members of the labor force with nearly perfect cushioning against the instabilities and uncertainties of the market place. The seamy side of this picture is that large bureaucratized associations and corporations tend to escape society's "natural"—that is, nongovernmental—control mechanisms. Whether the natural control mechanisms are doing an "adequate" job in any particular situation is, of course, a matter for the political system to determine. In practice, it determines that greater and greater governmental control is required with every passing decade.

---

[1] The term "political" appears five times in the above paragraph. What, precisely, does it mean? I have ventured a formal definition in my article, "The Study of American Public Administration," which appears in Section I. [See note 1, pages 14–15.]

Similar developments have occurred in the fields of welfare and national security, though in these the new bureaucracies are predominantly public. In the former, the decline of the extended family as a welfare institution, the demise of the locality as a self-sufficient economy, the increasing mobility of the nation's population, and rapidly rising welfare expectations have produced immense bureaucracies devoted to caring for the poor and helpless, to insuring workers against the financial perils of old age and unemployment, to educating the nation's youth, and to maintaining the national economy on a vigorous upward course. In the latter, the demise of the European balance of power, the declining value of the oceans as protectors, and the Communist revolutions in Russia and China have compelled the nation to maintain huge standing military forces—supplemented by such trimmings as a vast intelligence establishment and a five billion dollar a year space program—for the first time in its history.

Thus, the federal government, though it lagged a bit until the presidency of Franklin Roosevelt, has grown at least as rapidly over the past century as its corporate and associational competitors for national dominance. Laissez faire has been superseded by the "mixed economy," and in it the role of government has become increasingly dominant. Within the public sector, the "old federalism" of states rights has increasingly given way to a "new federalism" of government by contract and grant-in-aid. Within the national government, the scales of dominance have shifted decisively from Congress to the executive branch. In recent decades, moreover, the same threats from abroad that have made defense the nation's biggest business have rendered plausible the idea that many of the fundamental bases of the government's most vital decisions should be kept secret, and that much other information should be released selectively with an eye to manipulating foreign—and by coincidental indirection, therefore, domestic public and congressional—opinion.

In view of these and countless related developments, there are many who believe that American society is moving inexorably toward a situation in which something like the following conditions will prevail: (1) most power will be wielded by a relatively few huge bureaucracies, whose top administrators will be meaningfully accountable only to their own consciences and each other; (2) among these bureaucracies, those which are private institutions, and those which are state and local, will have little power to balance the federal government in genuinely pluralistic fashion; (3) Congress and the public will have little capacity to control the activities of the executive branch, particularly when it is led by a master politician in the presidency; and (4) because of the decline both of the constitution's checks and balances *and* of the widespread diffusion of power in American society as a whole, democracy and liberty will at best remain pale shadows of their former selves.

This picture may or may not be overdrawn. Regardless, the popular definition of democracy as involving fairly detailed control of governmental decision making by the electorate becomes less descriptive each year of the way in which the American political system actually operates. Some would dismiss this observation as too obvious to be worth making. The plain fact is, however, that only the crudest beginnings have yet been made toward building a democratic theory that grapples seriously with the realities of the bureaucratic state—one which explains how "adequate" public control ought to be redefined in the light of modern conditions, and how the public can be rendered capable of exercising such control without the republic being rendered unable to meet the vital challenges that it faces from within and without.

The organization of this reader rests ultimately on my concern with these cardinal issues. They are generally in the background, however. The volume begins and concludes with sections devoted to them, but for the rest of its length it focuses on the most important specific conflicts that have swirled within and around the American federal bureaucracy in recent years. Its primary objectives are simple and four in number: (1) to introduce beginning students of public administration to the main actors in these areas of dispute, their opinions and interests, their sources of influence and weakness; (2) to indicate how the American governmental system typically deals with these conflicts—particularly where these ways differ from those that the average, legally oriented, introductory course in American government might lead one to expect; (3) to present a variety of provocative viewpoints on how it *ought* to deal with them; and (4) to spur students to think seriously about what they, as budding systematic theorists wishing to grasp the essential dynamics of the American political system, ought most to want to know about the federal bureaucracy and its patterns of interaction with the other major forces in American political life.

In short: this book of readings has no methodological or normative axe to grind; its central presupposition, however, is that American public administration can very fruitfully be studied as a branch of American politics. I have developed this latter theme a bit more fully—in the course of analyzing the intellectual history of public administration as a field of study—in a brief essay which appears [on pages 2–17]. I trust, however, that the utility of this volume will not be confined to those who agree with the opinions there expressed, nor, for that matter, even to those who are explicitly interested in the issues there explored.

ALAN A. ALTSHULER

The Politics of
the Federal Bureaucracy

The Nature and Study of American Public Administration

The two essays in this section deal with the intellectual history of public administration as a scholarly discipline. They are placed at the outset on the premise that the remaining selections can only be superficially understood without knowledge of the context from which they emerged and of the content and direction of recent developments. They are also intended to serve as a general guide to the content of this volume.

Alan Altshuler addresses himself primarily to the following questions: What subjects occupied the attention of students of American public administration over the eighty-year period, 1887–1967? Why? How well did these subjects mesh with the changing concerns of professional students of American politics? After reviewing this history, he concludes that a bold effort to redefine the boundaries and central questions of the subject "American public administration" is called for and he suggests the form that the redefinition ought to take.

In contrast to Altshuler, Dwight Waldo's orientation is more consciously contemporary. He views public administration as passing through a period of great stress and consequent change. He moves from examination of broad societal forces to a progressively more specific focus on the external and internal environments of public administrators as he describes and explains recent developments in the theory and practice of the field. Waldo's analysis suggests, although somewhat tentatively, that the academic discipline of public administration is moving toward a marriage of political science and economics in a modern version of the old field of political economy. He also observes, however, the emergence of a "new" public administration in which both practitioners and scholars are more activist than their predecessors and are committed to making bureaucracy increasingly responsive to human needs. Waldo's essay challenges us to define the principal forces and ideas that are shaping the future of public administration. Which trends that Waldo observed in 1972 are continuing? Which of his predictions need to be modified or discarded in the light of subsequent developments? Although public administration as a field of inquiry is in an untidy, rapidly changing condition, Waldo's analysis

1

should heighten our awareness of its continuing dynamism and of its increasing significance for those who would understand the workings of American government.

The Study of American Public Administration

Alan A. Altshuler

The study of American public administration developed in the late nineteenth century as a branch of American political science, then preoccupied with legal relationships, strongly oriented toward reform rather than research, and conceived simply by most of its tiny band of practitioners as "the study of government." It seemed obvious enough to political scientists of the day what governments were, and it was also clear that governments performed many noncontroversial service functions at any time in addition to their cardinal function, the management of social conflict.

By contrast, modern political scientists devote little attention to legal forms; they aim at understanding; and they concentrate on the sudy of distinctly political phenomena. Indeed, they have increasingly considered it irrelevant whether the institutions and processes chosen for analysis have been "governmental" in the formal sense at all; the test of relevance has become the significance of the political functions performed.[1]

Students of public administration have abandoned legalism, reform, and simple-minded notions of which institutions they ought to consider suitable for study. But they have regularly resisted the overall disciplinary trend toward concentration on politics. My purpose in this essay is to ask why, and to suggest a few highly tentative answers.

At the birth of public administration as an academic discipline, quite naturally a need was felt to explain with the greatest possible clarity what distinguished it from other subjects within the broad field of government. The constitutional distinction between legislative and executive institutions—which the post–Civil War Supreme Court was in process of reifying, and developing into a theory of distinct functions—provided an obvious foundation on which to build. The formulation that quickly won general acceptance was stated with stark simplicity by Woodrow Wilson. In his celebrated 1887 essay, "The Study of Administration," Wilson argued as follows:

> The field of administration is a field of business. It is removed from the hurry and strife of politics. . . . It is a part of political life only as the methods of the counting-house are a part of the life of a society; only as machinery is part of the manufactured product . . . [In other words], administrative questions are not political questions. Although politics sets the tasks for administration, it should not be suffered to manipulate its offices. . . . Policy does nothing without the aid of administration; but administration is not therefore politics. . . . This discrimina-

ED. NOTE: "The Study of American Public Administration" by Alan A. Altshuler was written especially for the first edition of this text.

tion between administration and politics is now, happily, too obvious to need further discussion.[2]

The object of public administration as a field of study, Wilson went on, should be to improve—through the application of scientific modes of analysis—the performance of public administrative activities. Another way of putting this might have been to say that public administration should follow the reformist bent of the rest of political science, but should focus on the noncontroversial activities of governments, those which political analysts had hitherto ignored.

Having thus defined the focus of public administration rather narrowly, Wilson made clear that his own interests were extremely broad. He placed his call for a science of administration within an analysis of the growing complexity and consequent bureaucratization of the function of governance. For the first time in history, he declared, "it is getting harder to *run* a constitution than to frame one." He wrote, moreover, as a partisan in a *political* movement: that for reform of the nineteenth century spoils system and substitution of a civil service merit system in its place. After issuing his call, Wilson did not consider devoting his scholarly life to the refinement of administrative techniques. He left that to more prosaic minds.

Many did take up where he had left off, however. For fifty years after he wrote, the dominant theme of writings on public administration was the pursuit of principles which, when applied sensitively, would produce "efficient" administration. Without seriously asking why, moreover, nearly all professional students of administration assumed that the "value-free science" of administration should take as its fundamental orientation the perspective of an organizational chief who, knowing his goals clearly, desires only additional knowledge of how to manipulate his subordinates and "customers" more effectively.[3]

Some of the most sophisticated writers of this period—for example, Leonard D. White and Luther Gulick—did regularly remind their readers that the discipline was still in its infancy, that the "principles of administration" discovered to date set only very general constraints and that therefore the practice of administration remained predominantly art rather than science. About the aim, however, they rarely wavered. Gulick articulated the consensus of the profession when he concluded a seminal volume of essays in 1937 as follows:

> In the science of administration, whether public or private, the basic "good" is efficiency. The fundamental objective of the science of administration is the accomplishment of the work in hand with the least expenditure of man-power and materials.[4]

This consensus was already beginning to be challenged as Gulick wrote, however. From Wilson's day to the early 1930's, the study of public administration had been unambiguously allied with the ideal—to use Herbert Kaufman's nomenclature[5]—of "neutral competence" for the public service. The experience of the early New Deal suggested, however, (1) that patronage might be of great value in aiding a vigorous President to push through programs of social and economic reform, and (2) that such a President might be justifiably reluctant to entrust his new programs to career bureaucrats who—though merit appointees—had grown deeply attached to the philosophies and procedures of the old order. FDR often chose to press for the establishment of new agencies to carry out programs that represented sharp breaks with the past,[6] and it was difficult for professional students of administration to fault him compellingly on "efficiency" grounds for doing so. Many were critical, of course, but others chose to reassess the academic dogmas on which they had been reared.

Thus, beginning in the mid-1930's a body of scholarship began to develop on the constant and apparently irrepressible penetration of administration by politics in the United States.[7] These studies were bound to be, and were, followed quickly by at least a few analyses hypothesizing the "functions" of the patterns observed. From here, particularly in view of the sympathy with which most members of the profession viewed the New Deal, it was only a brief step to extolling the virtues of these patterns. Some, at least, took that step. Even more significantly, no serious student of public administration could ignore the impact of these new descriptions and justifications. Even Gulick, in the very passage cited several paragraphs back, went on as follows:

> But both public administration and politics are branches of political science, so that we are in the end compelled to mitigate the pure concept of efficiency in the light of the value scale of politics and the social order.
>
> There are, for example, highly inefficient arrangements like citizen boards and small local governments which *may* be necessary in a democracy as educational devices. It has been argued also that the spoils system, which destroys efficiency in administration, is needed to maintain the political party, that the political party is needed to maintain the structure of government, and that without the structure of government, administration itself will disappear.
>
> While this chain of causation has been disproved under certain conditions, it nonetheless illustrates the point that the principles of politics may seriously affect efficiency. . . .

To illustrate the full extent of the discomfort that—as a theorist anxious to fit the new perspective into the context of the old—Gulick apparently felt during this transitional period, it should be added that after admitting the above he immediately pulled back to more orthodox ground. His next two sentences but one ran as follows:

> These interferences with efficiency [do not] in any way eliminate efficiency as the fundamental value upon which the science of administration may be erected. They serve to condition and to complicate, but not to change the single ultimate test of value in administration.[8]

The confusion might have been resolved, it seems clear today, by recognizing frankly that the objectives actually pursued by any administrative agency—the proper criteria against which to measure efficiency—were often not simply its stated objectives. They might, for example, include satisfying the psychological needs of individual employees, mollifying client interest groups, and providing jobs for members of the political party in power. A profession devoted for fifty years to defining efficiency in terms of universally acceptable, explicitly stated goals—and, in particular, to defining patronage and efficiency as polar opposites—was bound, however, to find this point extremely difficult to accept. Moreover, acceptance of it would only have brought Gulick (and the profession) to two even more embarrassing questions: (1) is it possible to construct a science of efficiency around organizations whose goals are in significant part unknowable? and (2) is the term "efficiency" meaningful even when organizational goals so elude attempts to define them with certainty and precision?

Despite this "crisis of the old order" in public administration, the controversies swirling around such epithets as "big government" and "the bureaucratic state" during the Roosevelt era fascinated American political scientists. Probably in consequence, this period was not only one in which "political" analyses of administrative subjects became fashionable; it was also one in which public administration attracted an extraordinary number of the ablest minds in political science. V. O. Key, Robert Dahl, Pendleton Herring, Herman Pritchett, Harvey Mansfield, Avery Leiserson, David Truman, Charles Hyneman, Norton Long, and Roland Pennock: all were beginning their careers in the thirties and early forties, and chose to focus at least major portions of their research energies on administrative subjects. They were joined, of course, by such as Herbert Simon, Dwight Waldo, Philip Selznick, and Reinhard Bendix—who carried their concerns with problems of bureaucracy into the fifties and sixties (though in progressively less "political" form), but who chose their specialties in the period under consideration.

Even as some students of administration were discovering and being provoked by "politics," however, others were attacking the traditional literature with a more orthodox end in view: that of pursuing efficiency more scientifically. Herbert Simon, who was to be its foremost spokesman and strategist, launched this school with a 1946 article entitled "The Proverbs of Administration."[9] "It is a fatal defect of the current principles of administration," he wrote:

> that, like proverbs, they occur in pairs. For almost every principle one can find an equally plausible and acceptable contradictory principle. Although the two principles of the pair will lead to exactly opposite organizational recommendations, there is nothing in the theory to indicate which is the proper one to apply.

He went on to document this apparently devastating charge with reference to four of the administrative literature's most frequently cited "principles."

He cited, for example, the doctrine that: "Administrative efficiency is increased by grouping the workers, for purposes of control, according to (a) purpose, (b) process, (c) clientele, or (d) place." These were clearly alternative criteria, Simon noted. The principle as stated offered administrators no help in deciding how to weigh or choose among them. Moreover, the terms themselves were ambiguous. Thus: "A health department conceived as a unit whose task it is to care for the health of the community is a purpose organization; the same department conceived as a unit which makes use of the medical arts to carry on its work is a process organization." Similarly: "A unit providing public health and medical services for school-age children in Multnomah county might be considered as (1) an 'area' organization . . . ; (2) a 'clientele' organization . . . ; (3) a purpose or process organization. . . ." And these, Simon made clear, were typical rather than unusual cases. The other principles discussed fared no more favorably.

Was the need, then, for a completely new beginning? Simon denied that it was. "Almost everything can be salvaged," he contended. What had been called "principles" of administration were in fact no more than criteria. As criteria, they were useful and important. The aim of the science of administration henceforth had to be to define them precisely, to list them exhaustively, and to weight them scientifically. In Simon's own words:

A valid approach to the study of administration requires that *all* the relevant diagnostic criteria be identified; that each administrative situation be analyzed in terms of the entire set of criteria; and that research be instituted to determine how weights can be assigned to the several criteria when they are, as they usually will be mutually incompatible.

In fact, Simon was being unfair to the most sophisticated among the students of administration who had written before him. Gulick, for example, had fully recognized the proverbial nature of the "principles of administration." In the course of the most authoritative exposition of them ever written, he had emphasized that:

> There is apparently no one most effective system of departmentalization. Each of the four basic systems of organization is intimately related to the other three, because in any enterprise all four elements are present in the doing of the work and are embodied in every individual workman. Each member of the enterprise is working for some major purpose, uses some major process, deals with some persons, and serves or works at some place.
>
> If an organization is erected about any of these four characteristics of work, it immediately becomes necessary to recognize the other characteristics in constructing the secondary and tertiary divisions of work. For example, a government . . . divided in the first instance by purpose, may well be divided next by process and then by place. While the first or primary division of any enterprise is of very great significance, it must none the less be said that there is no one most effective pattern for determining the priority and order for the introduction of these interdependent principles.

He had then discussed at length the kinds of circumstances in which each of the four "principles of departmentalization" might profitably be given top priority. And he had begun the section on these principles by confessing frankly that: "Unfortunately, we must rest our discussion primarily on limited observation and common sense, because little scientific research has been carried on in this field of administration."[10] The difference between Simon and Gulick, then, was not that the former could tell a proverbial from a scientific principle. It was rather that the latter considered some proverbs very useful—as checklists of factors worth considering, as handy cores around which to organize one's thoughts, and as the closest brief approximations of wisdom available in many circumstances. Gulick's thought had unquestionably been based on intuition and experience rather than science, but he had presented his observations with such clarity and elegance that even today, when one knows his arguments to be dated, one can almost count on remembering the "principles of administration" for years on the basis of one careful reading of his paper.

It should be kept in mind, moreover, that the "principles of administration" remain alive and kicking. Though scholars stress their limitations, no substitute body of normative ideas on how to organize a bureaucracy has taken their place. Consequently, consultants and committees charged with recommending large governmental reorganizations still regularly fall back upon them.

Simon undoubtedly served the profession well, however, by exposing the inadequacies of the "principles" in such memorable fashion. For most students of administration, they had become sacred dogmas, to be taught and applied rather than developed. They were stultifying thought rather than stimulating it. To cite one outstanding example, the "principles" focused almost exclusively on coordination as the key to efficiency; in consequence, virtually nothing had been written about the problems of infusing large bureaucracies with intelligence, innovative capacity, and zeal.

More generally, concentration on the goal of efficiency had long diverted attention from political phenomena. As noted previously, however, quite a few political scientists had attacked the politics-administration dichotomy by the time Simon wrote, and some had gone on to explore the patterns of political-administrative interaction that characterized the American system in detail. Simon ignored their work completely. His only major concession—and it was implicit—to their critique was to substitute for the politics-administration dichotomy a "fact-value" dichotomy.

While noting that one could not meaningfully distinguish political from administrative *decisions*, Simon emphasized that all decisions rested on both factual and value *premises*. Only the former, he contended, had any relevance to administrative science. Moreover, most values or goals were not "ends-in-themselves," but were rather "intermediate ends." That is, they were valued on the *factual* premise that they were instrumental to the achievement of ultimate ends. Thus, the applicability of science was extremely wide. One could ask scientifically whether intermediate ends were efficiently conducive to the ends-in-themselves from which they drew their appeal, even though scientists could have nothing to say about the "goodness" of these ultimate values themselves.

So long as the discussion remained abstract, these points contributed to conceptual clarity and were indisputable. When it came to practice, however, the fact-value dichotomy suspiciously took on the hue of the politics-administration dichotomy. For example, while disclaiming any wish to discuss the controversial issue of administrative responsibility at length,"[11] Simon contended that democracy, which nearly all Americans considered "good," would be strengthened by:

> procedural devices permitting a more effective separation of the factual and ethical elements in decisions. . . . The allocation of a question to a legislator or adminis-trator for decision should depend on the relative importance of the factual and ethical issues involved, and the degree to which the former are controversial. . . . Though the function of making value judgments may often be delegated to the administrator, especially where controversial issues are not involved, his complete answerability, in case of disagreement, must be retained.[12]

These sentences certainly appear to imply that *decisions*, and perhaps even *governmental functions*, can be divided into (1) those that are predominantly concerned with factual and intermediate value decisions, and (2) those that are predominantly concerned with ultimate or controversial value decisions. No sophisticated scholar had ever believed that the conceptual politics-administration distinction should be interpreted for practical purposes as suggesting more.[13]

Over the years, as it happens, Simon himself seems to have abandoned the idea that theorists of administration should focus on efficiency. In the index to *Organizations*, an analytical survey of the literature that he and James G. March published in 1958, the word "efficiency" appears only once—where it refers to the work of Gulick. This is quite understandable. The obstacles to building a science of administration upon the concept of efficiency have proven thus far to be insurmountable. In particular, as rigorous studies have been attempted, it has become increasingly apparent that:

(1) To be meaningful, evaluations of efficiency must rest upon a considera-tion of all an organization's values, not merely those which have been publicly stated, or those on which attention focused as any particular sequence of decisions was made.

(2) It is impossible to ascertain the true—as opposed to the explicit and announced—goals (together with appropriate weights thereof) of any organization with great precision or certainty.

(3) Decision-makers themselves discover many of their value priorities only in the course of choosing among concrete alternatives.[14]

(4) It would be an extraordinarily foolish administrator who searched end-lessly for the absolute optimal alternative in any situation.

In view of (4), Simon has suggested, reasonable decision-makers "satisfice" rather than "maximize." To put it more simply, they cease searching for proposals when they come across "satisfactory" alternatives. So stated, the satisficing concept expresses a significant and frequently neglected insight; and it is a truism. Simon has sought to develop it into more, however. He has defined "satisficing" in opera-tional terms and written of it as an important scientific hypothesis to be tested. "An alternative is *satisfactory*," according to Simon, "if: (a) there exists a set of criteria that describes minimally satisfactory alternatives, and (b) the alternative meets or exceeds all these criteria."[15] Thus, an administrator can be said to have satisfied if he has listed his minimal criteria exhaustively and then chosen the first alternative presented to him which met them.

This is certainly an operational definitoin. It is unlikely, however, to provide the operational criterion of efficiency that might make possible a genuine "science" of administrative efficiency. Rare indeed, after all, is the administrator who decides by going through the formal steps of listing criteria exhaustively and then com-paring alternatives with them. Moreover, anyone who wished meaningfully to evaluate the efficiency of an administrator seeking "satisfactory" solutions would have to begin by judging whether the criteria that he listed were sufficiently ambitious or imaginative—in view of the obstacles to greater optimality facing him. In this age of innovation, quite clearly, the "efficiency" of the unimaginative and unambitious administrator who achieves all the goals he sets for himself can lead quickly to the decline of his organization.

With considerations such as these no doubt in mind, Simon formally abjured his program of raising the old "principles of administration" from proverbial to true scientific status in his 1957 introduction to the (otherwise unrevised) second edition of *Administrative Behavior*. "Organizations," he wrote,

> are complex structures, and the importance of any particular factor in the design of such a structure will depend on many circumstances. Hence we can hardly hope for a set of invariant "weights" to apply to the design problem. I expect that for a long time to come, research in administration will be more concerned with identifying and understanding the basic mechanisms that are present in systems of organizational behavior than with assigning numbers to designate the importance of these mechanisms.[16]

Simon's vigorous reaffirmation of the ideal of a value-free science of adminis-tration has had a tremendous impact, nonetheless, probably because it coincided with the postwar behavioral revolution in American social science. Controversy still rages about the proper way to define behavioralism, but clearly its single most significant *influence* has been to enhance the valuation placed upon certainty—as opposed, for example, to provocativeness and profundity—as a quality of research conclusions. Scholars who have wished to earn the esteem of their behaviorally oriented colleagues have been spurred to define their concepts operationally (which is to say, so as to be susceptible of measurement), and to base their conclusions upon the measurement of observed actions or characteristics. Those *most* sensitive to the behavioral influence have been driven to do controlled experiments; others have been content to control their data analyses through the use of reputable statistical techniques; still others have tried by a variety of review procedures to reduce the element of arbitrariness in the writing of case studies to an absolute minimum.[17]

Of these three techniques, the first is almost never applicable to subjects of high political interest. The second, statistical analysis, is applicable most notably to political processes in which voting is an important factor. Thus, the past two decades have witnessed a flowering of studies of elections, legislative roll call patterns, and even judicial voting consistencies. They have also witnessed the production of numerous sophisticated studies of the opinions and background characteristics of all sorts of groups in American society, including, of course, both public and private bureaucratic leaders.

The third technique, case description, has also been employed in a great number of works. It has had its greatest impact, however, when complementing rather than substituting for more general analyses.[18] The major deficiency of the case study is that it necessarily deals with a very limited set of facts. Statistical research findings are also reliable only for the data with which they deal, of course, but these data may be of wide scope and immense intrinsic interest: national voting or opinion patterns, patterns of cohesion and conflict in Congress or the Supreme Court, background differences between the nation's political and business leaders, and so on. If one tries to deal with comparably large subjects via the case method, it obviously becomes impossible to interview all important actors, to give all a chance to read the case and have their reactions reported, or to examine all the publications, memoranda, and files that might shed light on the action described.

In other words, as the subject becomes larger, the aim of exhaustiveness in research becomes more clearly elusive. Moreover, as the subject matter becomes more controversial, charges that the researcher observed with biased eyes become progressively more difficult to refute. Hence, those anxious to enhance the case method's reputation for scientific reliability have been driven to describe quite small decision-making sequences or systems; and the case studies themselves have generally been most useful for illustrative and teaching rather than theory-testing purposes.

What has been the impact of the behavioral revolution on the study of public administration? One cannot be at all certain, but I believe it has been two-fold. First, it has contributed to the decline of public administration as a subfield within political science. Second, it has encouraged a boom in social psychological studies of men in organizations. Let us consider these two developments in order.

Public administration has become a rather peripheral subfield of political science, lingering in the teaching curriculum but having little impact on advanced scholarly thought. Those highly oriented toward the "scientific" study of politics have turned to studies of opinions, elections, communications, legislative roll call patterns, etc. They have been diverted from public administration by the fact that statistical analysis of administrative decisions is unusually difficult, for such reasons as the following.

First, most administrative decisions are informal. Second, a large proportion, even in the domestic agencies, are secret. Thus, one can almost never feel confident that the sample of decisions which can be analyzed is typical. Moreover, even where records of decisions are available, their classification for purposes of policy analysis often presents insoluble problems. Administrators normally stress the unique and technical—as opposed to the general policy—determinants of each decision, so as to maximize their future flexibility and to minimize the danger of broad press and congressional interest coming to center on their work. When analyzing congressional decisions, one can often bypass this problem by using the evaluations of particular roll call votes issued by easily labeled organizations, or by looking for voting patterns among the Congressmen themselves. Administrative decisions rarely have obvious labels, however, nor do large groups of administrators vote regularly on common sets of questions. (In contrast to their decisions, of course, the background characteristics and the opinions of administrators are highly amenable to statistical analysis, and numerous studies have focused on them in recent years.)

Even those willing to base their analyses upon case studies find public administration a particularly frustrating field in which to work. Case writers who describe major political disputes at least have intrinsically interesting and important stories to tell. Those who examine congressional processes or election campaigns can use their cases to complement rather than substitute for statistical analyses. Those who examine the politics of a particular city can hope to cover most of the major issues active in it during a given time period, thus eliminating much of the sample problem.[19] Moreover, major political disputes occur largely in the open; in the course of being blown up they come to symbolize general policy issues; and most of the leading participants in them (politicians, interest group leaders, etc.) tend to be anxious to help the case writer get their sides of the story in full.

By contrast, administrative agencies deal with enormous numbers of matters and, as noted previously, tend to minimize the symbolic importance of each. It is quite clear to all that research ought to deal with the great mass of secret, routine, and informal decisions as well as the few that become subjects of widespread public controversy. Thus, after investing several years preparing case studies in a given administrative area, a researcher is likely to find that the stories he has to tell are important only to the extent that they are typical, and that he has no basis for refuting changes that they are not.

So much for the reasons why highly behavioral students of politics may have turned away from public administration. Many other political scientists, however, have continued to choose research topics solely on the basis of political importance. Why have so few of these focused on public administration in recent years?

In part, of course, the answer is obvious. The research boom of the thirties in public administration was significantly due to the fact that this was the period in which big bureaucratizied government came to America. Its potential impact on American democracy was one of the hottest intellectual issues of the day. Since World War II, on the other hand, the interest of American intellectuals has increasingly shifted to such subjects as international relations and the politics of the underdeveloped areas.[20] Within the United States, the main focus has been on such "new" issues as race and the impact of the Cold War.

Quite clearly, however, this is only a partial answer. The Cold War has vastly accelerated the bureaucratization of American society and government,[21] and in fact the subject of national security policy making (including such attendant subtopics as science and government, news management, loyalty-security programs, and government contracting) has been the focus of substantial and constantly increasing research activity over the past fifteen years. The interesting question is why so few writers on national security policy making—even those dealing with such subjects as budgeting, interagency rivalries, the inner workings of the National Security Council, and the development of the position of Secretary of Defense—have chosen to present their work as falling within the traditional rubric of public administration.

One suspects that they have been put off by the traditional emphasis of public administration on efficiency, and that they have seen little reason in any event to associate with a specialization so widely considered moribund. Whatever their motives, however, their choice has had at least two unfortunate effects. First, it has served to discourage syntheses of the old literature with the new, and of the literature on domestic politics with that on national security politics. Second, it has served to delay incorporation of the new research on national security policy making into the teaching curriculum. Although it constituted the most interesting body of work published in the postwar period on American public administrative processes, many teachers of public administration have yet to make a significant place for it in their syllabi. Consequently, its presentation to students has often had to await the introduction of special courses on national security policy making. Such courses in turn have typically been taught as though their subject matter were *sui generis*, neither drawing sustenance from nor contributing to any larger body of theory about American governmental processes.

Before going on, a brief recapitulation may be helpful. Two major reasons for the decline of public administration as a political science subfield have been suggested. First, the increasing behavioral influence in American social science has spurred students of American politics to move from public administration into the study of subjects more amenable to "scientific" analysis. Second, public administration itself has failed to replace "efficiency"—a term which appears increasingly less precise, and a goal in which students of government are progressively less interested—with a set of concerns more closely related to the central concerns of modern political science. The problem, it should be emphasized, is not that contemporary students of public administration remain unswervingly devoted to efficiency. It is rather that, taken collectively, they have failed to become identified in the eyes of their colleagues with any more compelling set of governmental problems.

So much for the neglect of administration in recent years by students of American politics. One of the striking phenomena of the postwar period, however, has been a burgeoning of administrative research that is not politically (or even publicly) oriented. The interdisciplinary field of organizational behavior, with its focus on the social psychology of men in organizations, has enjoyed a boom of truly major proportions since World War II. Nearly all of the organizations examined have been nongovernmental, however, and few scholars working in the field have considered political relevance a noteworthy criterion of research significance. Formal organizations have been seized upon for their character as relatively well-defined social systems. Attention has focused predominantly on their internal lives, especially their relations with individual employees, small work units, and "customers."

The new discipline of organizational behavior has not emerged primarily, or even very significantly, from public administration. Three major "schools" of administrative study thrived in the first four decades of this century. Of these, only one, that exemplified by Wilson, Goodnow, and Gulick, focused mainly on public bureaucracies. It is today remembered as the "administrative management" school. The other two, which are remembered as the "scientific management" and "human relations" schools respectively, focused primarily on corporate bureaucracies—and the lowest levels of corporate bureaucracies at that.

Members of the scientific management school aimed at making optimal use of the human body in the performance of repetitive mechanical tasks. They produced numerous ingenious studies purporting to specify (1) how specific tasks could be done with minimal expenditures of time and effort, and (2) how maximal production could be obtained from well-motivated workers with minimal expenditures of time for eating, resting, and other nonproductive activities.

During the twenties and thirties a reaction to "scientific management" developed in the name of "human relations." Human relations theorists contended that the fundamental obstacle to industrial efficiency was the difficulty of motivating workers to strive for good performance. The scientific management school had assumed that the human material of bureaucracies was psychologically inert—that is, simply and almost limitlessly susceptible of being manipulated by those at the top charged with prescribing formal structures of authority and systems of compensation.[22] It had followed that the problem of motivation in manual work situations could be dealt with by any competent technician. The solution was to determine scientifically the rate at which "good" men could produce, and what they "deserved" to earn if they worked to capacity. Price rates could then be set accordingly. Human relations theorists, by contrast, maintained that men were primarily seekers after acceptance and approval, particularly from their peers, rather than money. They perceived the answer to the motivation problem to lie mainly in the area of cultivating group life within the factory—conceived ideally as a "community"—and influencing group social and moral norms.

The scientific management and human relations schools still flourish. The problems of showing manual laborers how to use their bodies efficiently and then of inducing them actually to do so remain of great interest to businessmen. Both schools, moreover, have made significant practical contributions to industrial efficiency in a wide variety of situations. In consequence, American corporations have increasingly provided them with testing grounds and money for their research. Over the past fifteen years the two schools have strengthened themselves by gradually integrating their orientations and theories. Their research has increasingly attracted the interest of sociologists and social psychologists interested solely in understanding (as opposed to practical applications). Out of this amalgam has come the half pure—half applied discipline, organizational behavior.

How is this relevant to an understanding of what has happened to public administration? The answer is simply that most of those in the "administrative management" tradition who have not left the study of administration altogether have progressively in recent years taken their bearings from the literature on organizational behavior. Herbert Simon himself has led the way in this direction, and indeed he had indicated in *Administrative Behavior* that he might. On page two of that volume he had declared that "the construction of an efficient administrative organization is a problem in social psychology." On its final page he had returned to this theme, contending that the science of administration might take either of two paths. On the one hand, it might pursue knowledge "as to how men would behave if they wished their activity to result in the greatest attainment of administrative objectives with scarce means." On the other hand, it might simply describe and analyze "the way in which human beings behave in organized groups." These alternatives, he concluded, found their analogies in other sciences, such as economics:

> First, economic theory and institutional economics are generalized descriptions of the behavior of men in the market. Second, business theory states those conditions of business behavior which will result in the maximization of profit.

Administrative Behavior had dealt with both, because its concern was the entire science of administration.

It was not surprising, then, that as the pursuit of principles of efficiency to guide top-level administrators came to appear fruitless, scholars who wished to achieve a high degree of certainty and yet to remain students of administration would turn to social psychological analyses of human behavior "in organized groups." This alternative was the more attractive because such scholars who happened to have received their training in political science could take their new bearings from, and more or less join, the growing fraternity of psychologists and sociologists already studying human behavior in organizations. They did not, in other words, have to strike out wholly on their own. They had simply to shift reference groups.

This is not to disparage the field of organizational behavior. Some of its recent fruits have been extremely interesting, and some of the older classics which are today accounted part of its literature are remarkably fruitful sources of hypotheses about the causes and political consequences of bureaucratization.[23] My purpose is rather to venture an explanation of the fact that those political scientists (defined in terms of graduate training and academic appointments) who have continued to specialize in administration have more and more taken their bearings from sociology and psychology—the most "behavioral" social sciences—rather than from the rest of political science. Their research has, no doubt in consequence, been of less and less *political* relevance.

It is not at all clear that the teaching of introductory public administration has followed suit to any great extent. Nonetheless, recent textbooks and books of readings have tended to replace or supplement the old material (left over from the thirties) on the techniques of financial and personnel administration primarily with new material on small group dynamics. The major exception to this picture is that there has been a great resurgence of interest during the 1960's in rational (now termed "cost effectiveness") budgeting. The new theories of budgeting are an outgrowth of economics, and behavioral students of administration feel at home with them. Part of their attraction is that they call for rigorous attempts to quantify and to employ mathematical techniques of analysis in the budget process. Unquestionably, they do constitute an important administrative innovation. In another sense, however, they are a throwback. Their aim is to aid organizations rationally to pursue explicit values determined at the top. They assume implicitly that pluralism and bargaining relationships within an organizational system are unfortunate (except, perhaps, as they are sources of ideas). In other words, they greatly resemble the principles of administrative management. What is politically interesting about them is the ways in which their application can alter bargaining relationships within a political system. Textbook treatments to date, however, have simply expounded the theory. Analyses of its political consequences have been rare even in the scholarly literature.

With the history reviewed in this essay as background, permit me to conclude with a few words on the aims of the present volume. Few contemporary texts or readers focus on the political issues surrounding American public administration. (I have endeavored in these pages to explain why.) These few, moreover, are without exception abbreviated volumes aimed more at the basic American government course—which typically includes a week or so devoted to administrative subjects—than at the full-semester course in public administration. Hence, the first of this volume's aims is simply to make life a bit easier (1) for students, and (2) for those colleagues around the country who believe that public administration should be taught as an integral part of the study of American politics. The second is to serve and reinforce the still embryonic trend toward incorporating the literature on national security administrative politics into the public administration curriculum. Third, and finally, some hope is entertained that this volume may have a modest influence on research, by reminding political scientists specializing in administration of the need for politically oriented studies, and by reminding students of American politics more generally of the potential for vital and exciting research that remains in public administration.[24]

NOTES

1. A definitional note may be helpful. I understand "politics" to be those activities in a society having to do with the expression of conflicts among social groups within it, and with attempts to resolve or manage such conflicts. I specify "group" conflict (1) on the premise that one ought to exclude from a definition whatever one can without severely aggravating the difficulty of relating actual phenomena to it, and (2) because it seems clear that conflicts among individuals rarely challenge the governmental capacities of a society unless fairly large groups (measured against the standard of the society under consideration) begin to take sides. The group conflicts which I term *distinctly* political are those which in the time period being analyzed are deemed (by at least some of the interested groups) unsuitable for resolution by the mere application of legal or technical expertise—both of which assume the preexistence of authoritative, applicable and clear decision rules.

Three related points deserve to be made.

First, the political importance of any dispute is a matter for judgment, not measurement. It depends on opinion about the significance of the issues at stake. A political scientist does not have to depend solely on his own opinion, however. He can seek also to ascertain the opinions of active participants in the dispute, members of the general public, governmental officials, and panels of expert outside observers.

Second, political science is concerned with potential as well as actual conflicts. The sources of consensus in a society on issues that have disrupted other societies is a typical and highly legitimate subject for political analysis.

Third, my inclination is to specify that "political" means are nonviolent, though they often involve the threat of violence unless compliance is forthcoming. There is nothing political about securing compliance by direct physical force; political science departments do not offer courses in jujitsu, or even in military tactics. One hastens to add that two of the most vital functions of any society's political systems are (1) to determine the purposes for which violence may be used in the society, and (2) to determine the procedures by which it should be called upon and applied in appropriate circumstances. One certainly cannot grasp the essential character of a political system without having a profound understanding of its provisions for the regulation of violence. It should be kept in mind, nonetheless, that the actual use of violence indicates a failure of politics.

2. Woodrow Wilson, "The Study of Administration," reprinted, *Political Science Quarterly*, XVI (December 1941), 481–506. The quotations are from pages 493–495.
3. My language here follows Chester Barnard, who noted that many of the essential contributors to any organization's survival and prosperity are not employees. The organization is a system of cooperative activity which must induce possessors of money and materiel to participate as well as workers. Barnard emphasized that the buyers of a business organization's product were fully as important members of its cooperative system as employees. I employ the term "customer" a bit more broadly, to include the investors in and creditors of a business enterprise as well as those to whom it sells, the constituencies (all whose political support is important to it) of a political organization, and the contributors (of energy, time, and materiel as well as money) to a voluntary association.
4. Luther Gulick, "Science, Values and Public Administration," in Luther Gulick and L. Urwick, eds., *Papers on the Science of Administration* (New York: Institute of Public Administration, 1937), p. 192. These were not the volume's final sentences, but they were the key sentences of its concluding essay.
5. See his article, "Emerging Conflicts in the Doctrine of Public Administration," *American Political Science Review*, Vol. 50 (December 1956), pp. 1057–1073.
6. By way of illustration, see Arthur Schlesinger, Jr., *The Coming of the New Deal* (Boston: Houghton Mifflin, 1958), pp. 534–536; and Grant McConnell, *The Decline of Agrarian Democracy* (Berkeley: University of California Press, 1953), pp. 84–89, 93–111.
7. See, for one of the earliest and finest examples of the genre, E. Pendleton Herring's *Public Administration and the Public Interest* (New York: McGraw-Hill, 1936).
8. Gulick, *op. cit.*, p. 193.
9. The article appeared originally in the *Public Administration Review*, Vol. VI (1946), pp. 53–67; and subsequently as chapter two of Simon's book, *Administrative Behavior* (New York: Macmillan, 1947). The quotations which follow (in the text) are from *Administrative Behavior*, pp. 20, 21, 28, 30, 35, 36.
10. Luther Gulick, "Notes on the Theory of Organization," in Gulick and Urwick, eds., *op. cit.*, pp. 1–45. The above quotation is from page 21. The previous quotation was from pages 31–32.
11. The dimensions of this issue are explored in Section VII of this text.
12. Simon, *Administrative Behavior, op. cit.*, pp. 57–58.
13. Frank Goodnow, for example, whose book, *Politics and Administration*, published in 1900, occupies as prominent a place in the history of public administration as Wilson's essay cited previously, emphasized with great clarity that he understood the politics-administration dichotomy to be one of ideal type "functions," not of governmental activities or agencies. Goodnow never used the phrase "ideal type," but he distinguished politics from administration as follows:

. . . Politics has to do with the guiding or influencing of government policy, while administration has to do with the execution of that policy. . . . The use of the word "administration" in this connection is unfortunately somewhat misleading, for the word . . . means popularly the most important executive or administrative authorities. "Administration," therefore, when used as indicative of function, is apt to promote the idea that this function of government is to be found exclusively in the work of what are commonly referred to as executive or administrative authorities. . . . Such, however, is rarely the case in any political system, and is particularly not the case in the American governmental system.

He considered a rigid separation of powers along these abstract functional lines, moreover, to be clearly unfeasible:

. . . The separation of powers and authorities has proven . . . to be unworkable as a legal principle. The courts have made many exceptions to it, all in the direction of recognizing what one of them calls "a common vicinage" bordering on the domains of each authority, in the occupancy of which each authority must tolerate the others. Thus, the organ of government whose main function is the execution of the will of the state is often, and indeed usually intrusted with the expression of that will in its details. . . . That is, the authority called executive has, in almost all cases, considerable ordinance or legislative power.

On the other hand, the organ whose main duty is to express the will of the state, i.e., the legislature, has usually the power to control in one way or another the execution of the state will by that organ to which such execution is in the main intrusted. That is, while the two primary functions of government are susceptible of differentiation, the organs of government to which the discharge of these functions is intrusted cannot be clearly defined.

At the same time, like Wilson and Simon, Goodnow believed *normatively* that Congress should confine its control of the executive branch to matters of general policy interest. His reasons were less formalistic and more interesting, I believe, than Simon's. If political controls were extended further than was absolutely necessary to ensure the execution of the "state will," he thought, the administration was likely to become an instrument of the party in power. To the extent that this occurred, he wrote, "the spontaneous expression of the real state will tends to become more difficult and the execution of that will becomes inefficient." "On the other hand," he noted:

if the attempt is made to strengthen the administrative system unduly in the hope of securing efficient administration, there is danger that, if the party organization is weak, the administrative organization may be made use of to influence the expression of the will of the state through its power over elections.

He concluded that the only solution lay in "frankly recognizing" that a balance between the conflicting ideals of political control and administrative independence had to be sought. Involved political man that he was, he then went on to specify in detail what he thought would constitute a desirable balance for the American governmental system of his day.

The above quotations are from Frank J. Goodnow, *Politics and Administration* (New York: Macmillan, 1900), pp. 14–16, 28, 92–93.

14. The most provocative analyst of this phenomenon has been Charles E. Lindblom. See his article, "The Science of Muddling Through," which appears in section III of this text, and his book, *The Intelligence of Democracy* (New York: The Free Press, 1965).

15. James G. March and Herbert Simon, *Organizations* (New York: John Wiley and Sons, 1958), p. 140.

16. Herbert Simon, *Administrative Behavior: A Study of Decision-Making Processes in Administrative Organizations* (New York: The Free Press, 1957), p. xxxiv.

17. I should add that there had been another—and less precisely describable, but more indisputably healthy—impact of the drive to make the study of politics more genuinely "scientific." This has been to spur all the social science professions to do more research and less armchair theorizing, to refrain more scrupulously from offering recommendations unaccompanied by careful analyses of the unintended consequences they may entail, and in general to evaluate evidence more critically. David Truman elegantly stated the case for defining social "science" with reference to values such as these in his 1965 Presidential address to the American Political Science Association:

. . . To specify that "science" requires the hypothetico-deductive procedures and the integrated form of systematic explanation exemplified by the science of mechanics . . . is probably to deny that the discipline can be scientific or at best to confine it to problems of the most trivial character.

It is not necessary, however, so to restrict the definition or even to espouse that form of science as a goal or an ideal . . . If one accepts Nagel's characterization that . . . "The practice of scientific method is the persistent critique of arguments, in the light of tried canons for judging the reliability of the procedures by which evidential data are obtained, and for assessing the probative force of the evidence on which the conclusions are based," then the recommitment in the discipline becomes sensible and, at least presumptively, manageable.

Science so conceived requires generality of statement but not in a specified degree, nor does it require a particular level of precision, or a limited set of techniques. It does not assure the truth of every conclusion that it reaches or the absence of bias deriving, for example, from the value commitments of the investigator. It does not suggest that a precise line divides knowledge or beliefs that can be labelled "common sense" from knowledge that claims to be "scientific" . . .

David Truman, "Disillusion and Regeneration: The Quest for a Discipline," *American Political Science Review*, LIX, No. 4 (December 1965), pp. 865–873. The quotation is from pages 870–871.

18. See, for example, Raymond A. Bauer, Ithiel de Sola Pool, and Lewis Anthony Dexter, *American Business and Public Policy* (New York: Atherton Press, 1963) and Robert Dahl, *Who Governs?* (New Haven: Yale University Press, 1961).

19. Critics will still argue that the issues which are active in a stable political system at any time may be less relevant to a profound understanding of it than those which have been resolved, those which have been tabled, and those which no one has ever thought to raise. One of the historic functions of social science, of course, has been to point up general issues and trends where the active participants in social processes had previously been only masses of detail.

20. Increasingly in recent years, it should be noted, political scientists concerned with underdeveloped countries have written about their administrative problems and institutions. This is an important development, and it would deserve a prominent place in any comprehensive history of the study of public administration. The present essay, however, is concerned with public administration as a branch of the study of *American* politics and society.

21. National security spending—defined here to include the U.S. budget categories of National Defense, International Affairs and Finance, and Space Research and Technology—rose from one-eighth of the federal administrative budget in 1939 to three-fifths in 1965. The absolute increase was fifty-six times. National security employment increased from two-fifths of total federal employment (civilian and military combined) to three quarters in the same period. The absolute increase was seven times. These employment figures are artificially deflated, it should be noted, because they fail to take into account the millions of civilians now employed in the private sector under government contracts. Government by contract is essentially a postwar phenomenon.

22. It should be noted that this assumption was borrowed from classical economics, and that it was shared by the administrative management school. Administrative management theorists carried it to less absurd limits than their scientific management counterparts, however, and by the mid-1930s the more subtle among them were endeavoring to take account of recent writings on both "human relations" and American Administrative politics. The result, as noted previously, was never a genuine reconciliation of old and new, but it *was* a tempering of the old with a good deal of sophistication about its limited applicability.

23. See, for example, the relevant works of Henri de Saint Simon, Emile Durkheim, Max Weber, Robert Michels, and Karl Mannheim.

24. Is it totally fanciful to imagine a textbook (broadly defined) influencing research? I think not, and I suspect that they do quite regularly. Most scholars are teachers, and their ideas for research emerge significantly out of their teaching experiences. These experiences in turn are shaped significantly by the material that they assign their students to read. Textbooks at times purport merely to summarize the literature on a subject, but their authors unavoidably make numerous decisions about what to highlight and what to leave out entirely. When a consensus on many of the judgments emerges among the textbook writers, the neglect of certain subjects by researchers may be greatly reinforced. For a forceful statement of much the same point in another context, see Lawrence J. R. Herson, "The Lost World of Municipal Government," *American Political Science Review*, LI, No. 2 (June 1957), pp. 330–345.

Developments in Public Administration

Dwight Waldo

This report on recent and contemporary developments is centrally concerned with self-conscious Public Administration, that is, the academically centered area of inquiry and teaching that knows itself by this name. It is concerned with the institutions and activities of public administration chiefly as these relate to Public Administration.

A vexing terminological problem has already presented itself. Economics is little likely to be mistaken for the economy, political science for politics, sociology for society. But "public administration" can mean (1) the institutions and

Reprinted from "Developments in Public Administration" by Dwight Waldo in volume no. 404 of *The Annals* of The American Academy of Political and Social Science (November 1972), pp. 217–245. Copyright © 1972 by The American Academy of Political and Social Science. Extensive footnotes have been omitted by permission of the author.

activity of public agencies; (2) self-conscious inquiry and teaching focused upon such public agencies; or (3) both (1) and (2) as a total field of institutions, activities, inquiry, and teaching. In this discussion the style Public Administration will be used in referring to self-conscious inquiry and teaching. The style public administration will refer sometimes to the public institutions and activities, sometimes to the total field of institutions, activities, inquiry, and teaching. The reader will have to do his best to decide, from contextual clues, which of the two is meant.

Public Administration is in a period of stress and change. It is responding to many and often conflicting forces in a complex, sometimes turbulent environment. In the attempt to understand what is happening to and in Public Administration, attention is directed first to some aspects of the total field of societal forces to which it is responding. Then, narrowing the scope, I shall discuss interaction with its immediate "external" environment of public administration and with its "internal" environment of academically centered institutions and ideas. Finally, I shall try to decide what further observations are needed to complete the review and what speculations appear reasonable.

THE SOCIETAL CONTEXT OF CONFLICT AND TURBULENCE: ANTINOMIES AND PARADOXES

The plethora of problems with which public administration seeks to cope and the extraordinary level of societal conflict and turbulence which presently constitute its environment can hardly be ignored in any attempt to report on recent and contemporary Public Administration. These matters have of course been noted, analyzed, discussed, and debated at great length; and no brief treatment can pretend to add important new information. Perhaps, however, the relevance for public administration of some of the antinomies and paradoxes in the situation can be more clearly delineated. In any event that is the object of what follows.

Public–Private

Conflicting ideas on the proper division between the public and the private realms are hardly new. Neither is a measure of overlapping and intermixture. However, in the present period the conflict between the two principles has not only great intensity, but new aspects; and the growth of a "gray" area of public-private admixture, in its size and complexity, is creating a new situation in societal organization and administration.

Reaction against governmental institutions and solutions is massive, varied, and intricate. Manifestations abound: taxpayers' revolts, anti-busing movements, draft evasion, militancy of public employee unions, citizen vigilante organizations, withdrawn communal groups, and so forth. As well observed, the liberal consensus that formed about the New Deal has been greatly weakened; no longer is it easily presumed that a national problem can be solved by creating a national program with a matching bureaucracy. Much evidence indicates that belief in the intelligence, the justice, the honesty, and the efficiency of public officials and employees has declined during recent years. The reaction against government spans the social-economic spectrum. Right, Center, and Left, with different motives and for different objectives, speak in concert in this regard.

Yet for all the crying of the "sickness of government," government grows, and it grows because society asks it to grow. It remains by the logic of circumstances society's "chosen instrument" to deal with problems of large scope and great complexity. It could hardly be otherwise short of societal disintegration, or reconstruction in some very different form. The area of *public* problems, that is, the area in which the actions of one or a few affect many, steadily expands; and government, for all its faults, was created to deal with public problems—and there is no obvious and accepted alternative. Except for those whose alienation has led to a "drop out" status, there is no other important "game."

The result of conflicting sentiments is conflicting actions: toward government and away from government. Simultaneously there is movement toward the publicization of the private and the privatization—"reprivatization," as some would have it—of the public. The result, when combined with important technological and social changes, is the expansion of an area in which public and private, as these have been conventionally conceived, are intermingled in new and often exceedingly intricate ways.

To be sure, the line of division between public and private was never clear and simple, as even a cursory view of American history indicates (as with respect to such areas as defense, transportation, and banking, but also including farming and—even—general "business"). But with the first measures—even pre–New Deal—to deal with the economic collapse of 1929, an upward curve in the size and intricacy of a "gray" area began. Every important program to raise income, employment, and productivity, ameliorate social distress, correct abuses, and protect rights has entailed the creation of new and complex arrangements in which the distinction between public and private has become more blurred.

. . .

Rising Expectations–Lowering Expectations

In the 1950s, the idea of a worldwide "revolution of rising expectations" was widely publicized. Around the world, we were told, peoples by the hundreds of millions who had accepted poverty as a part of the natural order had now come to realize that poverty is man-made and unnecessary. Now they had come not only to expect a rising standard of living, they looked forward—with varying degrees of confidence and differing time scales—to a standard of living essentially comparable to that of advanced industrial countries.

It is not necessary to agree with all that was said about the revolution of rising expectations—some of which was exaggerated or in error—to recognize that it concerns something true and important: A new, volatile element has been added to the world and national situations. "Development" has, since World War II, become something of a worldwide ideology and movement; "to develop" is to do something eminently desirable, and while development is susceptible to differing interpretations, its customary meaning is given by such concepts as productivity, industrialization, and standard of living. Undoubtedly, the fervor with which development was embraced—having some religious qualities, however secular its core objectives—has affected our domestic politics as well as our international role: We have had our own revolution of rising expectations, among and concerning the poor and disadvantaged generally, but centering upon racial-ethnic minorities.

Meanwhile, a revolution of quite different characteristics has come upon us, one which appears to dictate in many ways and for many people a lowering of expectations. This second revolution is centered in the concept of ecology. It concerns such matters as: environmental pollution, exhaustion of nonrenewable resources, limiting population, de-emphasizing productivity as a goal, "quality of life" as against "standard of living." Ultimately it concerns preservation of the biosphere itself.

To picture two monolithic forces in direct conflict would, of course, be over-simplification. But that the two streams of ideas and activities do already conflict and that the potential for much greater conflict exists is beyond cavil.

. . .

Industrialism—Post-industrialism

Closely related is another antinomy. Obviously, industrialization has been so far the heart of development; and a de-emphasis of the production of material goods is viewed by many as essential to adjusting man to a supportable environment. Yet however intertwined, the two antinomies are neither equivalents nor opposites. Many now argue that the development with which disadvantaged people are concerned, or *ought* to be concerned, can be conceived in nonindustrial terms; and post-industrialism can be conceived as a condition in which production of goods is decreased relatively and perhaps even absolutely.

A long shelf could now be filled with the works discussing the movement of modern man from an industrial period into a post-industrial period. In general they argue: that scientific and technical advances make possible and perhaps inevitable a new socio-economic condition of man; that organized and codified knowledge is becoming increasingly important as against the conventional factors of production, land, labor, and capital; that new knowledge and new technologies enable us to produce goods with such efficiency and in such abundance that the archetypical industrial institution, the "factory," is being transformed, evolving into new techno-social patterns; that the new efficiencies in production of goods (the solu-tion of the ancient problem of scarcity) make it possible—and in some ways necessary—for society to emphasize the rendering of services and the enjoyment of leisure as against production of material goods; that these changes, at base technical and economic, have profound implications for total societal organization and style of life, as evidenced by the fact that as the economy of the United States becomes increasingly a service-rendering economy, we experience institutional and psycho-social crises.

To the extent such analyses and projections are correct, they are of course highly relevant to the several other antinomies here sketched. Can other societies—can parts of our society—move directly from pre-industrialism to post-industrialism? Is it realistic or humane to decry productivity while hundreds of millions are in dire need? If productivity as a goal and measure is inappropriate for a post-industrial, service-rendering economy, what—if anything—takes its place? What are the implications of the new modes of production and life-styles for the intermixture of public and private, and beyond that for the functions and organization of government?

Nationalism–Post-nationalism

Nationalism–post-nationalism may not be the proper choice of terms. Though some of the phenomena to which attention is called undoubtedly can be so designated, others probably deserve another designation. Be that as it may, the purpose is to note the conflicting forces bearing on the establishment, the permeability, and the disappearance of political boundaries.

The thesis developed by Hans Kohn and others that nationalism is not a universal phenomenon, but one peculiar to the modern period, has a corollary; namely, that it may wither and disappear. Reasonable evidence suggests that nationalism has suffered a decline in some of the older nation-states: a growing disinterest in patriotic observances, a neglect of the duties of citizenship, growing estrangement from or hostility toward governmental institutions. Taken by themselves these signs would seem to trend toward the emergence of a—what to call it?—human homogenization or universalism. More, this trend would seem in concert with trends based upon and emerging from various economic, functional, and technical considerations. The growth of transnational and sometimes world-encircling organizations, associated organizations, and complex systems of associated organizations, clearly is one of the important trends of the century.

But at the same time it seems indisputable that there are contrary trends in the direction of greater group self-consciousness and discreteness. This is manifest in the rise in the number of "new nations," of political entities that are nominally independent in terms of international law, a quadrupling in the fairly recent past. It is evidenced also in the rise of new, or renewed, racial-ethnic identities, often strident and militant: older nationalisms may become moribund; some countries may—from the evidence one may guess *will*—disappear, that is, lose their present identity; but the result may well be a progressive fractionalization of mankind instead of movement toward a common world culture and order.

Violence–Nonviolence

The mid- and latter-twentieth century presents a new condition of man with respect to the interaction of violence and nonviolence.

As to violence, The Bomb is not only an instrument beyond all past imaginings, it serves as symbol for a vast array of instruments either created afresh or reshaped and sharpened by modern science and technology. Paradoxically, both our successes and our failures in social organization act, according to circumstances, either to create violence or to enlarge its threat. Actual violence between nations, and within nations, as represented by crime, civil disorder, and repression, is high and probably trending higher; and the possibility of vastly accentuated violence, perhaps even holocaust, seems ever near.

In counteraction, sentiments and movements for nonviolence are high and also perhaps trending higher. To be sure, paradoxes and ironies abound. Some movements for peace and brotherhood take violence as a means; Right and Left, conservative, centrist, and radical find themselves in varying stances, either by their own recognition or in the perception of their opponents; vast confusion and much controversy concern means and ends, instruments and objectives. For violence—nonviolence are seldom pure issues, but come entwined with issues of right and equity. In any case, the fear of dire consequences is high, and the longing for some state of relative nonviolence is strong across the wide social-ideological spectrum and around the world.

. . .

Implications for Public Administration

The five fields of contesting forces noted . . . represent an attempt to probe beneath the surface of the rapid change and frequent turbulence of the day . . . with the object in view of understanding the context of public administration, and thus understanding public administration itself.

Fortunately, the moral that is about to be drawn will stand whether or not the best choice of force-fields has been made or whether their explication has been skillful. The moral is that since public administration, by lack of alternatives if not by enthusiastic choice, is government's central instrument for dealing with general social problems, it is located in or between whatever force-fields exist. It is affected by whatever forces and turbulence there are; and it attempts also to *act*, to restrain or to increase the direction or the degree of change.

. . .

THE EXTERNAL ENVIRONMENT OF PUBLIC ADMINISTRATION

I now narrow the focus, to note some of the events and developments of the recent past and present which "impact" public administration: to which it responds and with which it interacts. I shall then observe how some central and predurable aspects of public administration are affected by the larger societal forces noted above and by particular developments.

. . .

Anti-poverty

As noted, the revolution of rising expectations has been a domestic as well as a foreign phenomenon. In the sixties poverty was rediscovered in the United States. Notable works exposed the depth and breadth of domestic poverty, low-income groups became more politically active, and a "war against poverty" became an official national cause.

Much legislation and administration from the beginning of the Republic has been in some sense anti-poverty, and major programmatic additions, especially dealing with income maintenance for agriculture and labor, were made in the New Deal period. No great changes have been made in historically given programs; nor has much debate concerning the establishment of a national income floor yet resulted in legislation. The result of the so-called war against poverty has been rather a variety of special programs designed to improve living conditions, raise incomes, foster employability, and increase employment opportunities. The recently formed Department of Health, Education and Welfare and the newly created Office of Economic Opportunity have been centrally involved. The administrative problems encountered have often been novel and always extremely difficult; by and large only limited successes in reaching objectives and solving the administrative problems can be claimed.

Racial-ethnic Equality

The movement of the early sixties to effect the civil rights of blacks in the South of course broadened in many directions. Equality for blacks in all respects quickly became an ardently sought goal. Chicanos, Puerto Ricans, and Indians, stimulated more or less by the black example, began to assert their identity and to press for more equality in education, housing, employment, and income. There have been many reactive results, including something of a resurgence of ethnic self-identity among European populations that had seemed all but assimilated. To what extent the equality that is sought by all will, in the long run, entail separateness of racial-ethnic identity and culture is at this point quite unforeseeable.

Historically, much governmental action in the United States has been not simply discriminatory, but massively and harshly so. Much governmental action has also, however, been directed toward achieving equality; paradoxically, action to secure assimilation and uniformity also has sometimes been insensitive and coercive. This is not the place to analyze a complex national experience. What needs to be noted is that in recent years the goal of equality has been taken with more seriousness, however contentious it remains and however ineffective the results. In large part, the story involves legislatures and courts; no large government agencies have been established of which the *primary* mission is achievement of racial-ethnic equality. But the issue of equality of treatment, especially for blacks, is nevertheless centrally and intimately involved in programs in such areas as education, housing, and employment; smaller agencies are created that do have equality of treatment as their central mission; and in the administration of government personnel programs, the issue of equal treatment is, as such, an increasingly important issue. Altogether, the matter of racial-ethnic equality is central to the understanding of much of recent and contemporary public administration.

Urban Problems

The shift from an agricultural economy to an industrial economy, with accompanying growth of the city, was reflected in American public administration well before the end of the nineteenth century, as in the civil service reform movement and the shaping of formulas for structural rationalization. After World War I the generations-old migration to the city was accentuated by technological developments and by agricultural policies; rapid population growth helped to increase city size; various policies, particularly with respect to housing, contributed to an expansion of suburban growth at the expense of the central city. For these and for many other reasons, by the sixties the city had become a problem center of a new order of magnitude for public policy and public administration.

In a formal sense one can distinguish between city problems and problems that find their chief location and severest manifestations in the city. The former concern the location and specifications of urban artifacts; they pertain to such matters as physical planning, industrial and commercial location, housing, street layout, and public transportation. The latter concern the problems of an industrial society in transition to a new condition designated (negatively, because its defining characteristics are only emergent) as post-industrial—in any event, the worrisome problems of *this* society at this time: racial inequality, increasing crime, drug abuse, and so forth. In some measure these have a city focus simply because our national life now has a city focus. But such a formal distinction has only a limited relevance. In the city, problems meet, mingle, and meld; physical problems have human dimensions, and human problems are inseparable from physical problems, as of course only a superficial knowledge of any typical urban problem, such as educational inequality or central-city renewal makes clear. The incredibly complex mixture of differing problems and different kinds of problems is the essence of the matter. Few public problems are not now city problems.

The implications for public administration are most visible in the creation of a new federal department, the Department of Housing and Urban Development. But the implications run far beyond the easily visible, into the problems of the organization and administration of all recent or emerging national programs, and to every level and type of governmental jurisdiction.

Ferment and Change

Space does not permit extended discussion of many other themes and events relevant to recent and contemporary public administration. Brief notice of some of the more important must suffice. Again, it should be understood that separate notice does not imply separate existence. On the contrary, a complex pattern of overlapping and interaction—which would be beyond tracing even in book-length treatment—obtains.

PARTICIPATION. A prominent theme and movement of the late sixties and early seventies has been participation. The participation movement has manifested itself in public administration in two ways: (1) internally, in actions directed both toward greater personnel involvement in decisions affecting the conditions of employment and toward rank and file involvement in decisions on agency programs; and (2) externally, in actions aimed at greater community or clientele participation in both decisions on agency programs and the implementation of these programs.

DEVOLUTION. In some measure related to the participation movement, but in some respects quite different, has been a movement aimed at bringing public programs more under control of the states and of local governmental jurisdictions. Typically, but not always, participation is associated with liberal or even radical sentiments; typically, but not always, devolution is associated with conservative or even reactionary sentiments. Both are responses to a feeling of powerlessness, even alienation; both manifest a distrust of bigness, and distance; both represent an attempt to gain control of decisions affecting vital personal concerns. Both movements, alone or in combination, have resulted in various types of action with the avowed objective of returning power to the people—or at least keeping it from further concentrating in the federal government.

NEW LEVELS AND JURISDICTIONS. Related both to participation and to devolution, but also to the programs mounted against poverty—and to other matters—has been the creation of more or less experimental jurisdictions operating in unconventional ways. These include regional organizations created as a part of a national program to raise the economic and social level of backward or depressed regions of the country; and community action organizations, particularly in the central-city areas, created as a part of the war against poverty. The participation motives as well as those ascribed to devolution have been operative in the creation of new levels and jurisdictions, in addition to administrative and economic considerations.

MANAGEMENT TECHNIQUES AND INSTRUMENTALITIES. Recent years have witnessed the growth and spread of various more or less new management techniques and instrumentalities in public administration. Characteristically, the techniques and instrumentalities involved are shared with business administration, and in some cases were invented or first developed there. But some of these have been, in the public administration context, refined, adapted, and expanded.

The techniques and instrumentalities involved cannot here be catalogued and explained, or their usage examined. The term "management science" would comprehend many of the specific techniques, especially those that make use of quantitative methods and have a relation to the newer means of data gathering, storage, and manipulation which center on the computer. The related term, "operations research," also denotes a perspective and a cluster of techniques of considerable importance. Some techniques, especially perhaps project management, have been notably expanded and refined in the public sector.

UNIONIZATION AND COLLECTIVE BARGAINING. The growth of public employee unionization and collective bargaining, at all levels of government, has been a major development in public administration during the past decade—this at a time in which unionization in some private sectors has been stationary or even declining. Public employee unions are hardly new, but their memberships have been comparatively small, and they have not been, characteristically, bargaining units. The growth of public sector unionism has various types of causes. These would include causes related to the national shift from a predominately goods-producing to a predominately service-rendering economy and an accompanying growth in the proportion of the working population in public employment; a relaxation of laws and regulations which have restrained public sector unionization; and the social-ideological ferment and economic recession of recent years.

Increasing unionization, together with a new assertiveness—in some cases, even militancy—poses knotty new problems and has implications for much of traditional public administration. The traditional area of personnel administration obviously is most immediately affected; but the implications run to all of public organization and management. Indeed, they run to the role of the government in the country's economic and social affairs, and ultimately to the status and nature of government as a sovereign power.

PRODUCTIVITY AND EVALUATION. An issue that is rapidly coming to the fore is productivity in the public sector. Productivity is always an issue with respect to a modern economy, and the transition to a predominantly service-rendering economy has changed and sharpened productivity problems: What is the nature and what are the indices of productivity when there is no tangible product? (Sometimes, even, the object of a program is to prevent something from occurring.) With the public sector of the economy steadily enlarging, the problems become more complicated and controversial. Various factors will operate to bring contesting forces into controversy and confrontation: the demands of unions not only for greater economic benefits, but for shorter hours and control of the conditions of labor—perhaps also some policy role; increases in taxes coupled with widespread sentiment that the public services are unresponsive, inefficient, unproductive, and wasteful; still further demands on government, such as subsidization of corporate enterprises that have become closely government-related—"Lockheed issues"; the rationalization and further public funding of medical care delivery; and programs that make government the employer of last resort.

A sharpening of controversy over productivity issues will increase the importance of what is already an important problem of current public administration: evaluation. Evaluation is hardly a new problem in public administration. It is, in many respects, but a new term for many of the issues that have been involved in dealing with the perennial and often central issues of economy and efficiency. But now the nonmarket area grows in absolute and relative terms, and the mixture of economic rationality, political rationality, and social equity which must be addressed becomes more intricate and tangled.

Two somewhat linked developments in public administration have a close relationship to productivity-evaluation issues and illustrate their importance. One is the attempt to install Planning, Programming, Budgeting Systems (PPBS). Cost-benefit and input-output studies are at the heart of this enterprise. Such studies essentially attempt to deal with productivity-evaluation problems; and so intractable are the problems, that PPBS has faltered and, often, been turned back. The other is the burgeoning of evaluation studies. (These take many forms: Some are in-house, some are inter-agency, some are contracted out to consulting firms, think tanks and research institutes, universities, and even individuals.) The increase in number and complexity of social-economic programs that came with the sixties has greatly intensified problems of judging effectiveness. Typically, the immediate output of the programs involved—as in education—are intangible, immeasurable, and controversial; and typically the difficulties in trying to assess effectiveness and comparative worth are complicated by the intricate administrative means: complex interrelations between public organizations and/or public-private organizations.

ENVIRONMENTALISM AND CONSUMERISM. The greatly increased concern for pollution of the environment and an increasing, more generalized interest in the quality of life have significantly affected public administration and may be expected to affect it more with passing time. The most obvious results to date have been the establishment of the Environmental Protection Agency, together with programs of action aimed at pollution control directed both externally—for example, automobile exhaust emissions—and internally—the requirement of the environmental impact studies for new federal programs. But the new currents affect many areas where public administration intersects an aspect of national life, including resource extraction, public works, transportation, recreation, and even the arts.

Governmental concern for the consumer, it is often observed, tends to be minuscule or half-hearted in comparison with concern for economic growth and productivity. Nevertheless, a sizable apparatus of regulation and control has been built up during the past several generations, some parts of which have at least significant consumer obligations in their mandates and some parts of which, as the Food and Drug Administration, have as their primary mission the protection of the consumer from fraud and direct harm.

. . .

OTHER VECTORS. The events, situations, movements, and so forth, with which public administration is presently concerned and to which it is more or less responsive are beyond even brief explication. But some of the other matters of import should at least be noted. One of these is the rising tide of domestic violence, with its implications for such matters as police and correctional administration, social-economic policies, and judicial administration. Another is the economic-financial difficulties which came to the fore in the late sixties; while no major new economy management devices have resulted, still the repercussions in public administration have been far from insignificant. Another is the Women's Liberation movement, which has been taken seriously in personnel administration—how seriously depending on jurisdiction and point of view. Another is continued movement toward specialization and professionalization in American life and the public service; a simultaneous, complicated, recently accentuated counter-movement, which attacks credentialism, seeks to broaden decision-making, to decrease rigidities, to increase lateral communication—generally, to debureaucratize. Still another is President Nixon's proposals with respect to the restructuring of federal administration and his proposals concerning, directly or indirectly, the allocation of responsibilities and functions as between the federal government, the states, and the cities.

Finally, it may be noted that some of the important currents of recent years have slowed or reversed: It has been widely noted that a mood, if not a movement, of neo-isolationism has followed the international experiments and global activism of the post–World War II decades. It is thus not surprising that no report is necessary on new creativity in international organization; nor that aid to developing countries does not present recent administrative developments worthy of note. The Planning, Programming, Budgeting System, which may have been the major event in public administration in the sixties—and certainly was the central new item in the literature of Public Administration in that decade—has recently suffered a severe decline: given wide publicity for its putative successes in the Department of Defense in the early sixties, ordered broadly applied in federal agencies in the mid-sixties, it has been recently "non-required" in federal budgeting. This is not, however, to say that PPBS has suddenly disappeared. It continues, as such, in many state and local jurisdictions. It leaves, even where it is formally disestablished, a residue of techniques and altered perspectives; its impact will prove to have been permanent. Above all, the problems to which it was addressed remain.

THE INTERNAL ENVIRONMENT OF PUBLIC ADMINISTRATION

A distinction between the external and the internal environments of Public Administration may be more literary convenience than reflection of reality. Certainly the matters I now address are inextricably related to events and trends in the outside world. But in any case, Public Administration interacts not only with the world of public affairs, but with the shifting currents of ideas and the changing institutional arrangements of academia. Attention is now directed to some of these.

A Change in Mood

Paradoxically, though academia is the fount of much societal change, the university is in many ways remarkably conservative. It yields only slowly to demands for change in its own values, procedures, and organization. Revolutionary ideas become tenacious traditions; reforms tend to fade and be supplanted by older ways. So one generalizes at considerable risk.

Nevertheless, it may be noted at the outset that the recent period has been one of extraordinary ferment in the university. Society's turmoil has been reflected in the university; in fact, some of it has centered in the university, as the words Berkeley, Columbia, and Kent State signify. The result has been to weaken the hold of some dominant ideas, to further a research for and heighten receptivity to new ideas, to strengthen forces for change. Much of what is relevant for Public Administration is to be understood as an interaction between old and new, inertia and change, tradition and experiment. The interaction is extremely complex, however, and interpretation is difficult, since one man's progressive perspective is frequently another's philosophical-methodological sterility—or menace.

Two related matters deserve brief attention. One is the cry for relevance. The sentiment that the university is, at best, indifferent toward society's urgent problems has found wide and sometimes ardent expression within the university; and from outside the university has come a variety of pressures—social, political, and economic—for altered perspectives and shifts in emphasis in research and instruction. The result is a heightened malleability, a quickening of change. Public-oriented programs and curricula are of course affected above all.

The other matter concerns changing intellectual-emotional orientations. These are difficult to cover in brief compass, but several generalizations can be made. While there has been no wholesale abandonment of the view that it is the fundamental objective of the social sciences to achieve a true and thorough scientific status, nevertheless a significant softening has occurred. To some extent belief in accepted theories has been shaken by the seeming inadequacies of the theories: thus doubts about Keynesian economic theories created by its putative failures in treating recent economic problems. To a notable extent social scientists—for various reasons from the crassly economic to the moral and ideological—are more inclined toward addressing applied problems as against abstract theoretical problems; and since social problems typically ignore disciplinary lines, there is a corresponding rise in interdisciplinary interaction. Some movement is discernible toward more widespread acceptance of radical perspectives and ideologies. Philosophical orientations are shifting to some extent; logical positivism is no longer as widely and firmly espoused; neo-Marxism, existentialism, and phenomenology are frequently argued as bases or guides.

It is within the context of an altered academic-intellectual environment that the following matters are to be construed.

Movement Away from Political Science

It is hardly too much to say that self-conscious Public Administration was the creation of professors of political science, so prominent were the roles of men such as Woodrow Wilson, L. D. White, and W. F. Willoughby. Beginning in the twenties it was customary to regard Public Administration as one of the fields or sub-fields of political science, and in fact probably most persons, both in and out of political science, still so regard it. But at the present time it would appear that significant changes are under way. These changes move in different directions, and the outcome is far from clear. Some forces in motion suggest the outcome will be a closer, but different, relationship with political science; some suggest the achievement of independent status in department and school; some suggest the disappearance of Public Administration as such, its absorption in general management synthesis.

On logical grounds the case for regarding Public Administration as a part of political science is a strong one. Political science concerns the state, government, and the public realm. Public administration would thus seem by definition a part of the total concern of political science. Most professors of Public Administration have regarded themselves as first of all political scientists. Many have found departments of political science congenial environments; some still do.

But in many, many ways the relation has not been a satisfactory one. Two reasons seem pre-eminent. One concerns the customary liberal arts location and orientation of political science. To the extent Public Administration has perceived itself and been perceived as training for a career of government service, and not with scholarship and the values of a liberal education, it has been accorded a type of second-class citizenship in its customary academic home. The fact that much of what has constituted its curriculum has been drawn from outside sources, such as psychology, business administration, and management science, has accentuated the lack of rapport. The second reason concerns the rise and increasing predominance of behavioralism in the post–World War II period. Public Administration was one of the parts of political science that lagged in the behavioral movement. (The reasons for this are varied; probably some of them reflect favorably, some unfavorably, on Public Administration.) Thus to the disdain of the traditionalists was added the reproach, if not contempt, of the new men of political science.

For whatever reasons, Public Administrationists have become increasingly restive with an environment regarded as, at best, merely tolerant. But the problem of an effective remedy is not easy to solve. To muster the resources in money, manpower, and political support to achieve the status of an independent program, department, or school is usually difficult to the point of impossibility. To move, individually or collectively, to a school of business or management may or may not be feasible according to circumstances; but regardless, this solution may appear as merely exchanging one type of second-class citizenship for another.

Movements in ideas, the growth and spread of various management-related technologies with little relation to political science, and increasing interdisciplinary penetration in Public Administration accentuate feelings that political science is no longer an adequate base. Increasingly, it is felt that political science neglects the intellectual-professional needs of public administration. Contrariwise, it is felt that other disciplines and intellectual clusterings, such as economics, sociology, and management science, provide the appropriate ideas and techniques. Some feel that Public Administration, while not a profession in a strict sense, represents a focus of interests and occupations not unlike that represented by medicine or the health services; and that it deserves, somehow, an organizational status which will enable it to represent the realities and muster and combine the needed resources.

While the wish to escape from political science is widespread and growing, nevertheless it needs to be recognized that certain present and potential developments in political science might lead to changes which would make political science a more congenial and supportive environment. One of these concerns the emergence of a "post-behavioral" political science. The ferment of recent years has led, especially among younger political scientists, to something of a revolt against the behaviorally oriented establishment. Political science, and especially behaviorally oriented political science, it is charged, has been too much concerned with technique, too little with goals and values; too much concerned with science and too little concerned with society, with urgent public problems. Proper scientific concerns need not be abandoned—it is generally argued—but they need to be put to service in addressing real and urgent problems.

It is too early to assess the strength and effect of these new currents. But they at least suggest the possibility of a substantial reordering of interests and resources in political science, making it more relevant to public problems, more policy-oriented, and more concerned with delivery. A political science concerned deeply with public policy and not disdainful of the means by which policy is effectuated would be much more attractive to Public Administrationists than has been the political science of recent decades.

Movement Toward Political Economy

Another development in political science that holds the possibility of making it more attractive is the movement toward political economy. Two decades ago Robert A. Dahl and Charles E. Lindblom, in their *Politics, Economics and Welfare* (New York: Harper & Brothers, 1953), argued for the establishment of a new political economy, a joining of political science and economics in the interest of greater theoretical coherence and better policy guidance. No rush and certainly no concerted effort to establish a new political economy followed. But slowly at first, and lately with increasing speed and mass, movement in this direction has taken place. Economists, such as Anthony Downs and Gordon Tullock, crossed the boundary into political science, experimenting with the application of economic methods and models to political problems. Political scientists, including—perhaps especially including—those making Public Administration their specialty, have familiarized themselves with economics, seeking theories and techniques applicable to their interests. The movement toward a new political economy now has considerable force, its supporters include prominent political scientists such as William Mitchell. Economists, for their part, evidence a "have tools, will travel" policy. Their willingness, even eagerness, to help a putatively weaker discipline with its problems has been reinforced by various recent events, including—ironically—the embarrassments arising from the weakness of strictly economic policies in dealing with national economic problems.

Public administration, both as a part of political science and on its own, so to speak, has moved in the direction of liaison with economics. Of course the budgeting-fiscal-accounting complex of interests has always been an area of joint interest. But the wave of interest in Program Budgeting in the fifties, and especially the enthusiasm for Planning, Programming, Budgeting System in the sixties, did much to further interpenetration and foster mutual learning. . . .

To the extent that political science moves toward political economy, this might, as suggested, increase its attractiveness to a Public Administration moving in a like manner in the same general direction. But the implications with respect to the future are not clear. If Public Administration were to find itself allied with— conceivably a part of—a vigorous political economy, this might move it in quite different directions.

The "New" Public Administration

A significant development of recent years has been the emergence of a "new" Public Administration. The term that comes most readily to mind in describing the new Public Administration is "movement." But whether it now is, or indeed ever was, a movement is not clear: the appropriateness of the term is denied by some of the participants or exemplars. Also, the extent to which the positions taken and ideas espoused are in fact new is a matter of argument.

But in any case, events and writings usually referred to as "the new Public Administration" have been a part of the recent Public Administration scene. In general, new Public Administration is a reflection within the Public Administration community of the events and ideas of the recent period. Its participants—if this is the proper word—have been mainly the younger Public Administrationists. While none of them, by generally accepted usage of the term, could be called revolutionary—after all, as the most ardent point out, they want to change the system, not destroy it—in general they reflect in some degree the rebellion of youth, and certain ideas associated with the counter-culture and the non-Marxian Left.

In broad brush, the charges made against the old public administration are that it lacks a respectable and consistent ideological-philosophical frame and a sophisticated methodology; that in accepting an instrumentalist role it becomes a tool of a system or establishment that itself is in need of serious reform; that it is inefficient—or efficient in the wrong ways—unresponsive, and unimaginative. On one side the new Public Administration is linked to the forces in political science that have been responsible for the emergence of a post-behavioral mood; the acceptance of the critique of pluralism is, for example, prominent. On the other side the new Public Administration is linked, but only weakly, with certain radical movements within the public services.

On the positive side, new Public Administration urges a concern for social equity, a sensitivity to human suffering and social needs. It argues that public administration should be more activist: "proactive" and not simply "reactive." It professes not to be anti-scientific, but wishes advanced methodologies and proce- dures to be used in a context of concern and reform, not for their own sakes and certainly not as instruments of repression. It professes not to be anti-rational, but wishes the calculations of public administration to be more sensitive, subtle, and humane; the domain of public administration to be enlarged by recognition of the importance of affect. It has a special concern for the problems of the central city: racial inequality, poverty, violence, physical blight, and the like. It has a keen interest in and a receptivity toward organizational humanism and advanced techniques of organizational development. It reacts against logical positivism—it largely ignores pragmatism—and seeks philosophic guidance from such schools as existentialism and, especially, phenomenology.

As a movement—if it ever was one—new Public Administration has, within a few years of its attainment of self-consciousness, lost much of its coherence and identity. But this is not to deny it importance and impact. Its adherents were centrally involved in changes in the American Society for Public Administration designed to democratize its organization and procedures and to give it a more forward stance. The literature it has produced is widely read; its ideas and sentiments circulate in the public administration community, particularly in academia. As its adherents, both original and converts, are largely on the young side and still to reach positions of maximum influence, it is likely to exert a continuing, if unpredictable, influence. In brief, it is unlikely to transform radically Public Administration short run, but long run this is a possibility; and in any case it now is and will continue to be a yeasty addition to the entire complex of theories, techniques, and aspirations.

Organizational Humanism and Organizational Development

Even a brief survey of the academic-intellectual vectors affecting public administration should include some note of the complexes of interests and ideas represented by the terms "organizational humanism" and "organizational development."

Organizational humanism—not surprisingly—denotes the continuing movement to humanize—and democratize—organizations. What is sought is more knowledge about and sensitivity toward the human components. The aims are dual: greater organizational productivity or effectiveness; and greater human happiness and increased self-realization. In a sense, organizational humanism is but a continuation of the human relations movement rooted in the Hawthorne studies; and the issue of manipulation, which troubled human relations, remains. But organizational humanism is more subtle and sophisticated, and addresses itself with great seriousness and sympathy to the manipulation issue. The saint of organizational humanism is Abraham Maslow, and the "needs hierarchy," topped by self-actualization, is a paradigm-ideal for much of what takes place. . . .

More than with any other academic discipline, organizational humanism is associated with social psychology. Its most influential writers are associated in the main with business or general administration rather than public administration. But organizational humanism as a complex of ideas and techniques exerts a significant influence on public administration through various channels.

Organization development (OD) refers to conscious attempts to improve organizational output, performance, or health through study of and change in the organization, especially change in organizational members. Broadly construed, organization development consists of a rather wide spectrum of outlooks and techniques. One author lists seven currently popular approaches: (1) direct consultation, (2) survey feedback, (3) process consultation, (4) team building, (5) human relations training, (6) packaged programs, and (7) socio-technical systems. At one end of a spectrum, OD may be mostly concerned with hardware and systems, have no direct concern with interpersonal relations, and not be inclined to concern itself normatively with organization goals. But at the other end of the spectrum, the emphasis is strongly on the human components of the organization; interpersonal relations are of central concern; and there is a normative concern for organizational goals.

In its later and more popular forms, OD tends toward the second end of such a spectrum. It is closely related to organizational humanism, draws upon humanist psychologies as well as social psychology, and takes some variety of the training group as its characteristic methodology.

Organization development has many proponents and practitioners in and out of academia. While the great mass of all organizations remains unaffected by the movement, nevertheless its ideas and techniques now reach into many public as well as private organizations; and it appears at this point in time to be an incoming, not an outgoing, wave.

SOME SUMMARY OBSERVATIONS AND SPECULATIONS: TWO PERSPECTIVES

Patently, if the foregoing account is reasonably perceptive and accurate, what is happening to and in Public Administration hardly presents a clear and simple picture. Here is no discipline with a neat paradigm, no curriculum with agreed boundaries and stable subject matter. Rather, Public Administration appears as a loose cluster of research and teaching interests, focusing primary—but by no means exclusive—attention upon organizations defined—by law and convention—as public, drawing ideas and techniques from a wide range of sources, and interacting with changing, sometimes turbulent, environments of several kinds.

With the object of better understanding the complex of action and interaction, two perspectives are suggested. The first is the familiar one presented by the original, framing, and orienting ideas of Public Administration. The second views Public Administration as matrixed in and interacting with fundamental societal transformations. These are, in fact, related perspectives.

THE FRAMEWORK OF ORIENTING IDEAS

In the latter nineteenth century and early twentieth century, Public Administration was given definition by a cluster of beliefs. In brief, and to simplify, the main ones were as follows: Politics and administration—to decide and to execute—are the two basic aspects of the governmental process. In general, these two should be separated; politics should not meddle in administration. The objective of administration is to execute, with economy and efficiency, decisions reached in the political process. Free of politics, administration should be, and in important ways can be, scientific. The study of administration, approached in the proper scientific way, will yield principles that can be used to guide administration in becoming economical and efficient. In general the science of administration, and the principles it yields, are the same for all governments, democratic or autocratic; the difference between democratic and autocratic governments, that is, pertains chiefly to the way policies are made—decisions are reached—rather than to the way they are executed.

Much of this outlook is expressed in the definition at the opening of the first, and highly influential, textbook [L. D. White's *Introduction to the Study of Public Administration* (New York: Macmillan, 1926)]: "Public administration is the management of men and materials in the accomplishment of the purposes of the state." This definition indicates at least two other important facts. One is a concept of authority: men, no less than materials, are to be managed. The other is a concept of state: early conceptualizing, rooted in the political science of the day—much affected by Continental writings—regarded the state as unquestioned possessor of sovereignty. It should be added, however, that there was a firm belief in republican-democratic ideals. The emphasis on efficiency, science, and authority was not—as it was viewed—at the expense of democracy. On the contrary, the problem was seen as how to fulfill democratic ideals by insuring that decisions reached through the means of democratic politics would be effectively realized, not thwarted.

As is well known, these orienting and motivating ideas were seriously eroded in the mid-century decades. Sometimes they were directly challenged and disproved. Sometimes they were updated and revised. Sometimes the march of events seemed to refute them, or simply made them seem irrelevant. (The "state" all but disappeared in post–World War II political science.)

The result has been an indeterminate, even confusing, situation. The original, orienting beliefs remain, not exactly like the smile of the Cheshire cat after the disappearance of the cat, if for no other reason than the fact that some of the "cat" remains. The original, orienting ideas were an intelligent response to a new historical situation: a large polity trying to combine republican-democratic ideals with the situation created by industrialism, urbanism, science, and so forth; and that situation has not disappeared, it only further evolves. The original ideas thus continue to have a certain force and persuasiveness: It is difficult to be for political meddling and against efficiency and science in public administration. On the other hand, the original ideas are seen by all—or nearly all—as simplistic if not mischievous when addressed to many present realities. The challenge to them on empirical grounds and on moral-ideological grounds has been so thorough and effective, and the historical circumstances to which they were addressed have so altered, that they can no longer serve—it is judged—without serious modification.

A great deal of Public Administration since World War II has been concerned, one way or another, with attempting to work our way forward from the first firm framework of beliefs to a situation in which there might again be general agreement on a set of guiding beliefs. Up to this point no consensus approaching the original one has developed. What has united the Public Administration community has been, rather, the continuing force of the original ideas even in the presence of altered perspectives and problems; plus the fact that public administration *is:* its massive institutions are there, and the problems to which they are addressed are seen as real and crucial, whatever the differences concerning philosophy and methods.

If one views the attainment of a consensus in Public Administration similar to the original one as a desirable state of affairs—a problem to be solved—what conclusion is warranted in view of the above review of the societal-problem context, the external and the internal environments of Public Administration? Again assuming the above review to be reasonably perceptive and accurate, the necessary conclusion would appear to be that no consensus comparable to the old is in view. It seems highly unlikely that there will soon emerge any general agreement on what democracy means for and in administration; on what efficiency "is" and whether, how and to what extent, it is a proper goal or criteria in public administration; on what science dictates—or makes possible—in the study or practice of administration. No single school of philosophy, academic discipline, or type of methodology—or combination of these—would appear likely to persuade Public Administration to march under its banner.

This is not, of course, necessarily an unhappy conclusion. An untidy, swiftly changing world may be better addressed by an enterprise which contains many facets, perspectives, interests, and methodologies; one which is eclectic, experimental, open-ended.

Public Administration and Societal Transformation

A voluminous interpretative and speculative literature concerns our disturbed and anxious time. . . . It seems clear that more than public mood and literary-intellectual vogue are involved, that the rate of societal change is accelerating, and that the breadth and depth of change are increasing.

Accepting an increasing rate of change as a fact, and premising that the changes, cumulatively, will greatly transform historically received institutions, what are the implications for public administration? A large book could only begin to draw these out at any length, but this essay can appropriately end with some suggestions. To some extent this involves only restating what has already been said or implied.

First, public administration will be centrally involved in change and transformation. Administration is "the core of modern government"—in Carl Friedrich's oft-quoted phrase—and government itself is one of the basic societal institutions subject to change. But government is not merely acted upon, it acts; and public administration as its chief instrument is and will be a focal area for change and transformation in society generally. Much of the above review of recent and contemporary developments is, of course, commentary on this theme.

Second, what is patently implied is that public administration will itself be an area of stress, ferment, and accelerated change. Negatively, this means it is unlikely that any clear and generally accepted framework of orienting beliefs, comparable to that of the first generations, will soon evolve. The parameters are too indistinct, the variables too many—and too variable. Positively, this means philosophical, disciplinary, and methodological pluralism: continued proliferation of and competition between ideas and approaches in a continuing attempt to survive, adapt, and control change. What will hold Public Administration together —assuming it remains together as a self-conscious enterprise—will not be agreement on some one kit of tools or some one route into the future. Rather, it will be general agreement on the importance of the institutional area of public administration in making a societal transformation, a general interest in organizational phenomena, a comparatively high degree of "public regardingness" in outlook, and a wish to address—whether scientifically, professionally, "valuationally," or however—problems seen as problems in public administration.

Third, Public Administration, as represented by its curricula, its literature, and its organizations, will continue to change rapidly. For example, the old staples of personnel administration and budgetary-fiscal administration, now hardly recognizable as against their configuration of thirty years ago, will continue to enlarge their boundaries and respond to the many influences playing upon them. Fads, such as PPBS, will come and go—but in their coming they will be important, and even in their going they will have lasting effects. . . .

Fourth, public administration now is, and increasingly will be, concerned with administrative problems much different from those which it confronted even a generation ago. The administration of an organization is scarcely the center of the problem in many areas of activity. The continued increase in the demands—particularly with regard to "people" programs—placed upon public administration, the changes wrought by continued transition from a predominately goods-producing to a predominately service-rendering economy, the accelerating graying of the area between public and private and between governmental levels and jurisdictions: such phenomena have enlarged and transformed the nature of the administrative problem. The task now is the administration of systems—or at least complexes—of organizations, not single organizations; the establishment and monitoring of long, complicated chains as against single, bureaucratic pyramids; the creation and coordination of complex networks of subtle, shifting horizontal and/or diagonal interrelations as against neat, vertical command-obedience structures. In the words of the cliché, "It's a whole new ball game" for crucial areas of public administration.

Finally, the implications for public administration of its intimate involvement in societal transformation are beyond knowing, even beyond imagining. Beliefs and institutions that have given Western civilization its defining characteristics are under attack. The much discussed crisis of authority is real: traditional sources and loci, including family, religion, and law, exert diminishing influence. Ideas and institutions of modern vintage fare little better: industrialism and technology are under attack. Even science is now challenged as simply a "school of consciousness," not *the* approach to reality; only one way, and a limited or even dangerous way, of viewing and acting.

For one acquainted with the rise of the modern state out of feudalism, it sometimes appears that the film is now being run backwards: the sovereign state is being dissolved; its clear vertical authority structure is being replaced by complicated, contractual and informal, horizontal relationships—a new feudalism. Of course, the context is not medieval, and the comparison has but a limited value. It serves to remind us, however, that the modern state system is not necessarily the end of political evolution. In fact, it is now being transformed, and public administration is a part of the transformation process.

II

Bureaucratization and Liberal Democracy

A. The Nature of Bureaucracy

In his classic essay, "Bureaucracy,"[1] Max Weber (1864–1920) contended that the trend toward bureaucratization in the modern world was irreversible. His brief was simple. Bureaucracies are the most efficient mechanisms for mobilizing men and resources yet devised. Therefore, all nations, businesses, political parties, and other human associations that find themselves in competitive situations are driven to organize themselves bureaucratically. Those that do not tend to fall by the wayside.

This contention was striking enough, but Weber's thesis took on greatly added force from the stark simplicity with which he defined bureaucracy. The ideally efficient bureaucracy (which is to say, the ideally efficient mode for cooperative human activity), Weber wrote, is one characterized by a monocratic authority structure, by the elaborate articulation and recording of decision rules to guide subordinate officials in all their activities, by the making of personnel decisions on a strict merit basis, and by the total dependence of each official upon his job for his social status and livelihood.

Weber's image of bureaucracy and his sense of historical inevitability have dominated serious thought about bureaucracy until very recent years. Developing them, many scholars have concluded that liberal democracy is doomed. If history is characterized by the struggle of nations and lesser institutions for survival, they have reasoned, if the organizational form best adapted to this struggle is autocracy, and if the attribute most to be desired in individual bureaucrats is strict obedience, what basis for optimism about the future of democracy can there be?

The essential features of Weber's theory of bureaucracy and their manifestations is modern organizations are the subject of Victor A. Thompson's discussion. Thompson regards rationalism as the guiding spirit of modern

[1] H. H. Gerth and C. Wright Mills, eds., *From Max Weber: Essays in Sociology* (New York: Oxford University Press, 1946), pp. 196–244.

bureaucracy. The pursuit of the truth through reason and empirical verification have been the hallmark of the advance of science and technology based on specialization. Although there are substantial advantages that accrue through the use of bureaucracy—indeed, modern society is inconceivable without it— Thompson cautions that there are problems such as hardened resistance to change and the subordination of the needs of individuals to organizational goals.

In the United States, apprehension over bureaucratic power is fairly extensive. Most of this concern, however, is confined to governmental bureaucracies. In this context, the term "bureaucracy" conjures up the image of interminable procedures characterized by voluminous amounts of "red tape." This popular view of public administration contains many obvious misconceptions of the nature of bureaucracy as well as a lack of understanding of the function of government. Thompson points out that efficiency and inefficiency can be found in both private and public organizations.

In the article which follows Thompson's, Alvin Gouldner maintains that there is no empirical basis for pessimism about the future of democracy in a society heavily dependent on bureaucracy. He argues his case most persuasively, but you will do well to approach it with extreme skepticism. It is characteristically American, after all, to believe that all problems have solutions, that all objectives are compatible (or can be rendered so with a little innovative effort), and that man is master of his fate. These tenets may simply be manifestations of the arrogance of success, however. Other national traditions have been leavened by repeated experiences of failure, and the social analysts produced by them have generally taken very seriously indeed the idea that history has its tragic inevitabilities. Even if one accepts the case for determinism in principle, of course, it by no means follows that the Weberian vision of bureaucracy is valid. No one can say conclusively whether it is or not, but it is difficult to imagine anyone writing profoundly about bureaucracy without having reflected long and hard upon that question. Gouldner's article is an excellent starting point for such an analysis.

From the beginning of Franklin Roosevelt's administration to the end of Dwight Eisenhower's, American liberals were generally united in defending the federal bureaucracy against its critics. For much of this time, a public figure could expect that his rhetoric about the bureaucracy would be widely understood as a symbol of his position on most of the other great issues of the day: the welfare state, countercyclical fiscal and monetary policy, loyalty-security programs, foreign aid, etc. This situation has changed substantially in recent years. By failing to turn back the clock, the Eisenhower administration drastically reduced the range of controversy about big government. As this truth gradually sank in, and as just about all of the liberal agenda compiled in the forties and fifties became law in 1964 and 1965, patterns of political conflict began to shift. Many liberals felt free for the first time to take a hard critical look at the ways in which American big government actually operated. Of these, a significant proportion concluded that they had been too sanguine about the efficacy of existing programs and about the relationship between bureaucracy and individual freedom. Without curtailing their support for government efforts to improve upon the market's allocation of national resources, they began to think more and more seriously about administrative means. As their investigations have proceeded, they have "discovered" that a high proportion of contemporary bureaucratic activity is highly burdensome to the ordinary citizen and quite inessential (or even negatively related) to achievement of the government's basic objectives. Their action program has been to spur experimentation with methods of implementing society's collective goals that involve a bare minimum of bureaucratic regulation, discretion, and red tape. James Q. Wilson's article is a highly provocative example of this latest genre of American thought about bureaucracy.

Bureaucracy

Victor A. Thompson

1. MAX WEBER AND THE THEORY OF BUREAUCRACY

The great German sociologist, Max Weber, was the first to attempt a systematic theory of bureaucratic organization. His views remain important to us not only because of his enormous influence on American social scientists, but also because of the continuing validity of much of his analysis.

Weber pictured an evolution of organizational forms in terms of the kind of authority relations within them.[1] At one extreme is a simple, relatively non-specialized kind of organization in which followers give almost unqualified obedience to a leader endowed with "charisma"—presumed unusual, generally magical powers. Such organization was primitive in the sense that it was based upon belief in magic. Since their prerogatives depended upon their leader's charisma, his immediate staff felt insecure and sought a firmer legitimation of these prerogatives. Their fears came to a head at the time of succession in the leadership. Routinization of methods used to obtain a successor and thus to secure staff prerogatives resulted in the traditionalistic form of organization. Monarchy would be an example.[2]

Weber conceived of the world as becoming progressively rationalized and demystified, with corresponding change in organizational forms. Both charismatic and traditional authority become harder to maintain, and a new, rationalized, legalistic kind of authority and structure emerged. He called this kind of organization "bureaucracy."

Weber believed in a cycle of change from charismatic to traditionalistic and bureaucratic forms of organization against a background of increasing rationalization. Charisma disrupts and is antithetical to the process of rationalization. Charismatic leadership is needed when existing routines cannot cope with growing problems or crises. The charismatic personality emerges and overshadows routine and procedure.[3]

Weber specified a list of criteria for the fully developed bureaucratic form, including technical training of officials, merit appointments, fixed salaries and pensions, assured careers, the separation of organizational rights and duties from the private life of the employee, and a fixed and definite division of work into distinct offices or jobs. He noted that all offices were arranged in a clear hierarchy

From *Modern Organization* by Victor A. Thompson, pp. 10–23. Copyright © 1961 by Victor A. Thompson. Reprinted by permission of Alfred A. Knopf, Inc.

of subordination and superordination, that members of the organization were subject to strict and systematic control and discipline, and that a rationalized set of rules and regulations tied the whole organization together. He said that it should make no difference how these rules and regulations were adopted, whether they were autocratically imposed or adopted by consent. He also said that obedience to commands should be prompt, automatic, unquestioning.

He noted that the principal general social consequences of this organizational form were a tendency toward social leveling, resulting from the attempt to get the broadest possible basis for recruitment of technical competence; a tendency toward plutocracy, resulting from an interest in the greatest possible length of technical training; and the dominance of a spirit of formalistic impersonality, resulting in the minimization of hatred, of affection, and of enthusiasm.

He felt that the superiority over other forms of organization lay in its capacity to command and to utilize technical knowledge; or as we would say, in specialization. "The choice is only that between bureaucracy and dilettantism in the field of administration."[4]

2. SOME CHARACTERISTICS OF MODERN BUREAUCRACY

Although Weber sought to explain bureaucracy by means of a perhaps dubious historical law of increasing rationality, his description of bureaucratic organization seems, in effect, to be consistent with our own. Modern organization has evolved from earlier forms by incorporating advancing specialization. In an earlier period organizations could depend much more on the "line of command." The superior could tell others what to do because he could master the knowledge and techniques necessary to do so intelligently. As science and technology developed, the superior lost to experts the *ability* to command in one field after another, but he retained the *right* as part of his role.

A great structure of specialized competencies has grown up around the chain of command. Organizations have grown in size because they must be able fully to employ the new specialists and the specialized equipment associated with them if the organizations are to meet their competition. As more specialists appear and the organization continues to grow in size, it becomes necessary to group employees into units, and the units into larger units. Some of the larger of these units in government have been called "bureaus," and so the kind of organization resulting from this process has been called "bureaucracy." (These units were called "bureaus" from the French word for writing table or desk.)

The impact of specialization upon modern organization accounts for many of the latter's characteristic features. Because the modern organization evolves in response to modern science and technology, it reflects the guiding spirit of science and technology. This is the spirit of *rationalism*.[5] No longer are traditional or religious standards to be the guardians of knowledge. The quest for truth is to be limited and guided only by reason and empirical verification. Within the modern bureaucratic organization this rationalism expresses itself in constant self-scrutiny. The pragmatic test grows in importance. "How does it promote the organizational goal?" is the question most often heard. Although other evaluative criteria can be observed in modern bureaucracy, the pragmatic test seems to have become institutionalized. By this we mean that people seem to feel that they ought to apply that test to all arrangements.

The growing dominance of the spirit of rationalism in modern bureaucracy simply reflects the growing influence of scientific and technical specialists upon organizational decisions. The bureaucratic organization is the arena where science and technology are applied. With a few rapidly disappearing exceptions, such as medicine, we can say that the application and development of science and technology depend upon bureaucratic organization. As a consequence of the dominance of this spirit of rationalism and the influence of specialists on decisions, modern bureaucratic organization is the most productive arrangement of human effort that man has thus far contrived. Its ability to accomplish objective organizational goals has produced the highest standard of living yet achieved by man, while allowing populations to expand enormously at the same time. Not only has the poverty of the industrial worker been eliminated, but, as we shall see later, the industrial laborer is becoming a technically trained specialist.

Dependence upon highly trained specialists requires *appointment by merit* rather than election or political appointment. It requires *a system of assured careers*; otherwise, the individual would not invest the time needed to acquire specialized skill. It requires that the organization have a definite and reasonably assured division of work into defined jobs or offices. The trained specialist would not usually allow himself to be used as a jack-of-all-trades. In fact, the division of work in organizations for the most part simply follows the existing specializations in society at large.

As Weber said, charismatic forms of organization give way to bureaucracy because the former are inadequate for daily, regularized activity. Charisma functions in new situations and is not compatible with highly defined situations. Charismatic organization is dependent upon the reputed genius of individuals and is, therefore, unstable and precarious. To secure stability, continuity, and predictability of product, the activities of the organization are reduced to procedures or routines. *Routinization of organizational activity* is implicit in the process of specialization and is a characteristic of bureaucracy. Specialization requires a stable environment and a guarantee of continuity of function. Within the organization, the specialist must practice his specialty—a group of related routines. Although managerial ideology still strongly contains the charismatic image, bureaucratic organizations seek to avoid dependence upon individuals by reducing relevant information to classes, and organizational activity to routines which are activated when the appropriate class of information is perceived. It would seem, therefore, that the advance of specialization requires routinization, one of the central characteristics of bureaucratic organization.

Organizations as problem-solving mechanisms depend upon a *factoring of the general goal into subgoals* and these into sub-subgoals, and so on, until concrete routines are reached. These subgoals are allocated to organizational units and become the goals of those units. Individuals in the units are not given the impossible task, therefore, of evaluating their every action in terms of the general goal of the organization, but only in terms of the particular subgoal allocated to their unit. The definition of the situation is sufficiently simplified to bring it within the rational capacity of the human mind. If the factoring is accurate, rationality in terms of each unit will be rationality in terms of the organization as a whole. In this way, bureaucratic organizations achieve rationality far beyond the capacity of any individual.

In addition to accurate factoring, rationality in terms of the whole organization requires that individuals in the subunits accept their assigned subgoal as the end or objective of their activities. It must be the principal given value. Normally, individuals accept the assignment, since they accept the authority of the organization. Various forces, in addition, reinforce this identification with subgoals, particularly the fact that communication within the unit, and between it and the rest of the organization is heavily concerned with the subgoal. Looked at from our point of view, factoring of the organizational goal is simply differentiation of function—namely, specialization. People are to be concerned with a certain area of activities, not with all activities. Thus, specialization results in strong attachment to subgoals.

From a point of view outside a particular unit, the unit's goal is seen not as a goal, but as a means to a larger goal. From this external vantage point, therefore, the members of a unit seem to be attached to means rather than ends. One of the characteristics of bureaucratic organization based on specialization, consequently, in an *apparent inversion of ends and means*. For example, people outside a budget office frequently accuse budget officers of believing the organization exists for the purpose of operating budget procedures. From the point of view of a client interested in the general organizational goal, members of all subunits appear to have inverted means into ends. Such "inversion" may be a problem of factoring, of dividing up the work; and any necessary corrections may not be the direction of reducing subgoal identification but, rather, of reorganization.

A *formalistic impersonality* is a readily discernible characteristic of modern organization. In interpersonal relationships, total involvement probably never occurs. Each person is concerned with somewhat less than all of the actual or potential needs of the other. In specialist relationships, involvement is limited to the needs for which the specialized function is relevant. The relationship is partial, and functional; it is "secondary" rather than "primary." The specialist performs his function for many, and so he must limit his participation in the relationship to the area of his specialty. The resulting "impersonal" relationship need not be cold or painful. When both sides recognize their mutual interdependence—the client's dependence on the specialist for the fulfillment of some need, and the specialist's dependence on the client for the opportunity to work at his calling— the relationship is not necessarily without human warmth and mutual appreciation. Pleasant though impersonal relationships of mutual interdependence abound in everyday life—the motorist and the mechanic, the doctor and the patient, the householder and the postman. Impersonality is inevitably associated with bureaucratic organization, resting as it does on specialization.

An organization based on specialization must allow specialists to practice their specialties, to carry out the routines of which their specialties are composed. Specialists do not improvise for each unique event. Improvisation is charismatic, "dilettantish." Although there are unique aspects to all events, it is only to the repeated aspects that the routines of the specialty can be applied. Consequently, specialization requires that the raw data of reality be organized into classes or categories that often recur. Furthermore, enormous amounts of information needed in a specialized world can be summarized and communicated quickly by *categorization of data*, thereby greatly facilitating the solution of problems. Therefore, although an individual is to himself a total, complete person, in some ways unique, to the specialist he is a carrier of a class of data relevant to the practice of the specialty in question. He is a speeder, an income-tax evader, a disciplinary case, an applicant for a job, a coronary, etc. The reality of the specialist is created by his classes and categories. We are all specialists in some sense, so that the realities we perceive vary from person to person. In fact, language itself is a system of categories by which we organize the raw sensory data of experience. There would appear to be no basis, therefore, for criticizing bureaucratic organizations merely because they interpret reality through specialist categories and classes. What may be important, however, is to ensure through organization that differing conceptions of reality have ample opportunity to be heard and are not simply buried under an official reality.

Bureaucratic *classification of persons* for differential treatment is reinforced by the confusion in our culture between the norm of "evenhanded" justice, on the one hand, and on the other, the ideal conception of justice as giving to each man his due. People want equality before the law in general, but individualized treatment in particular. The grouping of individuals into classes is an attempt to come closer to ideal justice without losing equality before the law. Clientele behavior enforces classification. If one individual is treated out of class, many persons who feel similarly situated will insist on equal treatment. If they are denied, it is called "discrimination." This reaction shows that these classes do exist subjectively in the particular society. Frequently this process results in the creation of new classes. Elaboration of the system of client classification approaches the ideal of individual justice. Whether one's function is regulation or service, he disregards this social process of classification at his peril.

A final aspect of bureaucratic organizations, and one which often comes under criticism, is their *seeming slowness to act or to change*. In discussing this topic we must concede at the outset that bureaucratic organizations, in the face of emergencies, do often act with tremendous speed. A serious note is received from Russia, let us say, in the morning, and a reply with warlike implications is dispatched in the afternoon. A rush order is received, and all regular procedures are tacitly suspended, protocol is forgotten, and a busy, happy, problem-solving atmosphere pervades the organization until the order is out. Later in this book we shall consider this aspect of bureaucratic behavior. Here we shall point out merely that crisis situations, since they are by definition ones for which routines are not available, evoke a nonroutinized approach—a charismatic rather than a bureaucratic approach.

Under more normal conditions, organizations based upon specialization and its routines cannot be expected to react immediately to each stimulus. Great amounts of information must be accumulated if knowledge is to be substituted for impulse, thus assuring greater effectiveness of action and greater chance of success. Since action involves many interdependent specialists, co-ordination time must be expended. In order that all necessary parts of the organization act in co-ordinated fashion, clearances must be obtained, meetings held, many copies of proposals and information memoranda prepared and properly routed. In short, if the organization could act with the speed of an individual, the organization would not be needed.

With regard to *resistance to change*, it should be noted that this phenomenon is not uniquely related to bureaucratic organizations but is a characteristic of all institutions—hence the term "cultural lag." In the case of the bureaucratic organization, however, there is special need for caution with regard to change. As we have said before, specialization requires some guarantee of stability. Specialties must not soon go out of date, or people would not invest the time needed to acquire them.

Furthermore, the members of an organization become socially specialized. They become specialized in working with one another. It takes time to convert a number of abstract, related positions into a flesh-and-blood working organization. Consequently, any suggestion for change must be measured against its effect on the co-operative system as a whole. Bureaucratic organizations must plan and control changes. Although the persons urging change may feel that the resistances they encounter represent "bureaucratic" stubbornness, the desirability of any particular change, all things considered, is usually an open question.

Internally, the bureaucratic organization is a complex structure of technical interdependence superimposed upon a strict hierarchy of authority. The entire structure is characterized by a *preoccupation with the monistic ideal*. The hierarchical institution is monocratic. It is a system of superior and subordinate role-relationships in which the superior is the *only* source of legitimate influence upon the subordinate. Everyone in the organization finds himself in such a relationship. Since this was the original organizational relationship, it has dominated organizational theory and practice and still does so. This exclusive emphasis on hierarchy has produced our prevailing organizational theory and informed management practice. We shall refer to this theory as the monistic or monocratic conception of organization. Although conditions are undoubtedly changing, it is our prevailing organizational ideal. It is well illustrated by the following quotations from the first Hoover Commission report:

> The line of command and supervision from the President down through his department heads to every employee, and the line of responsibility from each employee . . . up to the President has been weakened, or actually broken, in many places and in many ways. . . . On some occasions the responsibility of an official to his superior is obscured by laws which require him, before acting, to clear his proposals with others. This breaks the line of responsibility. . . .
>
> Under the President, the heads of departments must hold full responsibility for the conduct of their departments. There must be a clear line of authority reaching down through every step of the organization and no subordinate should have authority independent from that of his superior.[6]

Under the influence of the primitive monistic ideal, modern organizations are modeled more on the parent-child relationship than on the adult relationships of specialist equals and colleagues. Attempts to maintain the legitimacy of the ideal lead to a great deal of hypocrisy and pretense and to the creation of myths, such as "the ignorance of the masses," "the indispensability of leadership," and "the magical power of fear."[7] Since a monocratic institution cannot admit the legitimacy of conflicts, the legitimacy of divergent goals and interests, much effort is spent securing the appearance of consensus and agreement—securing a "smooth-running organization." The modern organization wants converts as much as it wants workers. It is concerned with the thoughts of its members as well as their actions, and with the thoughts of its public about the thoughts and actions of its members. Consequently, it is concerned with its members' total lives, with what they think and do away from work as well as at work.

Preoccupation with hierarchy governs the distribution of rewards by modern organizations. Ranks of deference correspond to ranks of authority, and deference is manifested by the bestowal of good things. Success within our society means, for the most part, progression up an organizational hierarchy. Modern organizations, consequently, face a growing problem of rewarding specialists. To be socially regarded as successful, specialists must give up their technical fields and enter a hierarchy. Many do, leaving us with growing shortages of many kinds of technically trained people. A few entrepreneural specialists, such as medical doctors, have been able to avoid this dilemma, but the advance of specialization will force them all into organizations eventually—in the case of medical doctors because specialized equipment will be too costly for an individual to own, and because the health of the patient will require the co-ordinated services of many specialists.

3. PUBLIC VERSUS PRIVATE BUREAUCRACY

Whether the organization be public or private, the configurations of bureaucracy are sufficiently the same as to enable us to discuss them together in our analysis. There will still be some who object to this point of view. They will point to the alleged "inefficiency" of public organizations, and they will attribute different motivations to public and private officials.

The growth in size and capital requirements of modern industry has resulted in the separation of ownership and management. The people who run modern business corporations are professional salaried managers. Since their remuneration is not measured directly by the earnings of the corporations, it can hardly be said that their motivation is profit. With the growth in size of enterprises and the professionalization of management go bureaucratic patterns of organization and management, and bureaucratic motivations. Prestige, status, personal position, reduction of uncertainty, maintenance of the system of co-operation and the equilibrium of the organization—all these are important motives in the large corporation. "Satisficing" rather than maximizing criteria are usually applied, and the resulting slack or surplus in the system allows it to weather storms. This contributes to stability, if not to profits. Indeed, the motivations and behavior of public and private bureaucrats appear to be more and more the same.

The attempt to differentiate public from private bureaucracies may be prompted by ideological considerations. The blanket insistence that public bureaucracy is inefficient may help to stem the advance of expanding government, and it may give some show of legitimacy to insecure business leaders who no longer enjoy the charismatic legitimations of their owner-operator predecessors. The insistence that men are motivated to efficiency only by profit flies in the face of common sense and can no longer be used to differentiate and disparage the public bureaucrat. Finally, the disparagement of public bureaucracy may express the resentment of a recently alienated right wing in our society.

NOTES

1. Max Weber: *The Theory of Social and Economic Organization*, trans. A. M. Henderson and Talcott Parsons, ed. Talcott Parsons (New York: Oxford University Press, Inc.; 1947).
2. See Alvin W. Gouldner: *Studies in Leadership: Leadership and Democratic Action* (New York: Harper & Brothers; 1950), p. 645.
3. *Ibid.*
4. *Ibid.*, p. 336.
5. We are using the term "rationalism" and its various derivatives according to common usage—not in its philosophically technical sense as an antiempirical theory of knowledge.
6. Commission on Organization of the Executive Branch of the Government: *General Management of the Executive Branch* (Washington, D.C.: Government Printing Office; 1949), pp. 3–4, 34.
7. Peter Blau: *The Dynamics of Bureaucracy* (Chicago: University of Chicago Press; 1955), p. 219.

Metaphysical Pathos
and the Theory of Bureaucracy

Alvin W. Gouldner

The conduct of a polemic focusses attention on the differences between two points of view to the neglect of their continuity and convergences. No modern polemic better exemplifies this than the controversy between the proponents of capitalism and of socialism. Each tends to define itself as the antithesis of the other; even the uncommitted bystander, rare though he be, is likely to think of the two as if they were utterly alien systems.

There have always been some, however, who have taken exception to this sharp contrast between socialism and capitalism and who have insisted that there are significant similarities between the two. One of these, the French sociologist Emile Durkheim, maintained that socialism like capitalism involved an overbearing preoccupation with economic interests. In both socialist and capitalist societies, Durkheim argued, economic concerns were at the center of attention. In Durkheim's view, neither capitalism nor socialism deemed it necessary to bridle materialistic ends; neither society subordinated pecuniary interests to some higher, governing, moral norms. Therefore, "from Durkheim's point of view," writes Talcott Parsons, "socialism and laissez-faire individualism are of the same piece."[1]

Bertrand Russell came to similar conclusions on the basis of a trip to the then newly-established Soviet Republic: ". . . the practical difference between socialism and capitalism is not so great as politicians on both sides suppose. Certain features will appear in the early stages of industrialism under either system; and under either system certain other features will appear in its later stages."[2]

Without doubt, though, the most sophisticated formulation of this view was that conceived by the German sociologist, Max Weber. To Weber, the distinguishing characteristic of modern capitalism was the "rational organization of free labor." The pursuit of private gain, noted Weber, was well known in many earlier

From the *American Political Science Review*, Vol. 49 (June 1955), pp. 496–507. Reprinted by permission of the author and publisher.

societies; what distinguishes present-day capitalism, he held, is the peculiar organization of the production unit, an organization that is essentially bureaucratic. This conception of capitalism, writes Parsons, "has one important concrete result; in contradistinction to Marx and most 'liberal' theories, it strongly minimizes the differences between capitalism and socialism, emphasizing rather their continuity. Not only would socialistic organization leave the central fact of bureaucracy untouched, it would greatly accentuate its importance."[3]

While Marx had dwelt largely on the interrelations *among* production units, that is, their market ties, Weber focussed on the social relations *within* the industrial unit. If social relations inside of socialist and capitalist factories are fundamentally alike, in that they are both bureaucratic, then, asked Weber, does a socialist revolution yield very much of an improvement for the capitalist proletarian?

If Marx argued that the workers of the world had nothing to *lose* by revolting, Weber contended that they really had nothing to *gain*. "For the time being," he declared, "the dictatorship of the official and not that of the workers is on the march." Capitalism and socialism are thus placed under the same conceptual umbrella—bureaucracy—with the important practical result that the problem of choosing between them loses much of its point.

It is for this reason that the discussions of bureaucratic organization which are heir to the Weberian analysis must be understood as being, in part, a displacement of the controversy over socialism. Weber made it clear that questions of economic choice could no longer be treated in isolation from questions of administration. From Weber's time forward, administrative and economic choices were seen to be but two facets of the same hard problem. This has been recognized even by socialists, at least when they have been unencumbered by Communist party orthodoxy. For example, Oskar Lange once remarked, with a frankness that we hope he will never be compelled to regret, ". . . the real danger of socialism is that of bureaucratic organization of economic life. . . ."[4]

It is sometimes assumed today that the Weberian outlook is at bottom anti-socialist. In effect, the argument runs, Weber's viewpoint devitalizes the mythlike appeal of socialism, draining off its ability to muster immense enthusiasms. Weber's theses are therefore held to be an "ideology" serviceable for the survival of capitalism, while Weber himself is characterized as the "Marx of the bourgeoisie."

Now all this may be true, but it is only a partial truth; for, in actuality, Weber's theories cut two ways, not one. If it is correct that his theory of bureaucracy saps the fervor of the socialist offensive, it also undermines the stamina of the capitalist bastions. If socialism and capitalism are similar in being bureaucratic, then not only is there little *profit* in substituting one for the other, but there is also little *loss*.

Considered only from the standpoint of its political consequences then, the Weberian outlook is not anti-socialist alone, nor anti-capitalist alone, it is both. In the final analysis its political slogan becomes "a plague on both your houses." If Weber is to be regarded as an "ideologist," he is an ideologist not of counter-revolution but of quiescence and neutralism. For many intellectuals who have erected a theory of group organization on Weberian foundations, the world has been emptied of choice, leaving them disoriented and despairing.

That gifted historian of ideas, Arthur O. Lovejoy, astutely observed that every theory is associated with, or generates, a set of sentiments which those subscribing to the theory could only dimly sense. Lovejoy called this the "metaphysical pathos" of ideas, a pathos which is "exemplified in any description of the nature of things, any characterization of the world to which one belongs, in terms which, like the words of a poem, evoke through their associations and through a sort of empathy which they engender, a congenial mood or tone of feelings."[5]

As a result, a commitment to a theory often occurs by a process other than the one which its proponents believe and it is usually more consequential than they realize. A commitment to a theory may be made because the theory is congruent with the mood or deep-lying sentiments of its adherents, rather than merely because it has been cerebrally inspected and found valid. This is as true for the rigorous prose of social science as it is for the more lucid metaphor of creative literature, for each has its own silent appeal and its own metaphysical pathos.

Furthermore, those who have committed themselves to a theory always get more than they have bargained for. We do not make a commercial contract with a theory in which we agree to accept only the consignment of intellectual goods which has been expressly ordered; usually we take also the metaphysical pathos in which the theory comes packaged. In the end, the theory reinforces or induces in the adherent a subtle alteration in the structure of sentiments through which he views the world.

So too is it with the theory of organization. Paradoxically enough, some of the very theories which promise to make man's own work more intelligible to himself and more amenable to his intelligence are infused with an intangible metaphysical pathos which insinuates, in the very midst of new discoveries, that all is lost. For the metaphysical pathos of much of the modern theory of group organization is that of pessimism and fatalism.

I. EXPLANATIONS OF BUREAUCRACY

Nowhere does the fatalism of the theory of organization become more articulate than in its efforts to account for the development of bureaucratic behavior. One of the less challenging explanations, for example, premises a supposedly invariant human nature. Thus in an otherwise illuminating analysis, one political scientist remarks: "Civil servants are ordinary mortals; they have the defects and weaknesses typical of human nature. Each loves, as Shakespeare said, 'his brief moment of authority.' "

This, however, is difficult to reconcile with recurrent complaints, from civic leaders or business managers, that it is often hard to persuade people either to run for political office or to accept positions as foremen. Apparently there are some people who do not hanker after their brief moment of authority.

In any event, it does not seem possible to account for bureaucracy in any of its forms as an outgrowth of "human nature." This explanation cannot cope with the rudimentary fact that in some times and in some places there is much bureaucracy, but in other times and places there is little. Leaving aside the question of the validity of the argument, its practical results are again all too evident. For if bureaucracy is rooted in human nature then all hope for a remedy must be abandoned.

Much more serious as goads to pessimism are theories explaining bureaucracy as the end-product of increased size and complexity in organizations. This is by far the most popular of the interpretations. Marshall Dimock and Howard Hyde, for example, in their report to the Temporary National Economic Committee (TNEC), state: "The broadest structural cause of bureaucracy, whether in business or in government, is the tremendous size of the organization. Thus with capital or appropriations measured in hundreds of millions and in billions of dollars and personnel in tens and hundreds of thousands, it is difficult to avoid the obtrusion of the objectionable features of bureaucracy."[6]

While suggesting varied causes for the development of bureaucracy, Max Weber also interpreted it as a consequence of large size. For example, in discussing the ubiquity of bureaucratic forms Weber adds: "The same [bureaucratic] phenomena are found in the large-scale capitalistic enterprise; and the larger it is, the greater their role." He underscores the role of size by emphasizing that "only by reversion in every field—political, religious, economic, etc.—to small-scale organization would it be possible to escape its influence."[7] Despite his consideration of other possible sources of bureaucracy, these comments suggest that Weber regarded organizational size as the controlling factor in the development of bureaucracy.[8]

Weber's emphasis on size as the crucial determinant of bureaucratic development is unsatisfactory for several reasons. First, there are historic examples of human efforts carried out on an enormous scale which were not bureaucratic in any serious sense of the term. The building of the Egyptian pyramids is an obvious example. Second, Weber never considers the possibility that it is not "large size" as such that disposes to bureaucracy; large size may be important only because it generates other social forces which, in their turn, generate bureaucratic patterns.

Of course, in every analysis there are always intervening variables—the unknown "x"—which stand between any cause and effect. Scientific progress depends, in part, on moving away from the gross causes and coming closer to those which are more invariably connected with the object of interest. The point is that when a social scientist accepts "size" as an explanatory factor, instead of going on to ask what there is *about size* that makes for bureaucracy, he is making an analytic *decision*. It is not a formulation unavoidably dictated by the nature of the data itself.

Significantly, though, it is a decision that leads once again to bleak pessimism. For to inform members of our society that the only way out of the bureaucratic impasse is to return to the historical past and to trade in large for small-scale organizations is, in effect, to announce the practical impossibility of coping with bureaucracy. Moreover, many people in our society believe that "bigness" symbolizes progress; to tell them that it also creates bureaucracy is to place them on the horns of a dilemma which gores no matter which way they turn. In such a position the most painless response is inaction.

Underlying this conception of the matter there is a Hegelian dialectic in which "good" and "bad" are viewed as inseparably connected opposites; bureaucracy, "the bad thing," is represented as the inescapable price that has to be paid for the good things, the efficiency and abundance of modern life. One social scientist clearly puts it this way: "Assembly line techniques offer marked advantages over those of custom craftsmanship. They also have their price. They entail the imposition of an order of progression, the fixing of a rate or rhythm of operation, and the discipline of a regular routine. Set order, fixed pace, and adherence to routine—these are the very stuff of which red tape is made. Yet they are of the essence of system, too." However true or false, there can be little doubt that this is an outlook which is convenient and comfortable for bureaucrats—if not for many others.

II. THE STRUCTURAL-FUNCTIONALISTS

The fuller ramifications of this approach to bureaucracy can best be explained by turning to the analyses of industrial organization made by some of the "structural-functionalists." This is a comparatively new and vigorous school of American sociologists, which has grown directly out of the theories of Durkheim, Weber, and others, and whose most elaborate expression is to be found in the work of Talcott Parsons.

Parsons' recent analyses of industrial bureaucracy are of sufficient importance to be quoted in full. "Though with many individual exceptions [which he does not examine], *technological advance* almost always leads to increasingly *elaborate division of labor* and the concomitant requirement of increasingly elaborate organization." He continues:

> The fundamental reason for this is, of course, that with elaborate differentiation of functions the need for *minute coordination* of the different functions develops at the same time. . . . There must be a *complex organization of supervision* to make quite sure that exactly the right thing is done. . . . Feeding the various parts into the process, in such a way that a modern assembly line can operate smoothly, requires very *complex organization* to see that they are available in just the right quantities at the right times and places. . . . One of the most important phases of this process of change is concerned with the necessity for *formalization* when certain points of complexity are reached. . . .
>
> *Smaller* and simpler organizations are typically managed with a high degree of particularism (i.e., personal consideration) in the relations of persons in authority to their own subordinates. But when the "distance" between points of decision and of operation increases, and the number of operating units affected by decisions with it, uniformity and coordination can be attained *only* by a high degree of formalization. . . .[9]

Surprisingly enough, this is an atavistic recurrence of technological determinism in which characteristic bureaucratic traits—such as an elaborate division of labor, complex organization, and formalization—are held to stem directly from technological advance. This is a form of *technological* determinism because bureaucracy is seen as the result of technological change, without inquiring into the motives and meanings which these changes have for the people involved, and without wondering whether technological change would have a different impact on the formal organization of a group that had a high motivation to produce and therefore did not require close supervision. This is a form of technological *determinism,* because no alternative solutions are appraised or deemed possible and coordination is seen as attainable *"only* by a high degree of formalization. . . ."

Here once again we are invited to draw the conclusion that those who want modern technology must be prepared to pay for it with a minute and even stultifying division of labor.

All this, though, is a theoretical tapestry devoid of even the plainest empirical trimmings. Even on logical grounds, however, it is tenuous indeed. For it is evident that organizational patterns, such as a high division of labor, are found in spheres where modern technology has made comparatively little headway. This, in fact, is a point that Weber was at pains to insist upon. And if, as he maintained, bureaucratic forms are also found in charitable, political, or religious organizations—and not solely in industry—then they certainly cannot be explained as a consequence of modern machine technology.

Beyond these logical considerations, there are also some *empirical* grounds for questioning the adequacy of Parsons' analysis. Peter Drucker, for example, became extremely doubtful about the necessity of a minute division of labor while observing large-scale American industry during World War II. (This is crucial for Parsons' argument, because he holds that it is through increased specialization that technology evokes the other elements of bureaucratic organization.) Drucker comments that "we have learned that it is neither necessary nor always efficient to organize all mass production in such a manner as to have the majority of workers confine themselves to doing one and only one of the elementary manipulations. . . . It was impossible [because of wartime shortages of skilled labor] to 'lay out' the job in the usual assembly-line fashion in which one unskilled operation done by one unskilled man is followed by the next unskilled man. The operation was broken down into its unskilled components like any assembly-line job. *But then the unskilled components were put together again with the result that an unskilled worker actually performed the job of a highly skilled mechanic*—and did it as reliably and efficiently as had been done by skilled men."[10]

In short, lower degrees of specialization than those normally found in large-scale industry are not necessarily forbidden by modern technology. Drucker's observations must, at the very least, raise the question as to how much of the minute division of labor is attributable to technological causes. Parsons, though, gives no consideration to other factors contributing to an extreme division of labor. However, Carl Dreyfuss, a German industrial sociologist, has advanced an array of keen observations and hypotheses which meet this question directly. He writes: "the artificial complication of the rank order . . . permits numerous employees to feel that they hold high positions and are to a certain extent independent." Moreover, he notes that a complicated division of labor is "with its unwarranted differentiations, telescoped positions, and ramifications, diametrically opposed to efforts of rationalization." In other words, Dreyfuss suggests that much of the complex division of labor today is not to be explained by technological requirements, but rather in terms of the prestige satisfactions, the "psychic income," that it presumably provides workers.

In Dreyfuss' view, the "minute division of labor" also stems from management's needs to *control* workers and to make themselves independent of any specific individual or group of workers. A high division of labor, said Dreyfuss, means that "individual workers and employees can be exchanged and replaced at any time." Through its use, "dependence of the employee upon the employer is greatly increased. It is much more difficult for today's employee, trained in only one particular function, to find reemployment than it was for his predecessor, a many-sided, well-instructed business man, able and fitted to fill a variety of positions."[11]

A similar view is advanced in the more recent studies of industrial organization in Yankee City, which were made by W. L. Warner and J. O. Low. "While machine processes were adopted by shoe factories primarily to reduce costs and to speed the processing, the machine has other great advantages over the human worker from the managerial point of view," comment Warner and Low.

> Control problems are simplified . . . on two counts through mechanization: (1) machines are easier to control than human beings, and (2) mechanization tends to disrupt the social solidarity of the workers, who thereby become easier to control than they would if they were able to maintain close social relations during working hours . . . these factors tend to increase the subordination of the individual workers to management; from the management's viewpoint they are valuable means of social control over workers. . . . The routinization of jobs also simplifies control of workers in another way. The individual operative today does not have the feeling of security that the oldtime craftsman derived from his special technical abilities. In most cases, today's operative is aware that only a comparatively brief training period protects him in his job from a large number of untrained individuals. The members of the supervisory hierarchy are also well aware of this fact. The psychological effect of this result of the division of labor is to intensify the subordinate position of the individual operative and to make him submit the more readily to the limitations on his behavior required by the supervisory group.[12]

It is unnecessary for our purpose here to resolve this disparity between Warner and Dreyfuss, on the one hand, and Parsons, on the other. What may be suggested, however, is that there is considerable reason for holding Parsons' position to be both logically and empirically inadequate and to recognize that it has, without compelling scientific warrant, accommodated itself to the metaphysical pathos of organizational theory, which sees no escape from bureaucracy.

III. THE TRADITION OF MICHELS

There is another offshoot among the structural-functionalists which is distinguished by its concern for the problems bequeathed by Robert Michels and, as such, it is even more morosely pessimistic than others in the school. Michels, it will be remembered, focussed his empirical studies on the Social Democratic parties of pre-World War I Europe. He chose these, quite deliberately, because he wanted to see whether groups which stood for greater freedom and democracy, and were hostile to authoritarianism, were not themselves afflicted by the very organizational deformity to which they were opposed.

Michel's conclusions were, of course, formulated in his "iron law of oligarchy," in which he maintained that always and everywhere a "system of leadership is incompatible with the most essential postulates of democracy." Oligarchy, said Michels, "derives from the tactical and technical necessities which result from the consolidation of every disciplined political aggregate. . . . It is the outcome of organic necessity, and consequently affects every organization, be it socialist or even anarchist."

In concluding his study, Michels remarks with a flourish of defensive pathos, ". . . it seemed necessary to lay considerable stress upon the pessimist aspect of democracy which is forced upon us by historical study. . . ." "The democratic currents of history resemble successive waves. They break ever on the same shoals. . . . It is probable that this cruel game will continue without end."[13]

Focussing, as Michels did, on an apparently democratic group, Philip Selznick examined the TVA, which many Americans had long believed to be an advanced expression of democratic values. Like Michels, Selznick assumes that "wherever there is organization, whether formally democratic or not, there is a split between the leader and the led, between the agent and the initiator. The phenomenon of abdication to bureaucratic directives in corporations, in trade unions, in parties, and in cooperatives is so widespread that it indicates a fundamental weakness of democracy."

Selznick's study concludes that the TVA's emphasis on "decentralization" is to be best understood as a result of that agency's needs to adapt to suspicious local communities and to survive in competition with older governmental agencies based in Washington. "Decentralization" is viewed as a "halo that becomes especially useful in countries which prize the symbols of democracy." In its turn, the TVA's emphasis on "participation" is explained as a catchword, satisfying the agency's needs to transform "an unorganized citizenry into a reliable instrument for the achievement of administrative goals. . . ."

Selznick, like Michels, is impressed with the similarity in the organizational devices employed by different groups, whether they are democratic or authoritarian in ideology. He asserts ". . . there seems to be a continuum between the voluntary associations set up by the democratic (mass) state—such as committees of farmers to boost or control agricultural production—and the citizens' associations of the totalitarian (mass) state. Indeed the devices of corporatism emerge as relatively effective responses to the need to deal with the mass, and in time of war the administrative techniques of avowedly democratic countries and avowedly totalitarian countries tend to converge."

In Selznick's analysis human action involves a commitment to two sets of interests: first to the *goals* intended, and second to the organizational *instruments* through which these goals are pursued. These tools are, however, recalcitrant; they generate "needs" which cannot be neglected. Hence if men persist in their ends, they are forced to satisfy the needs of their organizational instruments. They are, therefore, as much committed to their tools as to their ends, and "these commitments may lead to unanticipated consequences resulting in a deflection of original ends."

For these reasons, organizational behavior must be interpreted not so much in terms of the *ends* that administrators deliberately seek, as in terms of the organizational "needs" which their pursuit engenders. "The needs in question are organizational, not individual, and include: the security of the organization as a whole in relation to social forces in its environment; the stability of the lines of authority and communication; the stability of informal relations within the organization; the continuity of policy and of the sources of its determination; a homogeneity of outlook with respect to the means and role of the organization."

"In general," writes Selznick, "we have been concerned to formulate some of the underlying tendencies which are likely to inhibit the democratic process. Like all conservative or pessimistic criticism, such a statement of inherent problems seems to cast doubt upon the possibility of complete democratic achievement. It does cast such a doubt. The alternative, however, is the transformation of democracy into a utopian notion which, unaware of its internal dangers, is unarmed to meet them." This, however, is an argument that rests upon assumptions which are not transparently self-evident and are acceptable without dispute only by those who are susceptible to its metaphysical pathos. Despite demagogic appeals to democratic symbols, there seem to be few places in either the Eastern or Western worlds in which there is a real and present danger of the "transformation of democracy into a utopian notion." Surely this is not to be expected among the class-conscious working classes of Europe, the laborite masses of England, the untutored peasants of China, or among the confused and often apathetic American electorate to whom politics is something of a dirty game, to be periodically enlivened with scandals and investigations. And if this appraisal is correct, then just who is there to be "armed" with this knowledge of the internal dangers of democracy?

For some reason Selznick has chosen—and this was not forced upon him by the data—to focus on the things which harry and impede democratic aspirations, rather than on those which strengthen and energize it. It is for this reason perhaps that he is led to reiterate Michel's apologia: "Attention being focussed on the structural conditions which influence behavior, we are directed to emphasize constraints, the limitation of alternatives imposed by the system upon its participants. This will tend to give pessimistic overtones to the analysis, since such factors as good will and intelligence will be de-emphasized."[14]

Selznick chose to focus on those social constraints that *thwart* democratic aspirations, but neglected to consider the constraints that enable them to be *realized*, and that foster and encourage "good will" and "intelligence." Are these, however, random occurrences, mere historic butterflies which flit through events with only ephemeral beauty? Or are they, as much as anything else, often the unanticipated products of our "commitments"? Why is it that "unanticipated consequences" are always tacitly assumed to be destructive of democratic values and "bad"; why can't they sometimes be "good"? Are there no constraints which *force* men to adhere valorously to their democratic beliefs, which *compel* them to be intelligent rather than blind, which leave them *no choice* but to be men of good will rather than predators? The neglect of these possibilities suggests the presence of a distorting pathos.

It is the pathos of pessimism, rather than the compulsions of rigorous analysis, that lead to the assumption that organizational constraints have stacked the deck against democracy. For on the face of it there is every reason to assume that "the underlying tendencies which are likely to inhibit the democratic process" are just as likely to impair authoritarian rule. It is only in the light of such a pessimistic pathos that the defeat of democratic values can be assumed to be probable, while their victory is seen as a slender thing, delicately constituted and precariously balanced.

When, for example, Michels spoke of the "iron law of oligarchy," he attended solely to the ways in which organizational needs inhibit democratic possibilities. But the very same evidence to which he called attention could enable us to formulate the very opposite theorem—the "iron law of democracy." Even as Michels himself saw, if oligarchical waves repeatedly wash away the bridges of democracy, this eternal recurrence can happen only because men doggedly rebuild them after each inundation. Michels chose to dwell on only one aspect of this process, neglecting to consider this other side. There cannot be an iron law of oligarchy, however, unless there is an iron law of democracy.

Much the same may be said for Selznick. He posits certain organizational needs: a need for the *security* of the organization, for *stable* lines of authority and communication, for *stable* informal relationships. But for each of the organizational needs which Selznick postulates, a set of contrary needs can also be posited, and the satisfaction of these would seem to be just as necessary for the survival of an organization. If, as Selznick says, an organization must have security in its environment, then certainly Toynbee's observations that too much security can be stultifying and corrosive is at least as well taken. To Selznick's security need, a Toynbee might counterpose a need for a moderate *challenge* or *threat*.

A similar analysis might also be made of Selznick's postulated need for homogeneity of outlook concerning the means and role of the organization. For unless there is some *heterogeneity* of outlook, then where is an organization to find the tools and flexibility to cope with changes in its environment? Underlying Selznick's need for homogeneity in outlook, is there not another "need," *a need that consent of the governed be given—at least in some measure—to their governors?* Indeed, this would seem to be at the very core of Selznick's empirical analysis, though it is obscured in his high-level theoretical statement of the needs of organizations. And if all organizations must adjust to such a need for consent, is there not built into the very marrow of organization a large element of what we mean by democracy? This would appear to be an organizational constraint that makes oligarchies, and all separation of leaders from those led, no less inherently unstable than democratic organization.[15]

These contrary needs are just as real and just as consequential for organizational behavior as those proposed by Selznick. But they point in a different direction. They are oriented to problems of change, of growth, of challenging contingencies, of provoking and unsettling encounters. Selznick's analysis seems almost to imply that survival is possible only in an icy stasis, in which "security," "continuity," and "stability" are the key terms. If anything, the opposite seems more likely to be true, and organizational survival is impossible in such a state.

Wrapping themselves in the shrouds of nineteenth-century political economy, some social scientists appear to be bent on resurrecting a dismal science. For the iron law of wages, which maintained that workers could never improve their material standards of life, some sociologists have substituted the iron law of oligarchy, which declares that men cannot improve their political standards of life. Woven to a great extent out of theoretical whole cloth, much of the discussion of bureaucracy and of organizational needs seems to have provided a screen onto which some intellectuals have projected their own despair and pessimism, reinforcing the despair of others.

Perhaps the situation can be illuminated with an analogy. For many years now, infantile paralysis has killed and maimed scores of people. For many years also doctors, biologists, and chemists have been searching for the causes and cure of this disease. Consider the public reaction if, instead of reporting on their newest vaccines, these scientists had issued the following announcement: "We have not reached any conclusions concerning the causes of the disease, nor has our research investigated defenses against it. The public seems to have perfectionist aspirations of flawless health, they have 'utopian' illusions concerning the possibilities of immortality and it is this—not the disease—that is the danger against which the public needs to be armed. We must remember that the human animal is not immortal and that for definite reasons his lifespan is finite." It is likely, of course, that such scientists would be castigated for having usurped the prerogatives and functions of clergymen.

This, however, seems to parallel the way in which some social scientists have approached the study of organizational pathology. Instead of telling men how bureaucracy might be mitigated, they insist that it is inevitable. Instead of explaining how democratic patterns may, to some extent, be fortified and extended, they warn us that democracy cannot be perfect. Instead of controlling the disease, they suggest that we are deluded, or more politely, incurably romantic, for hoping to control it. Instead of assuming responsibilities as realistic clinicians, striving to further democratic potentialities wherever they can, many social scientists have become morticians, all too eager to bury men's hopes.

NOTES

1. Talcott Parsons, *The Structure of Social Action* (New York, 1937), p. 341.
2. Bertrand and Dora Russell, *Prospects of Industrial Civilization* (New York, 1923), p. 14.
3. Parsons, p. 509.
4. Oskar Lange and Fred M. Taylor, *On the Economic Theory of Socialism*, ed. Lippincott (Minneapolis, 1948), p. 109.
5. Arthur O. Lovejoy, *The Great Chain of Being* (Cambridge, Mass., 1948), p. 11.
6. Monograph #11, Temporary National Economic Committee, *Bureaucracy and Trusteeship in Large Corporations* (Washington, D.C., 1940), p. 36.
7. *Max Weber: The Theory of Social and Economic Organization*, translated and edited by A. M. Henderson and Talcott Parsons (New York, 1947), pp. 334, 338.
8. [Ed. Note: It should be mentioned that Weber can also be read as a kind of Social Darwinian, contending that bureaucracy more and more holds sway because of its greater efficiency by comparison with alternative modes of organization. Consequently, those who pursue their aims bureaucratically tend to prevail in the never-ending social, economic, and political competition for survival. By the same token, it may be inferred, resourceful leaders of threatened organizations turn to bureaucratization as a highly useful tactic.]
9. Talcott Parsons, *The Social System* (Glencoe, Illinois, 1951), pp. 507–8. Italics added.
10. Peter Drucker, *Concept of the Corporation* (New York, 1946), pp. 183–84.
11. Carl Dreyfuss, *Occupation and Ideology of the Salaried Employee*, trans. Eva Abramovitch (New York, 1938), p. 17, 75, 77.
12. W. Lloyd Warner and J. O. Low, *The Social System of the Modern Factory* (New Haven, 1947), pp. 78, 80, 174.
13. Robert Michels, *Political Parties* (Glencoe, Ill., 1949), p. 400. Michel's work was first published in 1915, pp. 401, 402, 405, 408.
14. Philip Selznick, *TVA and the Grass Roots* (Berkeley and Los Angeles, 1949), pp. 9, 220, 252, 259, 265.
15. See Arthur Schweitzer, "Ideological Groups," *American Sociological Review*, Vol. 9, pp. 415–27 (Aug., 1944), particularly his discussion of factors inhibiting oligarchy. For example, "A leadership concentrating all power in its hands creates indifference among the func-

tionaries and sympathizers as well as decline in membership of the organization. This process of shrinkage, endangering the position of the leaders, is the best protection against the supposedly inevitable iron law of oligarchy" (p. 419). Much of the research deriving from the Lewinian tradition would seem to lend credence to this inference.

The Bureaucracy Problem

James Q. Wilson

The federal bureaucracy, whose growth and problems were once only the concern of the Right, has now become a major concern of the Left, the Center, and almost all points in between. Conservatives once feared that a powerful bureaucracy would work a social revolution. The Left now fears that this same bureaucracy is working a conservative reaction. And the Center fears that the bureaucracy isn't working at all.

Increasing federal power has always been seen by conservatives in terms of increasing *bureaucratic* power. If greater federal power merely meant, say, greater uniformity in government regulations—standardized trucking regulations, for example, or uniform professional licensing practices—a substantial segment of American businessmen would probably be pleased. But growing federal power means increased discretion vested in appointive officials whose behavior can neither be anticipated nor controlled. The behavior of state and local bureaucrats, by contrast, can often be anticipated *because* it can be controlled by businessmen and others.

Knowing this, liberals have always resolved most questions in favor of enhancing federal power. The "hacks" running local administrative agencies were too often, in liberal eyes, the agents of local political and economic forces—businessmen, party bosses, organized professions, and the like. A federal bureaucrat, because he was responsible to a national power center and to a single President elected by a nationwide constituency, could not so easily be bought off by local vested interests; in addition, he would take his policy guidance from a President elected by a process that gave heavy weight to the votes of urban, labor, and minority groups. The New Deal bureaucrats, especially those appointed to the new, "emergency" agencies, were expected by liberals to be free to chart a radically new program and to be competent to direct its implementation.

It was an understandable illusion. It frequently appears in history in the hopes of otherwise intelligent and far-sighted men. Henry II thought his clerks and scribes would help him subdue England's feudal barons; how was he to know that in time they would become the agents of Parliamentary authority directed at stripping the king of his prerogatives? And how were Parliament and its Cabinet ministers, in turn, to know that eventually these permanent undersecretaries would become an almost self-governing class whose day-to-day behavior would become virtually immune to scrutiny or control? Marxists thought that Soviet bureaucrats would work for the people, despite the fact that Max Weber had pointed out

From *The Public Interest*, No. 6 (Winter 1967), pp. 3–9. Reprinted by permission of the author and publisher.

why one could be almost certain they would work mostly for themselves. It is ironic that among today's members of the "New Left," the "Leninist problem"— i.e., the problem of over-organization and of self-perpetuating administrative power —should become a major preoccupation.

This apparent agreement among polemicists of the Right and Left that there is a bureaucracy problem accounts, one suspects, for the fact that nonbureaucratic solutions to contemporary problems seem to command support from both groups. The negative income tax as a strategy for dealing with poverty is endorsed by economists of such different persuasions as Milton Friedman and James Tobin, and has received favorable consideration among members of both the Goldwater brain trust and the Students for a Democratic Society. Though the interests of the two groups are somewhat divergent, one common element is a desire to scuttle the social workers and the public welfare bureaucracy, who are usually portrayed as prying busy-bodies with pursed lips and steel-rimmed glasses ordering midnight bedchecks in public housing projects. (Police officers who complain that television makes them look like fools in the eyes of their children will know just what the social workers are going through.)

Now that everybody seems to agree that we ought to do something about the problem of bureaucracy, one might suppose that something would get done. Perhaps a grand reorganization, accompanied by lots of "systems analysis," "citizen participation," "creative federalism," and "interdepartmental coordination." Merely to state this prospect is to deny it.

There is not one bureaucracy problem, there are several, and the solution to each is in some degree incompatible with the solution to every other. First, there is the problem of accountability or control—getting the bureaucracy to serve agreed-on national goals. Second is the problem of equity—getting bureaucrats to treat like cases alike and on the basis of clear rules, known in advance. Third is the problem of efficiency—maximizing output for a given expenditure, or minimizing expenditures for a given output. Fourth is the problem of responsiveness— inducing bureaucrats to meet, with alacrity and compassion, those cases which can never be brought under a single national rule and which, by common human standards of justice or benevolence, seem to require that an exception be made or a rule stretched. Fifth is the problem of fiscal integrity—properly spending and accounting for public money.

Each of these problems mobilizes a somewhat different segment of the public. The problem of power is the unending preoccupation of the President and his staff, especially during the first years of an administration. Equity concerns the lawyers and the courts, though increasingly the Supreme Court seems to act as if it thinks its job is to help set national goals as a kind of auxiliary White House. Efficiency has traditionally been the concern of businessmen who thought, mistakenly, that an efficient government was one that didn't spend very much money. (Of late, efficiency has come to have a broader and more accurate meaning as an optimal relationship between objectives and resources. Robert McNamara has shown that an "efficient" Department of Defense costs a lot more money than an "inefficient" one; his disciples are now carrying the message to all parts of a skeptical federal establishment.) Responsiveness has been the concern of individual citizens and of their political representatives, usually out of wholly proper motives, but sometimes out of corrupt ones. Congress, especially, has tried to retain some power over the bureaucracy by intervening on behalf of tens of thousands of immigrants, widows, businessmen, and mothers-of-soldiers, hoping that the collective effect of many individual interventions would be a bureaucracy that, on large matters as well as small, would do Congress's will. (Since Congress only occasionally has a clear will, this strategy only works occasionally.) Finally, fiscal integrity—especially its absence—is the concern of the political "outs" who want to get in and thus it becomes the concern of "ins" who want to keep them out.

Obviously the more a bureaucracy is responsive to its clients—whether those clients are organized by radicals into Mothers for Adequate Welfare or represented by Congressmen anxious to please constituents—the less it can be accountable to presidential directives. Similarly, the more equity, the less responsiveness. And a preoccupation with fiscal integrity can make the kind of program budgeting required by enthusiasts of efficiency difficult, if not impossible.

Indeed, of all the groups interested in bureaucracy, those concerned with fiscal integrity usually play the winning hand. To be efficient, one must have clearly stated goals, but goals are often hard to state at all, much less clearly. To be responsive, one must be willing to run risks, and the career civil service is not ordinarily attractive to people with a taste for risk. Equity is an abstraction, of concern for the most part only to people who haven't been given any. Accountability is "politics," and the bureaucracy itself is the first to resist that (unless, of course, it is the kind of politics that produces pay raises and greater job security). But an absence of fiscal integrity is welfare chiseling, sweetheart deals, windfall profits, conflict of interest, malfeasance in high places—in short, corruption. Everybody recognizes *that* when he sees it, and none but a few misguided academics have anything good to say about it. As a result, fiscal scandal typically becomes the standard by which a bureaucracy is judged (the FBI is good because it hasn't had any, the Internal Revenue Service is bad because it has) and thus the all-consuming fear of responsible executives.

If it is this hard to make up one's mind about how one wants the bureaucracy to behave, one might be forgiven if one threw up one's hands and let nature take its course. Though it may come to that in the end, it is possible—and important—to begin with a resolution to face the issue squarely and try to think through the choices. Facing the issue means admitting what, in our zeal for new programs, we usually ignore: *There are inherent limits to what can be accomplished by large hierarchical organizations.*

The opposite view is more often in vogue. If enough people don't like something, it becomes a problem; if the intellectuals agree with them, it becomes a crisis; any crisis must be solved; if it must be solved, then it can be solved—and creating a new organization is the way to do it. If the organization fails to solve the problem (and when the problem is a fundamental one, it will almost surely fail), then the reason is "politics," or "mismanagement," or "incompetent people," or "meddling," or "socialism," or "inertia."

Some problems cannot be solved and some government functions cannot, in principle, be done well. Notwithstanding, the effort must often be made. The rule of reason should be to try to do as few undoable things as possible. It is regrettable, for example, that any country must have a foreign office, since none can have a good one. The reason is simple: it is literally impossible to have a "policy" with respect to *all* relevant matters concerning *all* foreign countries, much less a consistent and reasonable policy. And the difficulty increases with the square of the number of countries, and probably with the cube of the speed of communications. The problem long ago became insoluble and any sensible Secretary of State will cease trying to solve it. He will divide his time instead between *ad hoc* responses to the crisis of the moment and appearances on Meet the Press.

The answer is not, it must be emphasized, one of simply finding good people, though it is at least that. Most professors don't think much of the State Department, but it is by no means clear that a department made up only of professors would be any better, and some reason to believe that it would be worse. One reason is that bringing in "good outsiders," especially good outsiders from universities, means bringing in men with little experience in dealing with the substantive problem but many large ideas about how to approach problems "in general." General ideas, no matter how soundly based in history or social science, rarely tell one what to do tomorrow about the visit from the foreign trade mission from Ruritania or the questions from the Congressional appropriations subcommittee.

Another reason is that good people are in very short supply, even assuming we knew how to recognize them. Some things literally cannot be done—or cannot be done well—because there is no one available to do them who knows how. *The supply of able, experienced executives is not increasing nearly as fast as the number of problems being addressed by public policy.* All the fellowships, internships, and "mid-career training programs" in the world aren't likely to increase that supply very much, simply because the essential qualities for an executive—judgment about men and events, a facility for making good guesses, a sensitivity to political realities, and an ability to motivate others—are things which, if they can be taught at all, cannot be taught systematically or to more than a handful of apprentices at one time.

This constraint deserves emphasis, for it is rarely recognized as a constraint at all. Anyone who opposed a bold new program on the grounds that there was nobody around able to run it would be accused of being a pettifogger at best and a reactionary do-nothing at worst. Everywhere except in government, it seems, the scarcity of talent is accepted as a fact of life. Nobody (or almost nobody) thinks seriously of setting up a great new university overnight, because anybody familiar with the university business knows that, for almost any professorship one would want to fill, there are rarely more than five (if that) really top-flight people in the country, and they are all quite happy—and certainly well-paid—right where they are. Lots of new business ideas don't become profit-making realities because good business executives are both hard to find and expensive to hire. The government—at least publicly—seems to act as if the supply of able political executives were infinitely elastic, though people setting up new agencies will often admit privately that they are so frustrated and appalled by the shortage of talent that the only wonder if why disaster is so long in coming. Much would be gained if this constraint were mentioned to Congress *before* the bill is passed and the hopes aroused, instead of being mentioned afterward as an excuse for failure or as a reason why higher pay scales for public servants are an urgent necessity. "Talent is Scarcer Than Money" should be the motto of the Budget Bureau.

If administrative feasibility is such a critical issue, what can be done about it? Not a great deal. If the bureaucracy problem is a major reason why so many programs are in trouble, it is also a reason why the problem itself cannot be "solved." But it can be mitigated—though not usually through the kinds of expedients we are fond of trying: Hoover Commissions, management studies, expensive consultants, co-ordinating committees, "czars," and the like. The only point at which very much leverage can be gained on the problem *is when we decide what it is we are trying to accomplish*. When we define our goals, we are implicitly deciding how much, or how little, of a bureaucracy problem we are going to have. A program with clear objectives, clearly stated, is a program with a fighting chance of coping with each of the many aspects of the bureaucracy problem. Controlling an agency is easier when you know what you want. Equity is more likely to be assured when over-all objectives can be stated, at least in part, in general rules to which people in and out of the agency are asked to conform. Efficiency is made possible when you know what you are buying with your money. Responsiveness is never easy or wholly desirable; if every person were treated in accordance with his special needs, there would be no program at all. (The only system that meets the responsiveness problem squarely is the free market.) But at least with clear objectives we would know what we are giving up in those cases when responsiveness seems necessary, and thus we would be able to decide how much we are willing to tolerate. And fiscal integrity is just as easy to insure in a system with clear objectives as in one with fuzzy ones; in the former case, moreover, we are less likely to judge success simply in terms of avoiding scandal. We might even be willing to accept a little looseness if we knew what we were getting for it.

The rejoinder to this argument is that there are many government functions which, by their nature, can never have clear objectives. I hope I have made it obvious by now that I am aware of that. We can't stop dealing with foreign nations just because we don't know what we want; after all, they may know what *they* want, and we had better find out. My argument is advanced, not as a panacea —there is no way to avoid the problem of administration—but as a guide to choice in those cases where choice is open to us, and as a criterion by which to evaluate proposals for coping with the bureaucracy problem.

Dealing with poverty—at least in part—by giving people money seems like an obvious strategy. Governments are very good at taking money from one person and giving it to another; the goals are not particularly difficult to state; measures are available to evaluate how well we are doing in achieving a predetermined income distribution. There may be many things wrong with this approach, but administrative difficulty is not one of them. And yet, paradoxically, it is the last approach we will probably try. We will try everything else first—case work, counseling, remedial education, community action, federally financed mass protests to end "alienation," etc. And whatever else might be said in their favor, the likelihood of smooth administration and ample talent can hardly be included.

Both the White House and the Congress seem eager to do something about the bureaucracy problem. All too often, however, the problem is described in terms of "digesting" the "glut" of new federal programs—as if solving administrative difficulties had something in common with treating heartburn. Perhaps those seriously concerned with this issue will put themselves on notice that they ought not to begin with the pain and reach for some administrative bicarbonate of soda; they ought instead to begin with what was swallowed and ask whether an emetic is necessary. *Coping with the bureaucracy problem is inseparable from rethinking the objectives of the programs in question.* Administrative reshuffling, budgetary cuts (or budgetary increases), and congressional investigation of lower-level boondoggling will not suffice and are likely, unless there are some happy accidents, to make matters worse. Thinking clearly about goals is a tough assignment for a political system that has been held together in great part by compromise, ambiguity, and contradiction. And if a choice must be made, any reasonable person would, I think, prefer the system to the clarity. But now that we have decided to intervene in such a wide range of human affairs, perhaps we ought to reassess that particular trade-off.

B. Expertise and Professionalism

As Max Weber pointed out, bureaucracy pervades modern society largely because it permits maximum utilization of technical expertise. In a society which stresses progress through the advancement of knowledge this places considerable power in the hands of bureaucrats. In this section, Francis S. Rourke examines the sources of bureaucratic expertise and the processes by which it is transformed into influence over the formulation and implementation of public policy. Rourke notes that the most important factor in the growth of bureaucratic power is the expanded exercise of discretionary authority by administrative officials. As the content of policy becomes more complex and dependence on expertise increases, it is necessary for legislatures to frame statutes in terms of general objectives and leave decisions about the selection of means and intermediate goals to the judgment of administrators. Rourke believes, however, that expertise plays a greater role in national security policy than in domestic policy arenas where officials are more involved in responding to and reconciling conflicting interests.

The mobilization of expertise is accomplished through the professions. The phenomenon of professionalism is the process whereby members of distinctive occupational fields undergo a specialized advanced education which equips them with knowledge and skills that accord them high prestige and the opportunity for lifetime careers.[1] Robert S. Friedman considers in his article the factors beyond expertise and prestige that explain the influence of professional groups and professionals generally in the political process. You might try to analyze

[1] This definition is based on Frederick C. Mosher, *Democracy and the Public Service* (New York: Oxford University Press, 1968), p. 106.

the factors that Friedman cites by applying them to various professional groups involved in public administration, for example, lawyers, engineers, etc.

Both Friedman and Rourke express a modest degree of uneasiness over our growing dependence on scientists, experts, and bureaucrats in public policy making. Don K. Price, one of America's foremost students of "science and public policy," is optimistic about the consequences of the growth of what he calls "the scientific estate." Price sees the new techniques of administration as very much within the American tradition and he believes that they are highly appropriate responses to the problem of nationalizing support for programs without sacrificing the benefits of political and social pluralism. There is nothing in the nature of the new administrative system, he writes, to determine whether power will be increasingly concentrated at the center, or the center will increasingly fall under the multiple influences of its "instruments." In practice, he concludes, there is much less danger of central bureaucratic dictatorship in the United States than of excessive fragmentation, inattention to the broader issues of policy, and disregard of the public interest. You will do well to evaluate the case he makes for this proposition with the utmost care.

In assessing the selections in this section, you should ask whether our dependence on experts and professionals poses a threat to the processes of democratic responsibility whereby elected officials and appointed "political executives" are periodically held accountable through elections and the consequent rotation in office. How are either the nonprofessional, inexpert officials chosen by the mass public or those persons directly appointed by elected officials able to evaluate the performance of bureaucratic professionals? How is the public to choose rationally between highly technical policy alternatives formulated and fully comprehended only by experts?

The Skills of Bureaucracy

Francis E. Rourke

From the perspective of administrative politics, an agency's influence in the policy process often appears to depend almost entirely on the constituency strength it commands, or upon its ability to maneuver successfully to advance its interests within the legislative or executive branch of government. To obtain a measure of the scope of an agency's power, it may thus be regarded as necessary only to determine how many followers the agency can muster in its own behalf.

This is not, however, an accurate picture of the bureaucratic role in the policy process. It is not adequate as a description of bureaucratic power in American administration, even though government agencies in this country have very wide-ranging involvements in the political process, and it is certainly not suitable as a description of bureaucracy in Western European government, where, by law and tradition, executive agencies are considerably more insulated from the play of ordinary political forces. Political activity such as the negotiation of alliances with outside groups can be a useful source of power for any administrative agency, but it is by no means the only source of administrative influence.

Of at least equal importance as a source of bureaucratic power is the expertise of executive agencies—the fact that administrators bring to the policy process a wide variety of skills necessary both for making decisions on policy and for carrying these decisions out. This is what Max Weber long ago saw as the distinctive attribute which gave bureaucracy its enormous influence in modern government.

> The decisive reason for the advance of bureaucratic organization has always been its purely technical superiority over any other form of organization. The fully developed bureaucratic mechanism compares with other organizations exactly as does the machine with the nonmechanical modes of production.
>
> . . .
>
> Under normal conditions, the power position of a fully developed bureaucracy is always overtowering. The "political master" finds himself in a position of the "dilettante" who stands opposite the "expert," facing the trained official who stands within the management of administration.[1]

. . .

THE SOURCES OF BUREAUCRATIC EXPERTISE

There are a variety of ways in which public bureaucracies acquire the expertise that is so important a source of their power in the governing process. For one thing a large organization is itself a mechanism for enhancing human competence. Men joined together in complex organizational systems can achieve results that individuals alone could never hope to accomplish—the construction of an atom bomb, the launching of a space vehicle into orbit, or the establishment of an educational system capable of meeting the intellectual needs of all citizens from primary school to post-doctoral training.

Organizations achieve this level of competence by taking complex problems and breaking them down into smaller and hence more manageable tasks. Once problems have been sub-factored in this way, each segment can be handled separately, and then by piecing the parts together, an organization can provide solutions to what may have originally seemed to be insoluble problems. This division of labor within large-scale organizations in addition allows groups of employees to acquire specialized expertise, even though they may not themselves have unusual technical qualifications. It is for these reasons that an organization is itself a source of expertise, quite apart from the skills which its members initially bring to the job.

A second way in which bureaucracies acquire expertise is through the concentrated attention they give to specific problems. Dealing day in and day out with the same tasks gives public agencies an invaluable kind of practical knowledge that comes from experience. This knowledge in time becomes part of the memory of a public organization and is transmitted to new employees by training and indoctrination programs. The task an agency performs may not on the surface appear terribly complex—the cleaning of streets or the removal of snow, for example—but the agency is the institution in society which by experience has come to know the most about it.

The sustained attention which bureaucrats can devote to specific problems gives them a decided advantage in framing policy decisions over political officials who deal with a wide variety of problems and confront each issue of public policy only at sporadic intervals. This advantage is characteristic of both democratic and nondemocratic societies. It is perhaps particularly important in the United States because American bureaucrats tend to specialize early and to remain in the service of a particular agency throughout their career. But in European as well as American bureaucracies, expertise reflects continuity in office as well as concentration of energy. Not only do bureaucrats focus their attention on specific problems but they also remain in office for longer periods of time than is customary for politicians.

The knowledge that agencies acquire by continuous attention to particular functions puts them in an especially advantageous position to influence policy when the facts they gather cannot be subject to independent verification or disproof. Intelligence units are especially well situated in this respect. . . . A monopolistic or near monopolistic control of the "facts" thus provides tremendous reinforcement to the power that bureaucrats possess from specialized and continuous attention to a particular set of responsibilities.

But while organizations have certain inherent assets which contribute greatly to their decision-making skills, it is not these organizational characteristics alone that account for the expertise which is the hallmark of modern bureaucracy. In the modern state this expertise comes pre-eminently from the fact that a variety of highly trained elites practice their trade in public organizations—physicists, economists, engineers—the roster of professions in American society could be called indefinitely without encountering a single skill that does not find extensive employment in one or more executive agencies. And there are several professions such as the military which are only employed in the public service. Moreover, the tendency for professionals to seek employment in public as well as private organizations is on the increase. Etzioni argues that as "the need for costly resources and auxiliary staff has grown, even the traditional professions face mounting pressures to transfer their work to organizational structures such as the hospital and the law firm."[2]

Of course not all public organizations exhibit the same degree of professionalism in their employment pattern. Some administrative units like the Post Office Department still hire mainly clerical employees. However, in other agencies, such as the National Institutes of Health, the level of professionalism is very high. Agencies like NIH are in fact often described as "professional organizations"— agencies dominated by individuals whose primary commitment is to the skill they practice rather than the institution by which they are employed.

. . .

In the early history of American bureaucracy, such claims to expertise as administration could make were based largely on the factor of continuity—the clerical employees who then staffed government agencies worked so continuously on particular problems that they acquired a kind of specialized knowledge as an inevitable result. Their expertise had its genesis in their organizational position. And it exacted little deference from politicians. President Andrew Jackson's statement in this regard is often taken as the classic expression of popular disdain for the skills of bureaucracy in early nineteenth-century America: "The duties of all public officers are, or at least admit of being made, so plain and simple that men of intelligence may readily qualify themselves for their performance; and I can not but believe that more is lost by the long continuance of men in office than is generally gained by their experience."[3]

However, since Jackson's day there has been a sharp up-grading in the skills required to run the modern state. As the innovations wrought by science and technology have increasingly complicated both the environment and the responsibilities of government, the duties of the public service are no longer so "plain and simple" as Jackson once regarded them. Moreover, with the abolition of spoils and the increasing acceptance of merit as the essential qualification necessary for public employment there has been a growing effort to recruit experts to the public service, to provide in-service training programs designed to improve the skills of public employees, and in a variety of other ways to encourage and enhance the development of bureaucratic expertise.

In summary, it can be seen that bureaucratic expertise is rooted in both the characteristics of public organizations and, increasingly, in the skills of their members. Each year the operation of executive agencies at all levels of government demands the employment of a more diverse and complex range of specialized personnel. In sharp contrast to President Jackson's belief in the simplicity of the administrator's task stands the following statement by President John F. Kennedy, delivered in support of an increase in pay for government employees: "The success of this Government, and thus the success of our Nation, depend in the last analysis on the quality of our career services. The legislation enacted by the Congress, as well as the decisions made by me and the Department and Agency heads, must all be implemented by the career men and women in the federal service. In foreign affairs, national defense, science and technology, and a host of other fields, they face unprecedented problems of unprecedented importance. We are all dependent on their sense of loyalty and responsibility as well as their competence and energy."[4]

EXPERTISE: CHANNELS OF INFLUENCE

Whether it stems from the characteristics of organizations or the skills of their members, bureaucratic expertise exercises influence over the development of public policy through two chief channels—the capacity of bureaucrats to give advice on policy decisions and the authority they are usually granted to exercise discretion in carrying out these decisions. In the case of advice, the power of bureaucrats is indirect, resting as it does upon their ability to persuade political officials that a certain course of action should be taken. Bureaucrats have influence only if politicians accept their advice. However, once bureaucrats have been granted the right to exercise discretion in the execution of policy, as is common practice in all political systems, their power is direct. The actual content of policy may in some instances become entirely a matter for bureaucratic determination.

THE POWER OF ADVICE. The agencies in which the power of advice can be seen in its clearest form in American administration are the staff agencies which surround the Presidency, administrative units like the Bureau of the Budget, the Council of Economic Advisers, and the President's Science Advisory Committee. These agencies have little operational authority of their own. They influence policy primarily by influencing the President. The economists who serve with the Bureau of the Budget and the Council of Economic Advisers can shape the President's perspective on fiscal policy, and hence his recommendations to Congress on tax and expenditure measures. The natural scientists who sit on the President's Science Advisory Committee are equally influential with the Chief Executive in the areas of their scientific and technical competence.

The relationship between the President and his advisers at this level of administration involves of course reciprocal benefits. Through their access to the President, professional groups like economists and natural scientists obtain a degree of influence in the policy process they would never otherwise enjoy. The members of most professional groups have neither the time, inclination, nor the capacity to win political office, and involvement in bureaucracy is, therefore, the only avenue to political power open to them.

At the same time, however, the President also derives tangible political benefits from his use of experts. The wisdom of his policy decisions can be greatly enhanced in the eyes of the electorate if he is in a position to assert that these decisions rest on the best professional advice he has been able to obtain. As has been said, for example, of the Council of Economic Advisers: "The acceptance of the Council's expertise as the President's economics increases the acceptance of his authority in matters of economic policy, and where applicable it adds economic persuasion to his strategies of influence. In return, the President provides the principal market for the Council's expertise."[5] The same point has been made with respect to the role of natural scientists in government: "The scientist may find himself on the political firing line, placed there by a politician interested in using the scientist's prestige as an 'expert' to disarm the critics of his (the politician's) choices."[6]

There are risks as well as benefits for the President in his relationship with his advisers. It is, for example, highly important to a President that no one adviser be allowed to exercise monopolistic influence over his decisions. . . .

. . .

In American government each of the major advisory institutions in the executive branch—the Joint Chiefs of Staff, the National Security Council, the Council of Economic Advisers, and the President's science advisory group—is in fact a committee. In the literature of public administration, committees are usually held in low regard as management instruments, since they disperse rather than focus executive leadership and control. But as an advisory institution, the committee has a great deal of utility, and with administrative agencies moving increasingly into the development as well as the execution of policy, committees have become as indispensable for deliberative purposes in the administrative process as they have long been in legislative decision-making.

. . .

Of course, an advisory group that is totally dependent upon the Chief Executive for its own survival may be highly reluctant to tell him unpleasant truths he ought to hear. In time the advice a President gets from these experts may do little more than mirror his own opinions. This is likely to be a particularly acute problem when the adviser is a career civil servant whose employment opportunities outside of government are limited. It contributes to candor in the advisory process if advisers are drawn from universities or other outside institutions to which they can return if need be—an option open to the members of both the Council of Economic Advisers and the President's Science Advisory Committee.

The impact of bureaucratic advice upon the policy process stands out very clearly not only in the activities of staff agencies which serve the Presidency, but also in the increasing tendency for the deliberations of Congress to be dominated by "agency bills"—legislation which has been originally drafted in the offices of executive agencies. This administrative initiative in drafting legislation has not received as much attention in recent years as was earlier the case. . . .

. . .

THE EXERCISE OF DISCRETION. No aspect of the growth of bureaucratic power in this century has been more important than the steady expansion in the scope of administrative discretion. As used in this context, the term "discretion" refers to the ability of an administrator to choose among alternatives—to decide in effect how the power of the state should be used in specific cases. The range of situations in which bureaucrats exercise discretion is virtually boundless. It includes the policeman deciding whether or not to make an arrest, a regulatory agency choosing either to issue or refuse a license or permit, or a selectvie service board determining whether to draft or defer a particular individual. These decisions may have a vital effect upon the fortunes or even the fate of the individual concerned. Whether or not discretion is, as has been asserted, the "life blood" of administration, its exercise may well have a life or death effect for the individual citizen.

In the traditional theory of public administration in the United States, it was assumed that the administrator's discretion extended only to decisions on means, while the ends or goals of administrative action were fixed by statute or by the directives of a responsible political official. This was the celebrated distinction between politics and administration presented by such early pioneers in the field as Woodrow Wilson and Frank J. Goodnow. This distinction was designed among other things to provide a rationale for insulating administrative agencies from exploitation by politicians bent on using administrative offices and powers as the "spoils" of victory at the polls. If bureaucrats did not shape policy, then there was no reason why administrative agencies could not be left in splendid isolation, free to make decisions on personnel, or on administrative organization and procedure, to attain maximum efficiency in carrying on the business of government. As Wilson puts it: "The broad plans of governmental action are not administrative; the detailed execution of such plans is administrative."[7]

This was a highly useful doctrine during the late nineteenth century and early twentieth century in the United States when public bureaucracy was an "infant industry" which needed a protective ideology behind which it could develop. It cannot, however, be regarded as valid doctrine today when the center of power in policy-making has shifted from the legislative to the executive branch and when all bureaucratic decisions are recognized as having at least some implications for policy.

The scope of this administrative discretion is vast with respect to both the everyday routine decisions of government agencies and the major innovative or trend-setting decisions of organizational life. These two broad types of administrative decision have been categorized by Herbert Simon as programmed and non-programmed decisions. In Simon's words: "Decisions are programmed to the extent that they are repetitive and routine, to the extent that a definite procedure has been worked out for handling them so that they don't have to be treated *de novo* each time they occur. . . . Decisions are non-programmed to the extent that they are novel, unstructured, and consequential."[8]

The policy impact of administrative discretion when it is exercised with respect to non-programmed decisions is clear and unmistakable. If the Federal Reserve Board abruptly changes the discount rate, or alters the reserve requirements for member banks to control inflationary tendencies in a booming economy, or to stimulate investment in the face of an impending economic recession, these are major policy decisions of obvious importance to the society at large. Or the Federal Communications Commission when it sets forth criteria for determining how many television stations are to be allowed in each section of the country is obviously taking the lead in designing a national communications policy through the exercise of its discretionary authority. . . .

What is perhaps not quite so clearly apparent is the power inherent in the capacity of bureaucrats to exercise discretion in the area of programmed or routine decision. The fact of the matter is, however, that decisions that may seem merely routine from the point of view of an administrative agency are often of critical importance to the parties affected by these administrative determinations. An individual denied the right to practice a profession as a result of a negative judgment on his qualifications by a licensing board has been grievously affected by the exercise of routine discretion in a situation in which the state controls entry into a profession.

Moreover, a government agency responsible for awarding defense contracts makes vital decisions for industries dependent upon these contracts for their survival, although the decisions may seem ordinary from the point of view of the agency. The exercise of discretion in an area of this kind has side-effects which reach far beyond the business firms immediately affected. The economy of an entire region may be heavily dependent upon the prosperity of a particular industry, and the denial of a defense contract or the closing of a military installation may represent an economic disaster for many communities.

. . .

Whatever the relative weight of politics and expertise as sources of bureaucratic power, all executive agencies in the United States recognize the value of political support, and . . . devote a great deal of energy to seeking out and nursing a constituency. The extent to which American bureaucracy is thus politicized reflects the fact that a democratic political system was already well established in this country when a bureaucracy of substantial size first began to emerge in the latter part of the nineteenth century. The development of political skills was part of the process by which executive agencies adapted to their environment in order to survive in the egalitarian democratic society in which they found themselves.

This American experience stands in stark contrast to the historical development of bureaucracy in European democratic states. There a highly developed bureaucratic apparatus commonly existed and played a large role in governing the state long before the advent of democratic political institutions. In Europe it was democracy which had to accommodate itself to the presence of a strongly entrenched bureaucratic system. Partly because they enjoyed a security of position that American bureaucracies lacked, and partly because of the conventions of the parliamentary system, executive agencies in European states have historically had less reason and less opportunity to engage in direct political activity of the sort that is so common in the United States.

But if a politicized bureaucracy is deeply rooted in the American political tradition, so too is a considerable degree of deference to expertise in the governing process. The creation of a variety of political institutions in the United States—including the council-manager form of government in urban communities, the special-authority device in both state and local government, and the independent regulatory commissions at the national level—testifies to the fact that it is very much in the American grain to attempt to de-fuse political controversy by transforming political issues into technical problems. The city and county managers are expected to furnish their local area with professional government based on non-political criteria, and the special authority and the independent regulatory commissions have both been set up to take government away from the politicians and put it in the hands of the experts.

The American political system thus reveals both an extremely high degree of political activity on the part of administrative agencies, and an equally firm commitment to the notion that referring a problem to the bureaucracy takes it out of politics. As a result administrative agencies in the United States are often able to have the best of both worlds. While exhibiting a stance of complete dedication to professional goals, they can simultaneously cultivate as broad a basis of political support as their circumstances will allow. The fabric of their power is thus woven out of both politics and expertise, but precisely in what pattern is often difficult to discern.

However, as a rough generalization applicable to the experience of American national government, it would be fair to say that expertise is the dominant source of bureaucratic authority in the area of foreign or national security policy while bureaucratic politics is much more salient in the administration of domestic activities. In national security policy, the involvement of domestic political groups usually takes place only after a decision has been made. Most decisions are reached in secret, and public opinion is acquainted with what has transpired only through "leaks"—which often come from executive officials who disapprove of what has been decided and are trying to reverse the decision by arousing public opinion against it.

Bureaucratic experts of various kinds thus exercise a pervasive influence over the framing of national security policy. These professional groups include diplomats, military officers, scientists, and what Bernard Brodie calls "scientific strategists." As Huntington describes the development of national defense strategy: "The relative absence of non-governmental groups concerned with strategy enhances the extent and the importance of the bargaining roles of governmental officials and agencies."[9] In this case public participation in actual policy decisions tends to be indirect. The public participates as the officials making the decisions take potential public reactions into account in reaching their own conclusions. While the public is not likely to question the competence of government officials to define the national interest, it is quite capable of eventual resentment against the sacrifices and burdens any international involvement may entail.

In domestic policy-making, on the other hand, a variety of non-governmental groups take a continuous interest in the policy-making processes of administrative agencies. As noted earlier, this relationship is in many instances initiated by the agencies themselves. The views of an agency's public can thus be incorporated into the initial design of policy. In fact bureaucratic policy-making in the domestic area commonly represents a reconciliation of conflicting group interests, as much as it does the application of expertise toward the solution of particular problems.

This distinction between policy-making in the administration of domestic and foreign affairs should not of course be exaggerated. Bureaucrats in the national security area enjoy somewhat more freedom from political pressures in their deliberations. But these pressures are never entirely absent from any area of bureaucratic decision in the United States, so wide and well-traveled are the channels of access between administrative agencies on the one hand and the community on the other.

NOTES

1. H. H. Gerth and C. Wright Mills, *From Max Weber: Essays in Sociology* (New York: Oxford University Press, 1946), pp. 214, 232.
2. Amitai Etzioni, *Modern Organizations* (Englewood Cliffs, N.J.: Prentice-Hall, 1964), p. 77.
3. James D. Richardson, *Messages and Papers of the Presidents* (New York: Bureau of National Literature, 1897), Vol. III, p. 1012.
4. *Congressional Quarterly Almanac*, 1962, p. 907.
5. Edward S. Flash, Jr., *Economic Advice and Presidential Leadership* (New York: Columbia University Press, 1965), pp. 309–310.
6. Warner R. Schilling, "Scientists, Foreign Policy, and Politics," in Robert Gilpin and Christopher Wright (eds.), *Scientists and National Policy-Making* (New York: Columbia University Press, 1964), p. 169.
7. Woodrow Wilson, "The Study of Administration," *Political Science Quarterly*, Vol. II (June, 1887), p. 212.
8. Herbert A. Simon, *The New Science of Management Decision* (New York: Harper & Row, 1960), pp. 5–6. *Cf.* also a similar distinction between "routine" and "critical" decisions in Philip Selznick, *Leadership in Administration* (Evanston, Ill.: Row, Peterson & Co., 1957), pp. 29–64.
9. Samuel P. Huntington, *The Common Defense* (New York: Columbia University Press, 1961), p. 147.

Professionalism: Expertise and Policy Making

Robert S. Friedman

Several prominent social critics have expressed alarm at what they consider the growing dominance of scientists, experts, and bureaucrats in public policy making. . . . They fear that a growing monopoly by "technocrats" is rapidly undermining democracy in Western industrial societies. Ironically, a number of distinguished

From Robert S. Friedman, *Professionalism: Expertise and Policy Making*. General Learning Press, Morristown, N.J., © 1971 General Learning Corporation. Reprinted by permission of Silver Burdett Company.

Bureaucratic Politics

For over a quarter of a century scholars have recognized the political character of public administration and regarded it as the feature that distinguishes it most sharply from private administration. No proposition is more generally accepted in the literature than that every domestic agency bears primary responsibility for coming to terms with its own constituency of interested groups and congressional committees. Most national security agencies, including the armed forces, are somewhat less "on their own," because Congress is more persuaded of the need for central planning and unified direction in the security area. Even national security agencies, however, compete with one another for funds and influence over policy.

The accommodations that all federal agencies reach in order to survive and prosper typically deflect them from their original conceptions of purpose and render them less amenable to control from above. To those who highly value comprehensiveness, coordination, and consistency, these outcomes generally seem most unfortunate. Others consider them reasonable prices to pay for building responsiveness into the national administrative system and for keeping it from confronting the rest of society as a monolith.

J. Lieper Freeman's study is one of the very few in the literature to focus upon an agency's effort to change its constituency base from one set of interests to another. He finds that the Indian Bureau was able to operate successfully as a protector of Indian interests so long as President Roosevelt had leisure to concentrate on domestic affairs and had adequate political resources to dominate Congress. When these conditions ceased to be fulfilled, Roosevelt's appointee as chief of the Bureau became expendable, and the agency had little choice but to lapse into the pre-1933 pattern of permitting congressmen from the affected areas (in which the great majority of voters were white, and frequently hostile to Indian interests) to set the limits of its commitment. This is not to say that in any period the bureau's chief was totally without room to maneuver. It is rather to indicate how the scope of his discretion varied with changes in the general political situation. You are urged to consider more systematically (and for a wide variety of circumstances) the determinants of a bureau chief's range of discretion, together with the risks that may guide him within that range.

Theodore J. Lowi has been one of the most articulate critics of the system of agency-constituency congressional committee relationships that Freeman describes. He labels it "interest group liberalism" and claims that it has been

elevated to the status of a "new public philosophy." Lowi's basic criticism
is that the conscious and unconscious involvement of private-interest organizations
in the processes of governmental decision making, including most critically
the implementation of programs by administrative agencies, has destroyed the
basis of public order—the electoral accountability of those who make policy.
Lowi suggests two additional consequences of the system of interest-group
liberalism beyond the erosion of popular control; it creates and maintains
"structures of privilege" and it is thoroughly conservative. His proposed remedies
are contrary to the thrust of the participative administration movement. He
would push group access back into Congress and out of the bureaucracy, and
he would place explicit limitations on the exercise of federal power while seeking
to strengthen the states. You should try to assess the accuracy of Lowi's
diagnosis and the appropriateness of his proposed remedies. He has fashioned
a strong intellectual challenge to American public administration that merits
careful attention.

Graham T. Allison examines national security policy making through a case
study of the Cuban missile crisis of 1962. He argues that the explanation of
a decision depends on the conceptual model employed by the analyst. The
decision may be conceived of as the action of a nation in the international
political system, it may be regarded as the output of an organizational process
within government, or it may be viewed as the result of bargaining between
individual officials. Allison shows that no analysis of a national security policy
decision can be fully adequate unless it employs models at the three analytical
levels. It is important to bear in mind that administrative politics occurs
simultaneously at the macro level of the national government, at the micro level
of the individual bureaucrat, and at the intermediate level of the various agencies.
Allison's article helps us to recognize the complex nature of governmental
decision making, which entails, as Pendleton Herring observed long ago, the
interaction of ideas, issues, individuals, and institutions.

The Political Ecology
of a Bureau

J. Lieper Freeman

In order to understand how issues are resolved and national policies are made,
one must view the system as something other than a well-geared monolith. . . .
Historically, although the federal government has accumulated great power and
reached huge proportions in the course of the nation's development, it has done
so relatively slowly and usually against considerable resistance from various special
interests. Many groups directly or indirectly urge specific expansions of power
favorable to themselves but oppose either general expansions or increases of
authority specifically favoring other groups. Furthermore, increases in federal
power have usually been realized only after limitations imposed by the federal

system, by the separation of powers, and by checks and balances have been reasonably satisfied. Perhaps the most significant point, in the last analysis, is that the growth of the federal government has most frequently occurred when new activities have been urged on Congress and the Administration by special segments of the population. If there is any creeping socialism in American government, it has come and is coming largely as an accompaniment of what might be called "creeping pluralism," that is, the gradual growth of political groups especially concerned with the protection and promotion of particular interests. The kind of government which has evolved is far from being a tightly knit leviathan.

THE AIMS AND UTILITY OF THIS STUDY

The present study endeavors to focus attention upon and to state some propositions about the interactions of certain key participants in this pluralisic leviathan. The actors are members of political subsystems centering upon executive bureaus and legislative committees. The chief value to be derived from the study should be a greater understanding of the patterns of policy-making *within* these subsystems. The major focus, beyond an examination of the relations between the general political setting and the participants in the subsystem, is upon relations among subsystem actors from the bureaucracy, from congressional committees, and from interested segments of the public. The value of studying the patterns of influence within executive-legislative subsystems has been well-stated by Professor Ernest S. Griffith, who called them "whirlpools." Griffith said, in part:

> . . . It is my opinion that ordinarily the relationship among these men—legislators, administrators, lobbyists, scholars—who are interested in a common problem is a much more real relationship than the relationship between congressmen generally or between administrators generally. In other words, he who would understand the prevailing pattern of our present governmental behavior, instead of studying the formal institutions or even generalizations in the relationships between these institutions or organs, important though all these are, may possibly obtain a better picture of the way things really happen if he would study these "whirlpools" of special social interest and problems.

In a recent most valuable book, Douglass Cater has similarly analyzed power in Washington in terms of "sub-governments" which are essentially the same as the whirlpools depicted by Griffith. These phenomena are neither new, surprising, nor devious. Rather they are so numerous and increasingly specialized that the mass of the citizenry has difficulty in following them. And as Cater points out, no part of the national political framework can effectively control all of them.

Similarly, a closely related additional value of the study may be a better understanding of the plural patterns of power and decision-making within the national government as they mirror the functional specialization and diversity of American society. This diversity of interests—of groups concerned with special values—has a host of sources deeply rooted in the nation's experience. Geographic dispersion, cultural heritage, religious belief, economic status, technological specialization, and traditions of individual and group self-seeking are but an important few of these sources. The groups arising from them have demanded the attention of special units of Congress and of the Administration and have thereby contributed to the diversity and complexity of the federal government while simultaneously attaining protection from it and niches for themselves within it. At the same time, Congress and the Administration, organized under legal norms which encourage permissiveness and particularism through their many sub-units, have tended to accommodate these interests. Furthermore, they have tended to encourage, aid, and abet their political activity and their very survival. The leaders from the official sub-units have become involved in relationships with leaders of the interest groups and have tended to take over major decision-making functions officially allotted to the government as a whole. By observing how and under what conditions specialists in certain areas of public policy are important determinants of that policy for the overall political system, one may sharpen his understanding of the importance of bureau-committee subsystems in the larger legislative-executive political setting. . . .

USING TOP-LEVEL SUPPORT. The proposals of bureau leaders . . . can be either endorsed or mediated by the higher echelons of the Administration of which the bureau is a part, especially in major issues of policy where the points under consideration are crucial to the Administration. In such an instance, the head of the department and other top leaders are likely to become involved. . . . Of course, the rule of limited intervention in lower echelon affairs usually applies to the Secretary and other top leaders of a department, as well as to the President, although in lesser degree. The Secretary does not intervene in every skirmish between one of his bureaus and a congressional committee any more than the President intervenes in every battle between a department and congressional leaders. Leaders of the Administration can be "supporting artillery" for a bureau chief, and the more crucial the target, the larger the "gun" that is brought to bear upon it.

The effect of the use of this strategy by a bureau leader was generally illustrated in the legislative relations of the Bureau of Indian Affairs during the New Deal, when high-level support from the Administration seemed to enhance the ability of the Bureau's leaders to gain acceptance of their recommendations and to defend themselves against attacks from committees and interest groups. During the earlier year of the New Deal, Commissioner Collier of the Bureau was successful on numerous occasions in getting Secretary of the Interior Ickes to communicate with or to testify before committees of Congress in support of the Bureau's viewpoint. In these instances the Secretary made the Commission's battles his own, with the characteristic Ickes vigor, and he usually helped to subdue critical committee members.

As has already been indicated, this state of mutual reinforcement does not appear uniformly in the relations of bureaus with the Administration. Yet every bureau chief to some degree has a choice as to the extent to which his efforts will be identified with the goals of the Administration and a choice as to how much he will exploit the power symbolized by the Secretary of his department or by the President. The case of Collier, Ickes, and Roosevelt was extreme, perhaps, in two ways: first, in the long span of their simultaneous incumbencies in office and second, in the degree of their interest and ideological proximity. All three men saw the New Deal through from its inception. All three were committed to the "progressive" point of view, sometimes looking with disdain upon the conventional political parties, but always strong for the "New Deal party." Ickes was put forward at first for the office of Commissioner of Indian Affairs under the New Deal, at which time he was supported by Collier and others. Roosevelt instead selected Ickes—almost sight unseen—to be Secretary of the Interior. Forthwith, Ickes, the party maverick in the Cabinet, gained the President's support and confidence, something he succeeded generally in holding for the next twelve years. The Secretary in turn got Roosevelt to appoint Collier as Commissioner, beginning a similar pattern of relations between the Bureau chief and the Department head. This was reinforced by the interest in Indians held by Anna Wilmarth Ickes, the Secretary's first wife, and by her assistance to Collier.

The Commissioner followed the strategy of using the backing of these leaders of the Administration to a maximum degree, and in turn utilized his own talents for promoting the New Deal in areas not particularly germane to his own Bureau. In securing the passage of the comprehensive Indian Reorganization Act of 1934, the Commissioner obtained the close support of the Secretary plus two endorsements from the President. He also used the prestige of the President in explaining the purposes of the bill to Indians in Oklahoma, telling them:

> You know that at the present time President Roosevelt controls both Houses of Congress. When the President wants a piece of legislation, he gets it from Congress. The bill we are going to discuss today is an Administration measure. It is a President Roosevelt measure. The majority of the members of Congress do not pretend to understand the Indian question in detail at all. The majority of the members of Congress have nothing to gain or lose by any Indian legislation. In other words, if the Administration had wanted to put this bill through quietly and quickly, understand they had the power, and they have the power to do it. The Administration, as I stated before, has adopted a new policy, which is the policy of bringing all the Indians into consultation on the bill, even though it entails, or may entail delay.

Needless to say, many committee members do not appreciate bureaucratic attempts to exploit the halo which sometimes attends presidential leadership, especially when the bureau spokesman infers that Congress can be pushed around by a strong President. Senator Elmer Thomas berated Collier for making the above statement. He said:

> You told *my* Indians down at *my* home that it made no difference what Congress thought about it, that you would pass the bill if you wanted to, and would do it quickly.

Also at issue here was another legislative norm: the sanctity of the local state or district against "outside" interference, especially "meddling" by the executive branch without consulting the lawmaker from that constituency. In using presidential support in this way the Commissioner evidently chose to bet that, given the popularity of the President, the exploitation of his support would in the long run more than offset the hostility aroused in the Senate Committee by violating some of the norms of its members. In this case the bill was passed, although Senator Thomas succeeded in delaying its application to his Indians in Oklahoma until he personally could investigate the need for it.

In the years between the advent of the New Deal and the advent of World War II the Commissioner secured the support of the Secretary in many other situations despite Ickes's preoccupation with Public Works and with the rarefied intrigues around the President. For example, Collier got the Secretary to issue a memorandum to Bureau employees telling them, in effect, either to quit criticizing the new policies in Indian affairs or to resign, and that if they persisted in their criticism without resigning, they would be dismissed. The Commissioner also cited the Secretary in standing up against congressional criticism of Indian Bureau publicity tactics and of the use of an official Indian Service periodical to organize support for the new policies. Collier told members of the House Committee on Indian Affairs:

> . . . We are promoting many things which, for their success, depend upon a friendly and informed opinion. We should properly cultivate public opinion, and we will continue to do that.
>
> I need only to add that I think this committee ought to know by this time that neither Secretary Ickes nor I hesitate to speak. We can always put out a release and we do so.

The two also joined in fighting certain groups which brought charges against them before the Dies Committee on Un-American Activities and before the Senate Committee on Indian Affairs. They also joined in warding off constant attempts to repeal the Indian Reorganization Act or to undermine it by cutting its appropriations. The Commissioner in turn extended his activities to take part not only in the propaganda battle in behalf of the President's Supreme Court plan, but also in the early attempts to counter the growth of the America First movement, two courses of action which reinforced strong interests of the Secretary's as well as of the President's.

In thus identifying with and using the endorsements of the Administration "above and beyond the call of duty," the Commissioner was often able to maximize his influence in the subsystem of Indian affairs by associating his recommendations with the prestige of higher officials. At the same time, however, he enlarged the range of controversy in the subsystem, and both he and his Bureau were recipients of retaliations that otherwise might not have come their way.

The other side of the coin of a bureau leader's attachment to higher symbols in the Administration and his exploitation of their prestige was demonstrated later when the support of Roosevelt and Ickes for Collier's Bureau was not so easily obtained and when it was not so effective, even though obtained. The Bureau headquarters were moved to Chicago during World War II to make room in Washington for wartime activities. Close communications with the Department of Interior and the White House were severely curtailed. The attention of the Administration was turned almost entirely from domestic policy to the war. In fact, it was doubtful if the New Deal was at that time the basis of the Administration's support so much as was the unifying objective of defense and victory.

During this period the Bureau chief became increasingly unable to stave off attacks from congressional committees. He was able to help the Bureau survive, but little else. Part of his difficulty in keeping committee members interested in Indian welfare and rehabilitation arose from the temporary mitigation of his Bureau's problems by the increase in Indian income due to wartime employment and by the relief furnished by the money sent home by many Indian servicemen. Part of the Commissioner's difficulty with some committees came from long-standing personal differences. Yet a crucial factor was his record of consistent fighting for the views of the New Deal and the use of the Administration's power to protect the policies installed in Indian affairs early in the New Deal. Lacking the continued strong reciprocal support of the Administration during the war period, the Commissioner was no longer able to maintain a favorable equilibrium. . . .

CHOOSING ALTERNATIVE COMMITTEES. Among the strategies of influence which a bureau leader can use is that of playing one committee against another. Every bureau deals with at least four committees of Congress, and frequently with more than four, giving the bureau leader a range of alternatives along this line. We have already observed the tendencies of the Senate Appropriations Committee to counterbalance the House Appropriations Committee. In addition, appropriations committees can and do alter policies enacted by substantive committees, both in setting the amount of money available for authorized programs and in altering the conditions under which money can be spent by the administrative unit. It is also possible that one investigating committee may counteract another in inquiries covering much of the same ground. All of these situations furnish possibilities in strategy for bureau leaders.

The last of these possibilities was used with some success by Commissioner Collier in the early 1940's. At that time the Investigating Subcommittee of the Senate Committee on Indian Affairs, which had been operating since 1928, brought out one of its most damaging indictments of the Bureau's policies and personnel. Shortly thereafter the Commissioner arranged with the leaders of the House Committee on Indian Affairs for a subcommittee of that unit also to investigate the Bureau, limiting its probe to specific, mutually acceptable points of inquiry to be covered in a stated length of time. Largely under the direction of Congressman Karl Mundt this was done, and a report was published which was considerably at variance with the Senate Subcommittee's report. Temporarily, the Bureau received some respite from the hostility emanating from the Senate Committee on Indian Affairs.

EXPLOITING COMMITTEE HEARINGS. Despite recognizable limitations, committee hearings furnish important channels of influence for participants in a subsystem, especially for bureau leaders. . . . Most hearings, especially those which are not televised and which are not given extensive press coverage, provide opportunities for some relatively unguarded communication among the policy-makers of the subsystem, as well as the opportunity to extend and exploit the proceedings for propaganda purposes.

Bureau leaders can frequently build up an impressive case for their side in the record. This furnishes documentation for those committee members who would be inclined to argue for the bureau's viewpoint, either in executive session where committee votes are taken, before the whole legislative body, or in public speeches. On occasion, a strong presentation in a hearing by bureau leaders may influence neutral or less-involved committee members. Yet often the most vital factors in communications in committee hearings, as in other small-group assemblages, are the methods and the disposition of the communicator plus his listeners' attitudes toward him and what he symbolizes, rather than the alleged facts presented and the logic used. Thus, among busy committee members who do not like to be snowed under by official or technical talk, bureau spokesmen can, by the strategies they employ, create or reinforce in the hearings sentiments about themselves and their organizations which have a lasting and controlling effect on the decisions of committees. It may be most important to the legislator whether he feels that the bureaucrat: (1) "knows what he's talking about" (e.g., speaks with confidence, answers questions simply and often categorically); (2) "plays it straight" (e.g., does not appear to evade, admits to imperfection, keeps the committee informed); and (3) "cooperates" (e.g., seems amenable to suggestions from committee members, shows them proper deference, does not try to put them on the spot with the press or with their constituents, and does not play his initiative too heavy-handedly). . . .

THE USE OF PUBLICITY. In addition to the opportunities for making news in committee hearings, there are other important facets of publicity (or propaganda) activities of bureau leaders which are critical. In general, these practices are natural outgrowths of needs for certain types of communications in our political system and overall legal attempts to limit them have been impracticable. Consequently there are usually abundant opportunities for bureau leaders to exploit the media of mass communication. A bureau's information office regularly gives out press releases (usually under departmental auspices) which, while dealing mainly with the facts of the bureau's business, nevertheless furnish a means of keeping the organization and its officials constantly on the news wires. If the bureau chief has an exceptional item to give out, he can usually get a reporter's ear without difficulty. From time to time radio and television opportunities come his way, as well as requests to write articles. Also, there is usually a network of friendly media only too willing to help carry the propaganda battle for the bureau leaders, to serve as vehicles of semiofficial tests of public sentiment, and to be favored in turn with inside stories. Finally, there is the array of official publications and reports, many of which can serve not only as information devices but as media supporting the bureau's policies and goals. . . .

The bureau leader may not have to propagandize a tremendous number of people in order to have an effect. First, the general public is not usually consistently interested in a subsystem. Second, the leading participants—committee members, clientele leaders, group leaders, and bureau employees—are the ones who are most sensitized to the propaganda of the subsystem. This means first that general-circulation media can usually be effectively used only to condition in a general, nontechnical way the sentiments of the public at large and their leaders toward the affairs of the subsystem, and second that "trade" or special-audience media will usually be more effective in mobilizing and sustaining the sentiments of the "insiders" or the informed and interested publics of the subsystem and their leaders.

In the publicity battle of Indian affairs, Commissioner Collier had either access to or considerable support from the following: *Indians at Work*, an official periodical of the Bureau in which he frequently editorialized about current issues of policy; the publications of the American Indian Defense Association, of which Collier had formerly been executive director, and the publications of its successor, the Association on American Indian Affairs; and *The Nation* and *New Republic*, two liberal periodicals which frequently devoted space to articles by friends of the

New Deal Indian program. Also, *Collier's* magazine occasionally presented articles by feature writers who tended to convey the Bureau's viewpoint in popularized form, and *The New York Times* and *The Washington Post*, in giving comprehensive coverage to national events, would devote space occasionally to Commissioner Collier's program. Moreover, releases from the Commissioner's office were sometimes printed in those local Western newspapers whose readers were likely to be involved. The above types of publicity were supplemented from time to time with various articles and addresses by the Commissioner. The Bureau and its chief were unusually well-fortified for the propaganda battle both among the general public and within the limited public of the subsystem.

There were counterparts of the Bureau's channels of publicity and propaganda in which the opposition could have its say—with the notable exception of official Bureau publications. Naturally enough, it was over the use of official publications that Collier had some of his greatest difficulty with committee members and with hostile group leaders. Frequently, they took statements from the Bureau's periodicals and introduced them as examples of unfair or unwarranted use of public facilities and of official status. Committee members warned Collier against such tactics, and subsequently on several occasions members took the matter of the Commissioner's publicity activities to the floor of the House or the Senate. Collier declined to alter his publicity activities, stating that he would never "hesitate to speak out." As a result, his capacity for exploiting the means of publicity seemed to reinforce his immediate influence in the subsystem; however, it also fed a smouldering resentment among those committee members who perceived him as "a good propagandist but a poor Commisisoner," and it probably contributed to their increased opposition to Collier in the long run.

INTERACTIONS BETWEEN BUREAU LEADERS AND GROUPS

Bureau leaders so often take the initiative in drafting and proposing policy changes that they must come to the committees of Congress buttressed by the favorable sentiments of significant groups represented in the subsystem, or at least of the spokesmen for these groups. The groups usually most intimately concerned with the affairs of a subsystem by virtue of their internal relationship with the bureau are its employees and its so-called clientele. Though the two are distinguishable, they often have much in common. In the first place, both depend upon the bureau: the employee for his livelihood and for other job-related satisfactions and the client for services, goods, or direction. Both in some measure are concerned about the organization's rules, goals, and resources. They are further likely to share certain loyalties, to have established certain particular mutual friendships, and perhaps to have identified with common symbols peculiar to that area of policy. Both groups will "know the lingo" of the organization, just as veterans come to know about the certificates of eligibility handled by Veterans Administration employees, or as both farm leaders and Agriculture Department personnel are conversant about parity and price supports. Finally, it is often the case that many employees of a bureau were, or are, clients as well.

Of course, neither the interests of clientele nor those of employees are uniform, and most bureau leaders are content to get major segments of each group, or perhaps only the most vocal ones to concur. This amount of employee and clientele support is well-nigh the crucial minimum for a bureau chief's success in dealing with committees. If he seems to lead and to represent these two groups, his case is likely to carry considerable weight with committee members, other things being equal, because the legislators often view the employees and the clients as considerable molders of what may be called the grass-roots sentiment in their constituencies as well as people who "know what it's all about." The employees are regarded as molders of sentiment partially because they represent the official side of the subsystem in the field. Often they can deliberately help (or fail to help) friends of committee members in the course of the performance of their duties for the bureau. Similarly, clientele leaders will be regarded as opinion molders insofar as they can voice satisfaction or dissatisfaction for the "folks back home" to hear.

Bureau attempts to mobilize employee support do not meet with uniform success, however. Committee members are likely to be highly suspicious of testimony or opinions conveyed to them under what appears to be some organized campaign from bureau headquarters. Furthermore, groups of employees themselves are likely to resist official attempts to coerce them. The case of the previously mentioned order handed down by Secretary Ickes at Commissioner Collier's request, directing employees of the Indian Bureau to refrain from criticizing new policies, was subsequently aired before a committee by certain unhappy employees, and it was used to cast the shadow of bureaucratic coercion over expressions of opinion by Bureau personnel. The cry of "gag rule" leveled at leaders of the bureaucracy has seldom helped their standing with legislators, and in this instance Ickes and Collier appeared to lose status.

Similarly, bureau leaders usually have to be circumspect about organizing the clientele. Congressmen resent this kind of "public relations," especially in their own territories, and more especially if they are not parties to it. Usually the clientele groups are sufficiently diverse so that some of the clientele who are opposed to the bureau will see to it that committee members are kept well-informed of their views as well as of the opinion-forming operations of the bureaucrats. . . .

RELATIONS BETWEEN BUREAU LEADERS AND NON-INTERNAL GROUPS. All groups participating in a subsystem are not necessarily so "internal" to the bureau as are the employees and the clientele. There are likely to be those who are simply in sympathy with the interests of the clientele and the services performed by the bureau. Others are likely to be in competition with or hostile to the clientele. In Indian affairs, a variety of non-Indian groups took interest in the policies of the Bureau apparently because they were primarily concerned about the welfare and the future of Indians as underprivileged people. Of course, other motives may have stirred their members, such as a desire to be socially active, to do good, to be identified with charitable enterprise, and so forth. Nevertheless, these groups were noted for their concern with the problem generally stated as "Indian welfare" or "Indian rights" or "Indian rehabilitation." Yet, despite this general bond of interest these groups often disagreed. For example, church and missionary groups felt that some Indian welfare organizations took too secular an attitude toward the definition of Indian advancement. However, all groups of the welfare type tended to oppose those groups which competed with Indian economic interests or which were actively engaged in trying to pry Indians loose from some of their property or privileges.

To a considerable extent, those non-clientele groups which were sympathetic toward the Bureau's clientele as a class were possessed of what may be called a cosmopolitan outlook. They drew their values from rather universal systems of ethics which were not generated primarily by particular relationships within the subsystem. They had memberships composed of people from diverse geographic and occupational categories. Some of their strongest bonds seemed to be ideological. On the other hand, the groups competing with the Indians or hostile toward the Bureau's protection of its clientele frequently seemed to be what may be characterized as more local or grass-roots in nature. Their systems of values arose from particular situations in "Indian Country." Their objectives were largely economic advantage for themselves and their kind, and their bonds were often geographic or occupational.

In gaining support for his policy views—especially to get backing before the congressional committees—the Commissioner of Indian Affairs found the cosmopolitan groups more amenable to his ideological approach. Insofar as his philosophy appealed to them, these groups were likely to support his concrete plans. The catch was, of course, that cosmopolitan groups lacked to some extent the ingredients for affecting non-Indian sentiment at the grass-roots where committee members might most likely be touched via the ballot box. Of course, cosmopolitan groups did have considerable field contact with Indians, with whom they could often make their views felt, but Indian opinion was often not the controlling one in a Western constituency, and most Committee of Indian Affairs members were from the West. Cosmopolitan groups were usually more skilled and effective in the battle of the mass media, the hearing room, and the colloquium than in the battle for local votes.

On the other hand, the local, anti-protection groups were usually less amenable to the Commissioner's views and were more likely to oppose him before the legislative committees as long as his major efforts were to guard energetically the economic interests of his clientele and to promote extensively their security through government aid. Frequently it was possible for leaders of these groups to convince committee members that they carried great weight in Western constituencies, since their memberships included more non-Indians of the West. Moreover, it was often characteristic of some grass-roots organizations that they would adopt ideological positions which would question basically the integrity of Bureau leaders and the philosophy behind their programs. Characteristic of the ideological warfare waged by these more extreme local interests was a weaving of examples of the Bureau's red tape and statements and actions of officials taken largely out of context into a pattern of interpretive innuendo. The result of this attack against the Bureau, somewhat irrespective of its intent or content, was basically to reduce congressional and public confidence in the Bureau's policies and personnel. To some extent this made it easier to assert local non-Indian interests over against those of Indians as seen by the Bureau, as well as to add strength to the anti-Administration forces in general. In fact, the more extreme members of certain of these local groups built up a considerable record of association with the more rabid, "super-patriotic," isolationist groups which fought the emerging internationalism of the New Deal from 1937 to 1941.

The Public Philosophy: Interest-Group Liberalism

Theodore Lowi

Until astonishingly recent times American national government played a marginal role in the life of the nation. Even as late as the eve of World War I, the State Department could support itself on consular fees. In most years revenues from tariffs supplied adequate financing, plus a surplus, from all other responsibilities. In 1800, there was less than one-half a federal bureaucrat per 1,000 citizens. On the eve of the Civil War there were only 1.5 federal bureaucrats per 1,000 citizens, and by 1900 that ratio had climbed to 2.7. This compares with 7 per 1,000 in 1940 and 13 per 1,000 in 1962—exclusive of military personnel.

The relatively small size of the public sphere was maintained in great part by the constitutional wall of separation between government and private life. The wall was occasionally scaled in both directions, but concern for the proper relation of private life and public order was always a serious and effective issue. Americans always talked pragmatism, in government as in all other things; but doctrine always deeply penetrated public dialogue. Power, even in the United States, needed justification.

Throughout the decades between the end of the Civil War and the Great Depression, almost every debate over a public policy became involved in the larger debate over the nature and consequences of larger and smaller spheres of government. This period was just as much a "constitutional period" as that of 1789–1820. Each period is distinguished by its effort to define (or redefine) and employ a "public philosophy."

. . .

In the constitutional epoch immediately preceding our own, ending in 1937, the perennial issue underlying all debate on public policy—and therefore the key to public philosophy in that period—was the question of the nature of government itself and whether expansion or contraction best produced public good. Liberal and conservative regimes derived their principles and rationalizations of governing and policy formulation from their positions on the question. Expansion of government was demanded by liberals as the only means of combating the injustices of a brutal physical and social world that would not change as long as it was taken as natural. Favoring government expansion became the mark of the contemporary

From the *American Political Science Review*, Vol. 61 (March 1967), pp. 5–24. Reprinted by permission of the author and publisher.

liberal. His underlying assumption was that the instruments of government provided the means for conscious induction of social change; without capacity for such change no experimentation with any new institutional forms or means of expanding rights would be possible. Opposition to such means, but not necessarily those forms or those rights, became the mark of the contemporary conservative.

There was unanimity on the criteria underlying the distinction between the adversaries. All agreed that a man's position was determined by his attitude toward government and his attitude toward deliberate social change or "planning." All agreed (and many persist in agreeing) that these two attitudes are consistent and reinforcing both as a guide for leaders in their choices among policies and as a criterion for followers in their choices among leaders. For example:

> Conservatism is committed to a discriminating defense of the social order against change and reform (liberalism). . . . By the Right, I mean generally those parties and movements that are skeptical of popular government, oppose the bright plans of the reformers and dogooders, and draw particular support from men with a sizable stake in the established order. By the Left, I mean generally those parties and movements that demand wider popular participation in government, push actively for reform, and draw particular support from the disinherited, dislocated and disgruntled. As a general rule, to which there are historic exceptions, the Right is conservative or reactionary, the Left is liberal or radical.[1]

These two criteria arose out of a particular constitutional period, were appropriate to that period, and provided a mutually reinforcing basis for doctrine during the period. After 1937, the Constitution did not die from the Revolution, as many had predicted it would. But the basis for the doctrine of that period did die. Liberalism-conservatism as the source of the public philosophy no longer made any sense. Once the principle of positive government in a growing and indeterminable political sphere was established, criteria arising out of the very issue of *whether* such a principle should be established became extinguished. They were extinguished by the total victory of one side of the old dialogue over the other.

The old dialogue has passed into the graveyard of consensus. Yet it persists. Since it has no real, operable meaning any more, it is almost purely ritualistic. However, its persistence has had its real effects. The persistence of this state of affairs so far beyond its own day, has been responsible for two pathological conditions in the 1960's. The first is that the empty rhetoric has produced a crisis of public authority. Without a basis for meaningful adversary proceedings, there has been little, if any, conflict among political actors at the level where each is forced regularly into formulating general rules, applicable to individual acts of state and at one and the same time ethically plausible to the individual citizen. The tendency of individuals to accept governmental decisions because they are good has probably at no time in this century been less intense and less widely distributed in the United States. This is producing many problems of political cynicism and irresponsibility in everyday political processes; and these problems, in turn, have tended toward the second pathological condition, the emergence of an ersatz public philosophy that seeks to justify power and to end the crisis of public authority by parceling out public authority to private parties. That is, the emerging public philosophy seeks to solve the problem of public authority by defining it away. A most maladaptive "political formula," it will inevitably exacerbate rather than end the crisis, even though its short-run effect is one of consensus and stabilization.

THE OLD FORMULA VERSUS THE NEW TIMES

A brief look at a few hard cases will be sufficient to show how little can really be drawn from the old public philosophy to justify the key modern policies and practices in either the public or the private spheres. Figure 1 helps to show at a glance just how irrelevant the old criteria are. . . . In Figure 1 are arranged a few selected public policies and private policies or widely established practices. They are placed in two dimensions according to the two basic attributes of liberalism-conservatism. Above the line are public policies; below the line are private policies or examples of established business and group practices. This vertical dimension is a simple dichotomy.[2] Therefore, above the line is the "liberal" dimension, and below the line the "conservative" dimension. The horizontal dimension is a continuum. Each policy or practice is placed along the line from left to right roughly according to its real or probable impact upon the society. To the left is the liberal direction, where policies are placed if they are likely to affect a direct change in things. To the right is the conservative direction, where policies and practices are placed if they tend directly to maintain one or another status quo.

If the two criteria—attitude toward government and attitude toward change—were consistent and if together they described and justified programs, then liberal policies would be concentrated in the upper left corner, and conservative policies would be concentrated below the line to the right. Little study of the Diagram is necessary to discover that the inconsistencies between the two criteria are extreme. And little reflection is necessary to see that policy makers are being guided by some other principles, if principles do guide at all. The fact that private and public policies range across the extremes of maintenance and change suggests the simple but significant proposition that no institution with the capacity and resources for affecting the society works always in the same direction.[3] Yet a public philosophy based upon public-private and change-maintenance criteria requires unidirectional institutions. Obviously, the liberal-conservative dialogue made sense only up until, but not after, the establishment of positive government.[4]

Analysis of the real or potential impact of public policies shows how incomplete is the fit between the earlier public philosophy and the policies it is supposed to support and justify. It shows that those who espouse social change in the abstract, especially government-engineered social change, are seldom peddling policies that would clearly effect any such change. Conversely, it shows that those who harangue on principle against government and change are frequently in real life pushing for strong doses of each. If these criteria do not really guide the leaders, they offer almost no plausible justification for the intelligent follower. A few examples in detail follow.

(1) The income tax. All taxes discriminate. The political question arises over the kind of discrimination the society desires. The graduated or progressive income tax is capable of effecting drastic changes in the relations among classes and between man and his property. According to the two criteria in question,

Figure 1 *Selected Public and Private Policies Arranged According to Probable Effect on Society*

Public policies (above the line) — liberal → conservative						
Graduated income tax (potential) Social Security programs based on graduated income tax Civil rights package Low tariffs	Luxury taxes Real antitrust "Yardstick" regulation (TVA)	Growth fiscal policies Graduated Income Tax (United States)	Counter-cyclical fiscal policies Sales taxes Aids to small business	Social Security programs based on insurance principles (U.S.) Direct regulation (e.g., FCC, ICC, CAB, etc.) Antitrust by consent decree	Existing farm programs Restraint of competition (NRA, fair trade, anti-price discrim.) Tax on colored margarine	(Kennedy-Freeman farm proposals) High tariffs Import quotas Utilities Group representation on boards Strict gold standard with no bank money

Private policies (below the line) — liberal → conservative						
Competition in agriculture New interest groups Corporate philanthropy Merit hiring and promotion	Competitive business	Oligopoly with research competition	Oligopoly without competition (steel, cigarettes.) Brand names Ethnic appeals of political campaigns	Trade associations Pools Basing points Price leadership Fair trade policies Union unemployment and automation policies		Monopoly Old interest groups (NAM, AFL-CIO, TWU, etc.)

Above the line: Public policies ("liberal")
Below the line: Private policies or practices ("conservative")

Toward the left side: Policies likely to produce change ("liberal")
Toward the right side: Policies likely to maintain existing practices ("conservative")

then, the steeply progressive income tax is "liberal" both because it is governmental and because it effects social change. Our own income tax structure can be called only mildly "liberal," if at all, because it is only mildly, if at all, progressive, allowing as it does full exemption on interest from public debt, fast write-offs, depletion allowances, host of "Louis B. Mayer Amendments," privileges on real estate transactions, and so on *ad nauseum*. It is generally understood that the effective ceiling on taxes is not 91% or 75% but a good deal less than 50%. And considering all taxes together, it seems fairly clear that they comprise a bastion against rather than a weapon for fluidity among classes and channels of opportunity. . . .

(2) The social security system. This is, of course, a bundle of policies, and accuracy would require classification of each. On balance, however, they are "liberal" only because they are governmental; they are conservative in their impact on social structure and opportunity. If they promote welfare, then, indeed, it is important to be able to say that a conservative policy *can* promote welfare. Above all else, old age insurance, unemployment compensation and the like are techniques of fiscal policy. They are, initially, important countercyclical devices, "automatic stabilizers," that work through the maintenance of demand throughout the business cycle and through the maintenance of existing economic relationships without dislocation. In this dimension, "liberals" are a good deal less willing to take chances than "conservatives."

At another dimension, social security in the United States is an even more interesting case of the gap between the old public philosophy and the real impact of established programs. For, social security programs are techniques of social as well as fiscal control, and as such they are clearly conservative. The American system of social security is based fairly strictly on an insurance principle, a principle of the spreading of risk through forced saving. Government's role is essentially paternalistic; speaking roughly, government raises the minimum wage by the amount of the employer's contribution, takes that plus about an equal amount from the employee's wages, and says, "This much of your income we'll not trust you to spend." This principle of contributory social security does not affect the class structure, the sum total of opportunity, or anything else; on the contrary, it tends to maintain existing patterns. It helps make people a little happier to be where they are doing what they are doing. The social security system is consistent with both criteria of liberalism only to the extent that it is based on a graduated income tax or to the extent that it supports those who did not contribute before entering the rolls. And that is a very small extent indeed.

The medicare program is significant as an addition to the scope and scale of social security, but in no important way does it change the social significance of social security. After President Kennedy proposed a medical care bill limited to the aged and based on "actuarial soundness," there was not even any need to debate the social significance of the bill. Actuarial soundness was a sufficient message that social security would remain altogether what it had been, except for the temporary addition of people who were already old and had made no contribution before entering the rolls. The only surprise in the medicare case was the difficulty of passage. But that was not due to a stalemate between liberalism and conservatism. It was due to a stalemate between the unorganized and apathetic elderly and the intensely felt and highly organized trade union interests of the American Medical Association. A program that originated with Bismarck was simply a while longer being needed in the United States.

(3) The farm programs provide an equally good case of the irrelevance of policy to the old public philosophy. High price supports with crop controls, the center of farm policy for a generation, are supported by "liberals"; but they are "liberal" because and only because they are governmental. The entire establishment escaped death in 1949–50 only with urban-labor support, but that support proves nothing about liberalism.

What has been the purpose and what is the impact of such a program? Basically, the aim was to restore and to maintain a pre-1914 agriculture in face of extremely strong contrary financial, industrial and technological developments. The effect of the program has clearly been as intended, for far larger numbers of farmers and subsistence farms remain than are supportable in strictly economic terms. And the program perpetuates the established sizes of a farm and relationships among farmers by basing present quotas and controls upon past outputs, state by state, county by county, and farm by farm. The New Frontier and Great Society proposals must be ranked as even more "conservative," despite their governmental base, because they would have delegated to a few leading farmers or farm group leaders in each surplus commodity area the power to determine the quotas, thus allowing those most involved to decide *for themselves* just what there is about agriculture worth conserving. This is elevation of government-by-conflict-of-interest to a virtuous principle. Early in his presidency, Lyndon Johnson called the leaders of the major agriculture interest groups to formulate new policy solutions to agriculture. This was the beginning of the Johnson round. In music, a round is a form in which everything is repeated over and over again.

(4) Business practices. The "conservative" side of the argument comes out no better upon examination. Competitive business enterprise is a highly dynamic force that usually makes change normal, innovation necessary, and influence by ordinary individuals over economic decisions possible. For these reasons many forms of competitive enterprise should be thought of as supported by real liberals despite the fact that government is only in a marginal way responsible for it. But, except for martyrs from Thurmond Arnold to Walter S. Adams who have sought vainly to use government to decentralize industry, the net impact of attitudes toward business from conservatives as well as liberals has been to restrain the system. One might say that the only difference between old-school liberals and conservatives is that the former would destroy the market through public means and the latter through private means. This is very largely due to the fact that, lacking any independent standards, all politicians depend upon those organized interests that already have access to government and to the media of communication. According to the second criterion of liberalism-conservatism, *all established interest groups are conservative.*[5] Government policy is one of many strategies organized interests feel free to pursue. In this respect it is useless to distinguish between NAM and AFL-CIO. Trade associations, for example, exist to "stabilize the market," in other words, to maintain existing relations among members despite any fluctuations in their respective sectors of the economy. They, in turn, are the primary determiners of private as well as public policies

toward business and business competition. Holding companies, pools, market sharing, information sharing, interlocking directorships, price leadership, competition through advertising and not prices, and collusion in bidding are typical nongovernmental policies, which become inevitable if they are not illegal. On the other hand, they are functionally in no way distinguishable from such governmental policies as basing points laws, fair trade laws, antiprice discrimination laws, NRA codes, and so on. To the extent that liberalism-conservatism is taken seriously as the source of public philosophy, liberals-conservatives become hemmed in by it, too rigid to withdraw their sentiments as new needs become old, vested interests. They are inevitably betrayed by the very groups that profited most by their support.

The enormous inconsistency between what public policy really is and what the old doctrine supposes it to be may turn out to be merely true but still inconsequential. This might be the case if it could be shown that American public men were the original pragmatists and were never in need of any doctrine other than the loose social code that binds us all. This possibility must be rejected. Stable countries, with their highly rationalized political order, have great need of legitimizing rituals, perhaps more so than transitional societies where expectations are not so high. Moreover, the very persistence of the old criteria so far beyond their appropriate hour can be taken as an index to the need American elites have for doctrinal support.

The old public philosophy became outmoded because in our time it applies to the wrong class of objects. Statesmen simply no longer disagree about whether government should be involved; therefore they neither seek out the old criteria for guidance through their disagreements, nor do they really have need of the criteria to justify the mere governmental character of policies. But this does not mean that public men are not now being guided by some other, widely shared, criteria that do apply to the relevant class of objects. The good functionalist must insist upon being guided by the hypothesis that some political formula or public philosophy does exist. If it is obvious that public men are no longer governed by the older public philosophy, then the next logical proposition is this, that there is some other public philosophy with which public policy behaviors are consistent, but it may be one not clearly enough formulated to be well known yet beyond public men themselves.

I contend that such criteria have emerged in a new and already well-developed public philosophy through which public men are attempting to grapple with the pathologies created by the persistence of the old formula. I contend, further, that the new public philosophy is the source of important new political pathologies in America. I contend, finally, that the new public philosophy is pathological because it emerged not out of an evolution of the older but out of the total and complete silence of the older upon those objects with which any new public philosophy had to deal.

INTEREST-GROUP LIBERALISM

The weaknesses of the old liberalism-conservatism were not altogether clear before the 1960's. This tardiness is due simply to the intervention of two wars and then an eight-year period of relative quiescence in policy making and in the saliency of politics and government to the masses. Truman's Fair Deal agenda, already left over from the end of the New Deal, held fire for over a decade until it became a major part of the Democratic agenda of the 1960's and comprised a very large proportion of the successful record of the 89th Congress, the most actively legislating Congress since 1933. Even the historic *Brown* v. *Board of Education* decision failed to bring about noticeable expansion and intensification of political activity until the Little Rock debacle of 1957. With increasing pace thereafter, new pressures began to be placed upon political institutions, and another round of governmental activity was in the making. In many ways the period that began in 1957 with Little Rock and Sputnik was as much a constitutional revolution as that of the 1930's. In this decade—as measured by Federal budgets, personnel, the sheer proliferation of service and other agencies, or the expansion of public regulatory authority—there have clearly been a civil rights revolution, an educational revolution, and a scientific and technological revolution.

All of this activity proves that there is no end to government responsibility. It is not possible to automate all the stabilizers. The new activity in the 1960's also proves that the political apparatus of democracy can respond promptly once the constitutional barriers to democratic choice have been lowered. However, that is only the beginning of the story, because the almost total democratization of the Constitution and the contemporary expansion of the public sector have been accompanied by expansion, not by contraction, of a sense of illegitimacy about public objects. Here is a spectacular paradox. We witness governmental effort of gigantic proportion to solve problems forthwith and directly. Yet we witness expressions of personal alienation and disorientation increasing, certainly not subsiding, in frequency and intensity; and we witness further weakening of informal controls in the family, neighborhood and groups. We witness a vast expansion of effort to bring the ordinary citizen into closer rapport with the democratic process, including unprecedented efforts to confer upon the poor and ineducable the power to make official decisions involving their own fate. Yet at the very same time we witness crisis after crisis in the very institutions in which the new methods of decision-making seemed most appropriate.

It is as though each new program or program expansion were admission of prior governmental inadequacy or failure without necessarily being a contribution to order and well-being. The War on Poverty programs have become as often as not instruments of social protest. The Watts riots, the movements for police review boards in many cities, the sit-ins and marches even where no specifically evil laws are being enforced against a special race or group, the strikes and protests by civil servants, nurses, doctors, teachers, transport and defense workers, and others in vital occupations—all these and many others are evidence of increasing impatience with established ways of resolving social conflict and dividing up society's values. Verbal and organizational attacks on that vague being, the "power structure," even in cities with histories of strong reform movements and imaginative social programs, reflect increasing rejection of pluralistic patterns in favor of more direct prosecution of claims against society. Far from insignificant as a sign of the times is emergence of a third and a fourth national party movement, one on either extreme but alike in their opposition to centrist parties, electoral politics, and pre-election compromise. Many of these new patterns and problems may have been generated by racial issues, but it is clear that that was only a precipitant. The ironic fact is that the post-1937 political economy, either because of or in spite of government policies and two wars, had produced unprecedented prosperity, and as the national output increased arithmetically the rate of rising expectation must have gone up geometrically—in a modern expression of the Malthusian Law. Public authority was left to grapple with this alienating gap between expectation and reality.

Prosperity might merely have produced a gigantic race among all to share in its benefits. The expansion of the public sector might have increased the legitimacy of government and other public objects through redistribution of opportunities to join the prosperity. Instead, the expansion of government that helped produce sustained prosperity also produced a crisis of public authority. Why? Because the old justification for that expansion had so little to say beyond the need for the expansion itself. The class of objects to which the new and appropriate public philosophy would have to apply should, it seems obvious, be the forms, structures and procedures of government control. There are vast technical, political and ethical questions involved in what are and what ought to be the consequences of the various ways in which power can be administered and employed. What constitutes "due process" in an age of positive government? What impact does one or another administrative process have upon society, upon the specific clientele whose compliance is sought, upon the capacity of the next generation to respond, governmentally and otherwise, to the problems of its own time?

Out of the developing crisis in public authority has developed an ersatz political formula that does, for all its problems, offer the public man some guidance and some justification in his efforts to shape, form and provide for the administration of positive laws in the positive state. There are several possible names for this contemporary replacement of liberalism-conservatism. A strong possibility would be *corporatism*, but its history as a concept gives it several unwanted connotations, such as conservative Catholicism or Italian fascism, that keep it from being quite suitable. Another is *syndicalism*, but among many objections is the connotation of anarchy too far removed from American experience or intentions. However, the new American public philosophy is a variant of those two alien philosophies.

The most clinically accurate term to describe the American variant is *interest-group liberalism*. It may be called liberalism because it expects to use government in a positive and expansive role, it is motivated by the highest sentiments, and it possesses strong faith that what is good for government is good for the society. It is "interest-group liberalism" because it sees as both necessary and good that the policy agenda and the public interest be defined in terms of the organized interests in society. In brief sketch, the working model of the interest group liberal is a vulgarized version of the pluralist model of modern political science. It assumes: (1) Organized interests are homogeneous and easy to define, sometimes monolithic. Any "duly elected" spokesman for any interest is taken as speaking in close approximation for each and every member. (2) Organized interests pretty much fill up and adequately represent most of the sectors of our lives, so that one organized group can be found effectively answering and checking some other organized group as it seeks to prosecute its claims against society.[6] And (3) the role of government is one of ensuring access particularly to the most effectively organized, and of ratifying the agreements and adjustments worked out among the competing leaders and their claims. This last assumption is supposed to be a statement of how our democracy works and how it ought to work. Taken together, these assumptions constitute the Adam Smith "hidden hand" model applied to groups. Ironically, it is embraced most strongly by the very people most likely to reject the Smith model applied in its original form to firms in the market.

These assumptions are the basis of the new public philosophy. The policy behaviors of old-school liberals and conservatives, of Republicans and Democrats, so inconsistent with liberalism-conservatism criteria, are fully consistent with the criteria drawn from interest-group liberalism: *The most important difference between liberals and conservatives, Republicans and Democrats—however they define themselves—is to be found in the interest groups they identify with. Congressmen are guided in their votes, Presidents in their programs, and administrators in their discretion, by whatever organized interests they have taken for themselves as the most legitimate; and that is the measure of the legitimacy of demands.*

The assumptions of the model and the concluding behavioral proposition constitute, for better or worse, an important part of the working methodology of modern, empirical political science. However, quite another story with quite different consequences is how all of this became elevated from an hypothesis about political behavior to an ideology about how the democratic system ought to work and then became ultimately elevated to that ideology most widely shared among contemporary public men.

INTEREST-GROUP LIBERALISM: AN INTELLECTUAL HISTORY. The opening of the national government to positive action on a large scale was inevitably to have an impact upon political justification just as on political technique. However, the inventors of technique were less than inventive for justification of particular policies at particular times. . . .

Nor was the doctrine of popular government and majority rule, which was so important in the victory of liberalism over conservatism, adequate guidance after the demise of liberalism-conservatism. If one reviews the New Deal period and thereafter he will see how little propensity Americans have had to use the majority rule justification. The reasons why are fairly apparent. Justification of positive government programs on the basis of popular rule required above all a proclamation of the supremacy of Congress. The abdication of Congress in the 1930's in the passage of the fundamental New Deal legislation could never have been justified in the name of popular government. With all due respect to Congressmen, little discernible effort was made to do so. Statutory and investigatory infringements on civil liberties during World War II and during the Cold War, plus the popular support of McCarthyism, produced further reluctance to fall back on Congress and majority rule as the fount of public policy wisdom. Many who wished to use this basis anyway sought support in the plebiscitary character of the Presidency. However, "presidential liberals" have had to blind themselves to many complications in the true basis of presidential authority and to the true—the bureaucratic—expression of presidential will.

The very practices that made convincing use of popular rule doctrine impossible—delegation of power to administrators, interest representation, outright delegation of power to trade associations, and so on—were what made interest-group liberalism so attractive an alternative. And because the larger interest groups did claim large memberships, they could be taken virtually as popular rule in modern dress. Interest-group liberalism simply corresponded impressively well with the realities of power. Thus, it possessed a little of science and some of the trappings of popular rule. Political scientists, after all, were pioneers in insisting upon recognition of the group, as well as in helping to elevate the pressure-group system from power to virtue. Political scientists had for a long time argued that the group is the necessary variable in political analysis for breaking through the formalisms of government. . . .

Following World War II, one easily notes among political scientists the widespread acceptance of the methodology and, more importantly here, the normative position. Among political scientists the best expression of interest-group liberalism was probably that of Wilfred Binkley and Malcolm Moos. The fact that it was so prominent in their American government basic textbook suggests that it tended to reflect conventional wisdom among political scientists even in 1948. Binkley and Moos argued that the "basic concept for understanding the dynamics of government is the multi-group nature of modern society or the modern state."[7] Political reality could be grasped scientifically as a "parallelogram of forces" among groups, and the public-interest is "determined and established" through the free competition of interest groups: "The necessary composing and compromising of their differences is the practical test of what constitutes the public interest."

The fact that a doctrine has some support in the realities of power certainly helps to explain its appeal as a doctrine. But there were also several strongly positive reasons for the emergence of this particular doctrine. The first, and once perhaps the only, is that it has helped flank the constitutional problems of federalism. Manifestations of the corporate state were once limited primarily to the Extension Service of the Department of Agriculture, with self-administration by the land grant colleges and the local farmers and commerce associations. Self-administration by organized groups was an attractive technique precisely because it could be justified as so decentralized and permissive as to be hardly federal at all. Here began the ethical and conceptual mingling of the notion of organized private groups with the notions of "local government" and "self-government." Ultimately direct interest group participation in government became synonymous with self-government, first for reasons of strategy, then by belief that the two were indeed synonymous. As a propaganda strategy it eased acceptance in the courts, then among the locals who still believed the farmer was and should be independent. Success as strategy increased usage; usage helped elevate strategy to doctrine. The users began to believe in their own symbols.

A second positive appeal of interest-group liberalism is strongly related to the first. Interest-group liberalism helps solve a problem for the democratic politician in the modern state where the stakes are so high. This is the problem of enhanced conflict and how to avoid it. The politician's contribution to society is his skill in resolving conflict. However, direct confrontations are sought only by the zealous ideologues and "outsiders." The typical American politician displaces and defers and delegates conflict where possible; he squarely faces conflict only when he must. Interest-group liberalism offers a justification for keeping major combatants apart. It provides a theoretical basis for giving to each according to his claim, the price for which is a reduction of concern for what others are claiming. In other words, it transforms logrolling from necessary evil to greater good. This is the basis for the "consensus" so often claimed these days. It is also the basis for President Kennedy's faith that in our day ideology has given over to administration. It is inconceivable that so sophisticated a person as he could believe, for example, that his setting of guidelines for wage and price increases was a purely administrative act. Here, in fact, is a policy that will never be "administered" in the ordinary sense of the word. The guidelines provide a basis for direct and regular policy-making between the President (or his agent) and the spokesmen for industry and the spokesmen for labor. This is a new phase of government relations with management and labor, and it is another step consistent with the interest-group liberal criterion of direct access.

The third positive appeal of interest-group liberalism is that it is a direct, even if pathological, response to the crisis of public authority. The practice of dealing only with organized claims in formulating policy, and of dealing exclusively through organized claims in implementing programs helps create the sense that power need not be power at all, nor control control. If sovereignty is parceled out among the groups, then who's out anything? . . .

President Eisenhower talked regularly about the desirability of business-government "partnerships," despite the misgivings in his farewell address about the "military-industrial complex." However, explicit and systematic expression of interest-group liberalism is much more the contribution of the Democrats. There is little reason to believe that one party believes more ardently than the other; but the best evidence can be found among the more articulate Democrats, especially in the words of two of the leading Democratic intellectuals, Professors John Kenneth Galbraith and Arthur Schlesinger, Jr.[8] To Professor Galbraith: "Private economic power is held in check by the countervailing power of those who are subject to it. The first begets the second."[9] Concentrated economic power stimulates other business interests (in contrast to the Smithian consumer), which organize against it. This results in a natural tendency toward equilibrium. But Galbraith is not really writing a theoretical alternative to Adam Smith; he is writing a program of government action. For he admits to the limited existence of effective countervailing power and proposes that where it is absent or too weak, government policy should seek out and support or, where necessary, create the organizations capable of countervailing. Government thereby pursues the public interest and makes itself superfluous at the same time. This is a sure-fire, nearly scientific, guide to interest-group liberalism. Professor Schlesinger's views are summarized for us in the campaign tract he wrote in 1960. To Schlesinger, the essential difference between the Democratic and Republican parties is that the

Democratic party is a truly multi-interest party in the grand tradition extending back to Federalist No. 10. In power, it offers multi-interest administration and therefore ought to be preferred over the Republican Party and:

> What is the essence of a multi-interest administration? It is surely that the leading interests in society are all represented in the interior processes of policy formation— which can be done only if members or advocates of these interests are included in key positions of government. . . .[10]

This theme Schlesinger repeated in his more serious and more recent work, *A Thousand Days*. Following his account of the 1962 confrontation of President Kennedy with the steel industry and the later decision to cut taxes and cast off for expansionary rather than stabilizing fiscal policy, Schlesinger concludes:

> The ideological debates of the past began to give way to a new agreement on the practicalities of managing a modern economy. There thus developed in the Kennedy years a national accord on economic policy—a new consensus which gave hope of harnessing government, business and labor in rational partnership for a steadily expanding American economy."[11]

INTEREST-GROUP LIBERALISM AND PUBLIC POLICIES IN THE 1960's. A significant point in the entire argument is that the Republicans would disagree with Schlesinger on the *facts* but not on the *basis* of his distinction. The Republican rejoinder would be, in effect, "Democratic Administrations are *not* more multi-interest than Republican." And, in my opinion, this would be almost the whole truth. This principle has been explicitly applied in the formulation of a large number of policies, especially since the return of the Democrats to power in 1961. That is, policy makers have in numerous new programs added elements of official group representation and have officially applied "participatory democracy" to the implementation as well as the formulation of law as part of the justification of their action. There are additional policies where evidence of the application of interest-group liberalism is clear even though not as consciously intended or as much a part of the record of self-praise.

President Kennedy provides an especially good starting point because his positions were clear and because justification was especially important to him. No attention need be paid to the elements of liberalism-conservatism in his program[12] but only to the consistency of his requests with interest-group liberalism. John Kennedy was bred to a politics of well-organized and autonomous units of power. Locally they were more likely ethnic, religious and neighborhood organizations, but they had to be reckoned with as powerful interest groups. The national party he set out to win in 1956 was also a congeries of autonomous factions and blocs; and it has been said that he succeeded by recreating the "New Deal coalition." But there is a vast difference between pluralism inside political parties and legitimized pluralism built into government programs. The one does not necessarily follow from the other, unless leaders believe it is desirable. President Kennedy's proposals and rhetoric mark his belief in that desirability. Many of his most important proposals mark his very real contribution to the corporatizing of the government-group nexus in the United States.

The agriculture problem, high and early on the New Frontier agenda, was to be solved somewhat differently from all earlier attempts, and that difference is much to the point. At local levels, federal agriculture programs had always been cooperative, with committees of local farm dignitaries applying the state and national standards to local conditions. President Kennedy proposed simply to bring this pattern to the center and to have the farmers, represented by group leaders, *set* the standards as well as apply them. Essentially, this was NRA applied to agriculture.

There was no attempt to reinstitute an industrial NRA pattern, but there were, just the same, moves toward recognition of the organized side of industry in the "interior process" of government. . . .

During the Johnson Administration the doctrines and policies of interest-group liberalism have been elevated to new highs of usage and rationalization. It is coming of age by being provided with new and appropriate halo words. The most important is "creative federalism," about which President Johnson and his Great Society team have spoken frequently and enthusiastically. This and related terms—such as partnership, maximum feasible participation, and, above all, consensus—seem to be very sincerely felt by present government leaders. The sentiments are coming to be shared widely among non-government leaders and are at the bottom of the extraordinary business support Johnson received during his most active period of legislative creativity. . . .

. . . President Johnson and his Administration have expanded the degree to which private organizations and local authorities become endowed with national sovereignty. Corporativistic programs inherited from the New Deal have been strengthened in the degree to which they can share in the new, explicit rationale. This has been particularly noticeable in the power and natural resources field, where policies are now quite explicitly left to the determination of those participants who know the "local situation" best. It is quite at the center of Great Society expansions of existing programs. When still Assistant Secretary for Education, Francis Keppel described federal education policy this way: "To speak of 'federal aid' [to education] simply confuses the issue. It is more appropriate to speak of federal support to special purposes . . . an investment made by a partner who has clearly in mind the investments of other partners—local, state and private."

The most significant contribution of the Great Society to the growing ratio such corporativistic programs bear to the sum total of federal activity is the War on Poverty, particularly the community action program. To the old progressive the elimination of poverty was a passionate dream, to the socialist a philosophic and historic necessity. To the interest-group liberal, poverty is becoming just another status around which power centers ought to organize. If one hasn't organized, then organize it. In so organizing it, poverty is not eliminated, but inconsistency in the manner of government's relation to society is reduced. Organizing the poor, something that once was done only in the Threepenny Opera, helps legitimize the interest-group liberal's preference for dealing only with organized claims. The "Peachum factor" in public affairs is best personified in Sargent Shriver. In getting the War on Poverty under way Shriver was misunderstood in many matters, particularly on any insistence that the poor be represented in some mathematically exact way. But one aspect of the doctrine was clear all the time. This was (and is) that certain types of groups should always be involved some way. As he listed them they are: "governmental groups," philanthropic, religious, business, and labor groups, and "the poor." The significance lies primarily in the equality of the listing. "Governmental groups" are simply one more type of participant.

Interest-group liberalism thus seems closer to being the established, operative ideology of the American elite than any other body of doctrine. The United States is far from 100 per cent a corporate state; but each administration, beginning with the New Deal revolution, has helped reduce the gap. And it is equally significant that few if any programs organized on the basis of direct interest representation or group self-administration have ever been eliminated. To the undoubted power of organized interests has now been added the belief in their virtue. There would always be delegation of sovereignty to interest groups in some proportion of the total body of governmental activities. The new context of justification simply means far more direct delegation than the realities of power, unsupported by legitimacy, would call for.

In sum, modern liberals are ambivalent about government. Government is obviously the most efficacious way of achieving good purposes in our age. But it is efficacious because it is involuntary; as one of the founders of modern social science put it, modern government possesses a monopoly of legal coercion in a society. To live with their ambivalence, modern policy makers have fallen into believing that public policy involves merely the identification of the problems toward which government ought to be aimed. It pretends, through "pluralism," "countervailing power," "creative federalism," "partnership," and "participatory democracy," that the unsentimental business of coercion is not involved and that the unsentimental decisions of how to employ coercion need not really be made at all. Stated in the extreme, the policies of interest-group liberalism are end-oriented. Few standards of implementation, if any, accompany delegations of power. The requirement of standards has been replaced by the requirement of participation. The requirement of law has been replaced by the requirement of contingency.

THE COSTS OF INTEREST-GROUP LIBERALISM

For all the political advantages interest-group liberals have in their ideology, there are high costs involved. Unfortunately, these costs are not strongly apparent at the time of the creation of a group-based program. As Wallace Sayre once observed, the gains of a change tend to be immediate, the costs to be cumulative. However, it takes no long-run patience or the spinning of fine webs to capture and assess the consequences of group-based policy solutions. Three major consequences are suggested and assessed here: (1) the atrophy of institutions of popular control; (2) the maintenance of old and creation of new structures of privilege; and (3) conservatism, in several senses of the word.

1. In his *The Public Philosophy*, Lippmann was rightfully concerned over the "derangement of power" whereby modern democracies tend first toward unchecked elective leadership and then toward drainage of public authority from elective leaders down into their constituencies. However, Lippmann erred if he thought of constituencies only as voting constituencies. Drainage has tended toward "support group constituencies," and with special consequence. Parceling out policy-

making power to the most interested parties destroys political responsibility. A program split off with a special imperium to govern itself is not merely an administrative unit. It is a structure of power with impressive capacities to resist central political control.

Besides making conflict-of-interest a principle of government rather than a criminal act, participatory programs shut out the public. To be more precise, programs of this sort tend to cut out all that part of the mass that is not specifically organized around values strongly salient to the goals of the program. They shut out the public, first, at the most creative phase of policy making—the phase where the problem is first defined. Once problems are defined, alliances form accordingly and the outcome is both a policy and a reflection of superior power. If the definition is laid out by groups along lines of established group organization, there is always great difficulty for an amorphous public to be organized in any other terms. The public is shut out, secondly, at the phase of accountability. In programs in which group self-administration is legitimate, the administrators are accountable primarily to the groups, only secondarily to President or Congress as institutions. In brief, to the extent that organized interests legitimately control a program there is functional rather than substantive accountability. . . .

Finally, the public is shut out by tendencies toward conspiracy to shut the public out. One of the assumptions underlying direct group representation is that on the boards and in the staff and among the recognized outside consultants there will be regular countervailing and checks and balances. In Schattschneider's terms, this would be expected to expand the "scope of conflict." But there is nothing inevitable about that, and the safer assumption might well be the converse. . . .

2. Programs following the principles of interest-group liberalism create privilege, and it is a type of privilege particularly hard to bear or combat because it is touched with the symbolism of the state. The large national interest groups that walk the terrains of national politics are already fairly tight structures of power. We need no more research to support Michels' iron tendency toward oligarchy in "private governments." Pluralists ease our problem of abiding the existence of organized interests by characterizing oligarchy as simply a negative name for organization: In combat people want and need to be organized and led. Another, somewhat less assuaging, assertion of pluralism is that the member approves the goals of the group or is free to leave it for another, or can turn his attention to one of his "overlapping memberships" in other groups. But however true these may be in pluralistic *politics*, everything changes when some of the groups are co-opted by the state in pluralistic *government*. The American Farm Bureau Federation is no "voluntary association" insofar as it is a legitimate functionary in Extension work. NAHB, NAREB, NAACP or NAM are no ordinary lobbies after they become part of the "interior processes of policy formation."

The more clear and legitimized the representation of a group or its leaders in policy formation, the less voluntary is membership in that group and the more necessary is loyalty to its leadership for people who share the interests in question. And, the more clear the official practice of recognizing only organized interests, the more hierarchy is introduced into the society. It is a well-recognized and widely appreciated function of formal groups in modern societies to provide much of the necessary every-day social control. However, when the very thought processes behind public policy are geared toward those groups they are bound to take on much of the involuntary character of *public* control. . . .

Even when the purpose of the program is the uplifting of the underprivileged, the administrative arrangement favored by interest-group liberalism tends toward creation of new privilege instead. Urban redevelopment programs based upon federal support of private plans do not necessarily, but do all too easily, become means by which the building industry regularizes itself. An FHA run essentially by the standards of the NAREB became a major escape route for middle class to leave the city for suburbia rather than a means of providing housing for all. Urban redevelopment, operating for nearly two decades on a principle of local government and local developer specification of federal policy, has been used in the South (and elsewhere) as an effective instrument for Negro removal. Organizing councils for the poverty program have become first and foremost means of elevating individual spokesmen for the poor and of determining which churches and neighborhood organizations shall be the duly recognized channels of legitimate demand. Encouragement of organization among Negroes and the White and non-White poor is important. Early recognition of a few among many emerging leaders and organizations as legitimate administrators or policy-makers takes a serious risk of destroying the process itself (more on this directly below).

3. Government by and through interest groups is in impact conservative in almost every sense of that term. Part of its conservatism can be seen in another look at the two foregoing objections: Weakening of popular government and support of privilege are, in other words, two aspects of conservatism. It is beside the point to argue that these consequences are not intended. A third dimension of conservatism, stressed here separately, is the simple conservatism of resistance to change. . . .

The war-on-poverty pattern, even in its early stages, provides a rich testing ground. I observed above that early official cooption of poverty leaders creates privilege before, and perhaps instead of, alleviating poverty. Another side of this war is the war the established welfare groups are waging against the emergence of the newly organizing social forces. Many reports are already remarking upon the opposition established welfare and church groups are putting up against the new groups.

. . . Old and established groups doing good works might naturally look fearfully upon the emergence of competing, perhaps hostile, groups. That is well and good—until their difference is one of "who shall be the government?" Conservatism then becomes necessary as a matter of survival.

The tendency toward the extreme conservatism of sharing legitimate power with private organizations is possibly stronger in programs more strictly economic. Adams and Gray reviewed figures on assignment of FM radio broadcasting licenses and found that as of 1955, 90 per cent of the FM stations were merely "little auxiliaries" of large AM networks. They also note that the same pattern was beginning to repeat itself in FCC licensing of UHF television channels.[13] The mythology may explain this as a case of "interest group power," but that begs the question. Whatever power was held by the networks was based largely on the commitment the FCC implied in the original grants of licenses. Having granted exclusive privileges to private groups in the public domain (in this case the original assignment of frequencies) without laying down practical conditions for perpetual public retention of the domain itself, the FCC had actually given over sovereignty. The companies acquired property rights and legally vested interests in the grant that interfere enormously with later efforts to affect the grant. Thus, any FCC attempt to expand the communications business through FM would deeply affect the positions and "property" of the established AM companies and networks. Issuing FM licenses to new organizations would have required an open assault on property as well as the established market relations. Leaving aside all other judgements of the practice, it is clearly conservative. Granting of licenses and other privileges unconditionally, and limiting sovereignty by allowing the marketing of properties to be influenced by the possession of the privilege, are practices also to be found in oil, in water power, in the newer sources of power, in transportation, in the "parity" programs of agriculture.

Wherever such practices are found there will also be found strong resistance to change. . . .

There are social and psychological mechanisms as well as economic and vested interests working against change. As programs are split off and allowed to establish self-governing relations with clientele groups, professional norms usually spring up, governing the proper ways of doing things. These rules-of-the-game heavily weight access and power in favor of the established interests, just as American parliamentary rules-of-the-game have always tended to make Congress a haven for classes in retreat.

INTEREST-GROUP LIBERALISM AND HOW TO SURVIVE IT

Quite possibly all of these developments are part of some irresistible historical process. In that case policy-makers would never really have had any alternative when they created group-based programs. And in that case the ideology of interest-group liberalism simply reflects and rationalizes the realities of power. However, the best test of a deterministic hypothesis is whether real-world efforts to deny it fail. Thus, a consideration of remedies is worthwhile.

. . .

. . . First, it is assumed that positive government is here to stay and expand. Thus, proposals for return to a principle of lesser government and for policies in the lower left-hand corner of the Diagram, while logical and perhaps desirable, are not acceptable. Second, it is assumed that *real* political pluralism is a desirable form of democracy and that it is a desirable democratic antidote to the "incorporated pluralism" which has been the object of criticism throughout this essay.

1. The first part of the remedy is attractive precisely because it is so obvious. This is to discredit interest-group liberalism as official ideology. Essentially, this is the effort of this paper. Unless we are locked in a predetermined secular trend, a change of ideology can affect the pattern of power just as the pattern of power can affect ideology. Certainly the egalitarian ideology has affected the distribution of power in every country where it has had any currency at all. A change of ide-

ology could keep to a minimum the number of programs that merely incorporate the forces responsible for passage. Some other ideology would provide a basis for resisting many of the most outrageous claims for patronage and privilege made by organized interests.

2. The second part of the remedy is institutional and also suggests the direction a new ideology ought to take. This is to push direct group access back one giant step in the political process, somehow to insulate administrative agencies from full group participation. This means restoration of the Federalist No. 10 ideology in which "factions" are necessary evils that require regulation, not accommodation. . . .

Pushing group representation and "participatory democracy" back into Congress and away from the executive requires several relatively traditional steps. The first would be revival of a constitutional doctrine that is still valid but widely disregarded. This is the rule that the delegation of legislative power to administrative agencies must be accompanied by clear standards of implementation.[14] This involves revival of the rule of law to replace the rule of bargaining as a principle of administration. It does not involve reduction of the public sphere. It *is* likely to make more difficult the framing and passage of some programs; but one wonders why any program should be acceptable if its partisans cannot clearly state purpose and means. Revival of the rule of law would also tend to dispel much of the cynicism with which the most active citizen views public authority.

Another way to restore competition to groups and ultimately push them back to Congress is to foster a truly independent executive. Development of a real Senior Civil Service is vital to this in the way it would tend to develop a profession of public administration, as distinct from a profession of a particular technology and a career within a specific agency. The makings of a Senior Civil Service lie already within the grasp of the Civil Service Commission if it has the wit to perceive its opportunity in its Career Executive Roster and its Office of Career Development and its Executive Seminar Center. The independent Senior Civil Servant, who could be designed for weakness in agency loyalty, combined with the imposition of clearer standards and rules governing administrative discretion, together would almost necessarily centralize and formalize, without denying, group access to agencies. In turn this would almost necessarily throw more groups together, increase their competition, expand the scope of that competition, and ultimately require open, public settlement of their differences. This would throw groups back more frequently into Congress and would also increase presidential opportunity to control the bureaucracies. The legitimacy of these institutions would be further confirmed.

3. A third part of the remedy has to do with programs themselves, although the recommendation overlaps No. 2 in that it has much to do with institutional roles. This is to set a Jeffersonian absolute limit of from five to ten years on every enabling act. As the end approaches, established relations between agency and clientele are likely to be shaken by exposure and opposition. This is as important as the need for regular evaluation of the existence of the program itself and of whether it should be abolished, expanded or merged with some other program. There is a myth that programs are evaluated at least once a year through the normal appropriations process and that specialized appropriations and authoriza-

program would be suitable for aggregation into an organizational, functional, or program budget. Not much progress has been made, however, and the various informational structures continue to be separate. One problem is that during the 1960's most major federal agencies invested heavily in the installation of their own management information systems, and these are not always compatible with the structures used by the central budgetary apparatus. A related problem is the clash between managerial and analytic perspectives, with the core categories appropriate for one purpose quite different from those helpful for the other.

Still another problem is the cost and technical difficulty of meshing the various structures for the government as a whole. Burned by the PPB experience and uncertain as to the direction it should take, OMB has been reluctant to commit itself fully to a new and costly approach. This reluctance has brought it into conflict with the Joint Committee on Congressional Operations which is monitoring implementation of the Legislative Reorganization Act of 1970. Section 202 of that Act directed OMB to work with the Treasury and GAO to "develop, establish, and maintain standard classifications of programs, activities, receipts, and expenditures of Federal agencies in order to meet the needs of the various branches of the Government." OMB's initial approach was very cautious:

> The evolution of the decisionmaking processes over time has created constituents for conflicting classification approaches. . . . Consequently, the transition from existing structures to any new concept will pose real challenge. A trend or movement to standardization must be "within reason."[13]

OMB set up four task forces with a handful of part-time staff persons to identify appropriate organization and fund codes, program structures, and supplementary classification systems. In effect, OMB merely continued the low-level information work it had commenced some years earlier.

The Joint Committee found these efforts "not reassuring," for they failed to take into account the informational needs of Congress or to move effectively toward the design of new standardized information systems. Under prodding by the Joint Committee, OMB finally admitted:

> that the scope of the system development effort as anticipated by the Congress is substantially greater than previously incorporated in our plans. . . . It is apparent that the limited part time involvement of staff . . . is grossly inadequate.[14]

OMB now estimates that over the next decade total development costs might reach $500 million and require 50 to 100 additional OMB personnel.

The clash between OMB and the Joint Committee arose in part from two old issues which plagued the installation of PPB. One has been OMB's reluctance to expand the kinds of budgetary and program information routinely available to Congress; another is OMB's reluctance to become the informational czar of the federal government. Until these are resolved, it is doubtful that congressional pressure will suffice to overcome OMB recalcitrance.

For OMB the main priority is to do something about the basic budget accounts and the methods for preparing the detailed budget and keeping track of expenditures. OMB finally has welcomed the computer into its chambers, though it has a long way to go before the computer is fully hitched to the routines of budgeting. OMB is aiming for a Rolling Budget System which would enable it to update the budget whenever changes occur as a consequence of departmental, presidential, or congressional action.

There is a significant difference between the informational ferment that was associated with PPB and that which now dominates OMB. Unlike PPB, current informational reforms are designed to improve the traditional budget process, to convert manual routines into computerized operations, to improve the accuracy of budget details, and to obtain current data on the status of all accounts. OMB has decided that the modernization of its core budget process must take precedence over the use of the budget for analytic purposes.

Performance Budgeting

PPB came on the scene before the aims of a previous reform—performance budgeting—had been realized. One of the chief purposes of performance budgeting was the use of work and cost measures in the preparation and execution of the budget. Cost and production goals would be established when the budget was formulated and these measures would be compared to actual performance. With only a few exceptions, performance budgeting failed in reaching these objectives. Consequently, when PPB arrived, most agencies lacked adequate work and cost reporting systems. The demise of PPB has spurred renewal of the performance budgeting efforts suspended in the mid 1960's.

OMB has been pilot testing a Performance Measurement System which combines features of performance budgeting and PPB. The system calls for pinpointing managerial responsibility and requires the manager to specify performance targets for this program. A reporting system shows variances from planned performance and enables program managers and OMB to take corrective action when variances exceed tolerance levels. Whether this system becomes a basis for a renewed PPB drive depends on at least two design features: the utility of the individual programs as building blocks for larger aggregations, and the types of output measures used.

The likelihood, however, is that this system will not mature into a PPB-type operation but will conform rather closely to the performance budgeting models which were in vogue during the 1950's. In testimony before the Joint Committee on Congressional Operations, an OMB spokesman described the system as based on "very fundamental, old-fashioned principles":

> Really, all we are trying to do is get a very explicit statement of exactly what it is he [a program manager] plans to accomplish, the time period for attaining specified results, and then let him prepare his own report card on how well he is doing in working toward the specified results.[15]

In sum, the performance measurement system is aimed at program managers rather than at top-level officials, and is oriented to work targets rather than to program objectives.

ON THE HILL

PPB was conceived almost exclusively from an executive perspective, as if Congress does not exist and that all it takes to make a budget is to review agency requests within an administrative setting. Moreover, PPB was engineered in a way that enabled the Bureau of the Budget to bypass Congress. The appropriation accounts were not restructured nor were significant alterations made in the budget submissions to Congress. The special PPB plans and analyses were destined for executive use and were not incorporated into the flow of data to Congress.

For its part, Congress generally preferred to continue in its accustomed ways, and the appropriations committee took little note of efforts to change the budget process. As a general rule, the closer a committee was to the appropriations process and to substantive power over spending, the less interest it showed in PPB. The only important PPB hearings were held by advisory committees, the Joint Economic Committee, and a Subcommittee of the Senate Government Operations Committee. On occasion, however, congressmen were piqued over the refusal of executive agencies to reveal the analytic and planning products of PPB. When it suits their purposes, congressmen want access to long-range cost projections and analytic studies. But they seem to have little interest in the overall PPB system.

Any inquiry into legislative attitudes toward PPB must reckon with Congress as an institution and with the division of labor and power among its members. To the extent that PPB would require Congress to trade away its control over the executive in favor of a larger policy role, it will be difficult to find many enthusiasts on Capitol Hill. However, if policy analysis can be fashioned into an instrument of legislative control over executive spending, the prospects become more favorable. For this reason there is bound to be a great disparity between executive and legislative uses of PPB. The President and program officials normally are willing to disclose the outcomes of their analyses and plans—that is, the programs and policies to be funded in the budget—but they are reluctant to reveal the alternatives which were considered and rejected, the analytic calculations which undergird their policy decisions, or the future costs of their policies. Congress, however, is as much interested in the alternatives as in the policies, and it looks to the analyses and projections as a means of challenging the executive's budget and program recommendations.

This tug of war explains recent congressional interest in budget innovation. Congress took the lead in the Legislative Reorganization Act of 1970. In addition to calling for a restructuring of budget classifications, that Act mandates five-year cost estimates for new programs and directs the Comptroller General "to review and analyze the results of Government programs and activities carried on under existing law, including the making of cost benefit studies," and it gives the GAO the go-ahead to recruit persons "who are expert in analyzing and conducting cost benefit studies of Government programs."

These requirements now written into law strive for the very objectives that executive PPB failed to accomplish. The parallel is strikingly complete because the federal PPB system that failed also gave top priority to a new program classification, multi-year plans, and program analysis. Knowledgeable persons do not expect the recent exuberance in Congress to transform federal budgeting or executive relations at once.

After all, GAO has had a broad mandate to evaluate administrative programs since its creation in 1921, but it has taken on this posture slowly and reluctantly. And the call for multi-year projections brings back memories of Public Law 84-801 enacted in 1956 which also prescribed long-range cost estimates, but has been honored infinitely more in the breach than in the practice. It will take much more than legislation to breathe vitality into program evaluation, but the 1970 Reorganization Act reflects the mood of Congress at this period in executive-legislative relations.

There is evidence that at least some congressmen or committee intend to take their new role seriously. The Family Planning Service and Population Research Act of 1970 delineates the types of information that Congress now wants. Section 5 might have been written for an executive's PPB system: it calls for a five-year plan specifying the number of individuals to be served, along with program goals and costs, as well as annual reports which compare results achieved during the preceding fiscal year with the objectives established under the plan and which indicate steps being taken to achieve the objectives of the plan.

It remains to be demonstrated whether Congress can accomplish via legislation that which PPB failed to accomplish by administrative order. However, the test of legislative success must be the same that I have applied to the executive; that is whether the central processes of budgeting are any different because of the availability of new analytic devices.

A RETURN TO PPB?

The failure of PPB in the federal government was not inevitable, though the traditions of budgeting and the manner of implementation made it likely. The few states which have achieved substantial budgetary renovation give evidence of what can be accomplished when resources are marshaled intelligently and forcefully. With so much of the business of PPB undone, it is probable that under a different label and with somewhat different approaches and techniques there eventually will be a return to the aims of PPB.

However, it is possible that the next wave of budget reform on the federal level will be directed toward one of the oldest issues of modern budgeting—the maintenance of financial control and accountability.[16] Contemporary issues of control fall into two categories. First is the reappearance of a very old problem—the ability of the government to control total spending. In current form, the problem is not of holding agencies to the spending limits established in law, but of "uncontrollable" forces that push total federal spending well above the figures estimated in the budget. A second cluster of issues pertains to the use of resources in instances where the normal internal controls are not effective. This situation prevails in intergovernmental fiscal relations and whenever there is a divorcement between spending authority and program delivery. As the granting government, the United States clearly has less effective control over the fiscal practices of recipient states and localities than it has over its own agencies.

. . .

All these are classical control problems in the sense that they pertain to the proper use of public resources. But their urgency derives from the enormous growth of government and the formation of new administrative institutions and relationships. The return of PPB will have to await the resolution of these problems, for control always is the first business of any budget process.

NOTES

1. Office of Management and Budget Transmittal Memorandum No. 38, June 21, 1971.
2. Alain C. Enthoven and K. Wayne Smith, *How Much is Enough?* (New York: Harper & Row, 1971).
3. Although Enthoven and Smith acknowledge that "between 1947 and 1961 substantial progress was made in improving the organization and legal structure of the U.S. Defense establishment" (p. 8), they do not recognize that the PPB developments in the 1960's would not have been possible without the organizational reforms of the 1960's.
4. See Frederick C. Mosher and John E. Harr, *Programming Systems and Foreign Affairs Leadership* (New York: Oxford University Press, 1970).
5. The first PPB guidance, Bulletin 66-3 (October 12, 1965) provided: "Specialized staff assistance is also essential in all but the smallest agencies. . . . Each agency will, therefore, establish an adequate central staff or staffs for analysis, planning and programming."
6. See Aaron Wildavsky, "The Political Economy of Efficiency: Cost-Benefit Analysis, Systems Analysis, and Program Budgeting," *Public Administration Review* (December 1966), pp. 292–310.
7. Victor A. Thompson, "Decision Theory, Pure and Applied," General Learning Press, 1971, p. 16.
8. See Aaron Wildavsky, "Rescuing Policy Analysis from PPBS," in Joint Economic Committee, *op. cit.*, pp. 835–852.
9. See Allen Schick, *Budget Innovation in the States* (Washington, D.C.: The Brookings Institution, 1971).
10. See Allen Schick, "The Budget Bureau that Was: Thoughts on the Rise, Decline, and Future of a Presidential Agency," *Law and Contemporary Problems* (Summer 1970), pp. 519–539.
11. Most of the changes in the Executive Office since 1939 were the addition of new units—such as the Central Intelligence Agency and the Office of Emergency Preparedness—rather than a shift in the functions of the existing units.
12. Reorganization Message of President Richard M. Nixon to Congress, March 12, 1970.
13. U.S. Congress, Joint Committee on Congressional Operations, Hearings on *Fiscal and Budgetary Information for the Congress*, 92nd Congress, 2nd Session, 1972, p. 163.
14. *Ibid.*, p. 63.
15. *Ibid.*, p. 31.
16. See Allen Schick, "The Road to PPB: The Stages of Budget Reform," *Public Administration Review* (December 1966), pp. 243–258.

Program Evaluation and Administrative Theory

Orville F. Poland

Program evaluation involves a retrospective examination of program operations. It looks to the past to provide a guide to the future. It asks questions of how well has the program been administered? Did it achieve its objectives? To what extent? Is it worth doing? Has it been done well? and at what cost? For many years program evaluation was the dark continent of public administration, a barely recognized function of administration.

The recent growth of evaluation has been closely linked with the flood of new programs in social policy enacted during the Johnson Administration. Many of these programs lacked the long gestation period associated with most important legislation and were, in the broad sense, experimental. In some areas parallel

From the *Public Administration Review*, Vol. 34 (July/August 1974), pp. 333–338. Reprinted by permission of the author and publisher.

programs were started, each dealing with the same problem. We hoped to learn from these; choose the most effective; downgrade or phase out the least effective. Evaluation was frequently linked with these experimental and new programs, and with social policy. Now a more conservative administration in a mood of retrenchment has questioned whether these programs are worth doing and has turned to evaluation to guide in reductions and abolition of programs.

There are three main themes in program evaluation. The first is the use of controlled experiments and other studies undertaken in the context of research designs of the social scientist. We have seen the widespread use of social scientists, especially sociologists and social psychologists, for evaluating educational and social programs of the federal government. They brought with them their methodological tools. These tools had not been used widely previously in public administration. One of the consequences of the participation of social scientists in evaluation is that public administration has gained yet another set of analytic tools. To the extent that this experience has been integrated into public administration, the academic field has moved another step toward an interdisciplinary one and away from its primary dependence upon political science.

The second theme in evaluation is the placement of evaluation in the context of cost-effectiveness analysis with a primary concern for program objectives. Policy analysts, influenced by their experience with PPBS and program budgeting, have structured program evaluations in terms of efficiency and effectiveness so that the basic questions asked are those of whether and to what extent did the program achieve its goals, and at what cost.

In the third place evaluations have been undertaken for many years in an eclectic fashion without much theoretical framework. These methods are dealt with most systematically by Yehezekel Dror in his *Public Policy Making Reexamined*.[1] Evaluations made in this vein consist largely of numerous analyses of the inputs, outputs, and processes of programs, so-called secondary criteria. These are used in place of net output of the program because of the difficulties surrounding measurement of net output. The evaluations made in these terms tend to be extensive and useful but somewhat diffuse.

Behavioral scientists brought the tools of the first theme to program evaluation. These are the controlled experiment, when possible, and when not possible *ex post facto* research with as rigorous research design as practicable. Ideally the behavioral scientist allocates individuals at random between the control group and the experimental one, measures each group before and after the experiment, and makes statistical comparisons. Failing to obtain the optimum design for his research, he uses a variety of methodological tools to make the best of the design he has. The concepts of good research design and the related methodological tools have been used in program evaluation, subject to many constraints. While they have shortcomings discussed below, they are becoming a regular part of public administration's research tools.

A review of the behavioralists' work emphasizes the very difficult methodological problems raised and exacerbated by political and administrative demands. Peter Rossi points out the following difficulties:[2] while research design favors the use of random allocation of individuals between the experimental and control groups, the public generally is quite uncomfortable with this arbitrary decision as to who shall be admitted to a new program. Congress, reflecting this feeling, forbade the use of randomization in some educational programs. Second, if administrators are convinced of the worth of the program, they are likely to influence the evaluation accordingly, and are unlikely to heed negative recommendations. Third, administrators resist the controls demanded of an experiment, for they are more concerned with getting results than with scientific testing. Moreover, administrators tend to change procedures and programs as they go along in order to attain better results. Fourth, programs administered in different jurisdictions are likely to differ so much that they cannot be compared as part of a controlled experiment. Alice Rivlin, in assessing the use of experimentation, notes that it is hard to get objective reports on results of projects that have not been successful, for administrators are often not willing to admit failure. Moreover, social experiments frequently take long periods of time to complete, while administrators usually must act in a shorter period.

Social scientists making program evaluations have been disappointed by their inability to undertake controlled experiments with "good design," including the assignment to experimental and control groups at random, and various devices to control variance. Instead social scientists frequently have had to settle for various forms of *ex post facto* research—with their methodological shortcomings.

However, even with good research designs, social scientists have had difficulty in showing scientifically that a given factor affects outcomes. Unfortunately for the scientist, social outcomes are influenced by a very large number of factors, no one of which usually has a very large influence. In some social research correlations of .20 are considered high enough to be important. Yet a correlation of .20 indicates that only 4 percent of the variation in the dependent variable is explained by variation in the independent variable. Because there are so many factors influencing dependent variables, it becomes difficult to identify and assess individual factors that have an influence. This being so it may be hard to show with methods of social science that programs effect intended changes.

For example, an analysis of the accident rate for auto drivers in Connecticut following the imposition of a lowered speed limit is instructive. The year following the imposition of the lower limit the number of fatalities declined from 324 to 284. Yet a careful statistical study was unable to conclude that the new speed limit caused the lower accident rate. Part of the analysts' difficulties were methodological, such as being faced with *ex post facto* research. Yet speed is only one of many factors that may influence the accident rate. Even with "good research design," it is difficult to determine what effect if any it has. These inherent problems in social science research make it difficult to assess the results of evaluations. In the study mentioned above, the findings do not indicate that the new speed limit did not reduce the accident rate, merely that with the evidence available and analysis undertaken one could not conclude that it did reduce it.

Two rather sobering possibilities may exist. First, relative to other factors our government programs may not have very much influence on events. Accident rate may be related to other factors than speed limits, such as the character of the driver, his experience, the weather, design of the highway, reliability of the automobile's parts, the automobile's design, the availability use of seat belts, chance, and many other factors. Second, social scientists may be very limited in their ability to provide useful evaluations. The second possibility has been noted by several observers. In addition to the methodological difficulties discussed above, social scientists, especially the behavioralists have focused on relatively narrow issues, leading to considerable disappointment among practitioners.

The second theme in program evolution, a concern with cost effectiveness and achievement of objectives, has come from PPB and program budgeting. Budget analysts had been assessing alternative means to attain goals as a part of PPB. The means they used were transferred to program evaluation by policy analysts.

Thus, contemporary program evaluation has inherited the intellectual framework of PPB. Emphasis has been placed upon (1) the efficiency of the program, that is, a measure of its output per unit of inputs; (2) its effectiveness, the extent to which the program achieves its objectives; and (3) its appropriateness, that is whether a program deserves to be done. Evaluators ask the questions how effective is the program in achieving its objective? How efficiently is the money spent? That is, what is the ratio of expenditures to output? and is the objective appropriate or worthwhile?

Analysis of effectiveness requires identification of goals and measurement of outcomes to determine how well goals have been achieved. This is a problem familiar to PPB analysts and students of cost-effectiveness. Inasmuch as some of the difficulties encountered in using PPB resulted from problems relating to goals, it is worth reviewing these. In the first place most or many programs have multiple goals. Disentangling and giving them weights is not easy. Moreover, objectives may not be entirely compatible. Second, objectives are frequently difficult to identify and make specific. Systems analysts have complained for a long time that they frequently must determine what results the decision maker really wants. Third, objectives change over time. Some years ago a colleague of mine evaluated 120 research and development projects for the military. Only one of these had been completed on schedule, but the goals of many of the rest had been changed during the project. In this and other ways, time is an important element in effectiveness analysis. Fourth, objectives are set in a political process with its compromising and log rolling; as a result objectives are not tidily stated. Politics may put goals in terms of an agreed upon distribution of power, influence, money, and/or resources among various interests. One of the objectives may be who gets what. This is difficult to accommodate in effectiveness evaluations that are based upon the values of marginal welfare economics. Fifth, goal achievement is difficult to measure even when the goals are identified. Sixth, frequently administrators wish to keep objectives stated in very general or ambiguous terms in order to increase their ability to maneuver, even to survive. These difficulties associated with objectives in PPB do not necessarily argue against the use of effectiveness analysis in program evaluation. They do warn up that its use will not be easy or free of problems.

The focus on goals required by the analysis is not always the focus of administrators. It is likely that many individuals, while aware of goals, are primarily concerned with process. They are concerned most of the time with the process they are undertaking, such as teaching students, or treating patients, not with abstract goals. Some social psychologists emphasize this concern with process, making self-actualization, an objective in administration, for self-actualization is achieved by focusing on the process of one's work instead of one's goal achievement. Decision theory which has directed attention to goals in PPB and program evaluation has introduced a value and a way of thinking that classes with a concentration on process. At the very least attention needs to be paid to the problem of accommodating the process orientation of the specialist providing services and the policy maker's concern with goal achievement.

It has been suggested that in this respect the goal orientation of policy science is not value free, but represents a new ideology. The examination of the ideological content, if any, of statistical decision theory and policy science entails extensive and technical rethinking of the field. Nevertheless, in view of our experience with benefit-cost analysis which appears to carry value biases in the methodology itself, the problem of values and goal orientation deserves exploration.

The first step in evaluation for effectiveness is the identification and conceptualization of goals; the second, to measure outputs in terms of these goals. However, it is not enough merely to measure outputs of the program; it is necessary to compare them with the output of no program or other alternatives. This is the familiar research program of establishing an experimental group and a control group. It has been the source of major methodological problems in program evaluation.

Because of its concern with objectives, effectiveness logically precedes efficiency as an aspect of evaluation. One needs to explore one's objectives before being concerned with efficiency. Efficiency is a measure of the relationship of outputs and inputs and focuses attention on management, motivation of employees, and use of capital equipment. It is closely related to the subject of productivity which has become a focal point for administrative concern. Productivity in economic literature has meant the relation of output to input, usually expressed as output per man. Recently administrative writers have transcended or ignored this restricted definition and have discussed productivity in terms of objectives as well as outputs. As a result, discussion of productivity has been confused with the larger area of program evaluation.[3]

Inasmuch as effectiveness and efficiency are quite different measures, programs may rate high on one and low on the other. A program might be highly effective in achieving its goal—keeping the streets clean, for example—but be inefficient in that it employs inordinate amounts of resources to achieve its results. A second program might be minimally effective in attaining goals, but use limited resources very efficiently. It is not clear which program is preferable in budgeting resources. To choose between them one needs to have a criterion for choice, or what is known as a decision rule, for the analysis does not give the answer.

Policy analysts also use a third measure in assessing programs—their appropriateness, that is the extent to which their objectives are desirable. This consists of measuring the program on a good-bad continuum and comparing it with other programs in terms of desirability. This type of evaluation involves the evaluator directly in policy.

The desire to reexamine policy even where established by statute is common. The second Hoover Commission explicitly was concerned with whether programs should be continued. Older programs need to be reexamined for current desirability. Grants-in-aid programs often are not subjected to regular scrutiny for policy in the budgeting process and thus may be particularly good candidates for appropriateness reviews.

Program budgeting and systems analysis have married program evaluation to ideas of effectiveness, efficiency, and appropriateness. Program evaluation is possible in other contexts and much takes place without regard to these concepts. Yehezkel Dror, writing some years ago, suggested that much evaluation is undertaken in terms of secondary criteria.[4] For example, one may wish to measure a program in terms of efficiency but be unable to conceptualize and measure outputs—or perhaps inputs. Instead of using a measure of efficiency one might then use a criterion that correlates with efficiency. Thus we judge school systems not in terms of net output, but by the pupil-teacher ratio which we assume to be correlated with net output, or at least with output. University academic programs are evaluated in terms of the jobs graduates obtain (an output), the student-faculty ratio (an input), the number of books in the library (an input), the faculty's publication record (output), the quality of course syllabi (a process), and so on. These are not measures of effectiveness, and they frequently lead to subjective judgments based on a combination of indicators. However, these evaluations identify problems that need attention, and often provide evaluators with important insights into programs. They do not provide the precision of effectiveness or efficiency evaluations, but often are easier to undertake and may give a better overall understanding of the program and its problems.

Much of the evaluation of social welfare programs has been dominated by behavioral scientists. As we have seen they have provided indifferent results for a variety of reasons. The behavioralists' techniques are frequently applicable to a relatively small number of the areas in which evaluation is desired. Managers wish evaluation of many other aspects of their programs than are susceptible to the use of new techniques or methods. The adminisrtator needs an assessment of many facets of his program, and the identification of its problems, successes, and failures. Only after such an evaluation may it be desirable to establish a controlled experiment. This suggests that we may be overemphasizing the role of the research experiment and that the broad-gaged approach to evaluation proposed by Dror some years ago and discussed above should not be rejected out of hand.

Program evaluation needs to be related to decision theory and our understanding of what constitutes a good decision. We are all aware that good management produces some bad outcomes, and poor management produces some good outcomes. If this is so, how can we link our evaluation of outcomes with the decision and future decisions to be taken? This puzzling situation requires some analysis. First, it is clear that we can never know the future with certainty. In most administrative situations there are major unknowns; factors change in unexpected ways. Ignorance of the future is called uncertainty by decision theorists. The prudent decision maker attempts to reduce this as much as possible and act rationally toward the remaining uncertainty. A second element to be considered is risk. This relates to decisions in which circumstances change, but with known probabilities. Weather records over the years, for example, indicate the probability of fog at an airport. Installation of equipment that permits airplanes to land during fog is not necessarily a bad decision because there was no fog during the month the evaluation team studied the airport's operations. We make the decision with regard to the probability of fog over many days. In many cases evaluation can deal with decision making under risk quite adequately. For example, the experimental addition on highways of holding lanes for drivers making left hand turns led to a significant reduction in the number of accidents per year. Here is a decision that affected a large number of individual actions over months. On the average each driver turning was safer than before. But what of the decision that is a one-shot affair, or at most is made only rarely? There are a good number of these. A decision rule for choosing 1,000 directors of agencies may not be of much help if we are to choose only one. If we make a poor choice, it is no consolation to know that the decision rule leads to this result only once in every ten choices. How do we cope with this in evaluation?

It is apparent that evaluation must be related to a theory of decision making and must incorporate some aspects of uncertainty and risk. The way in which evaluation treats these factors will influence decision making in practice. If bad outcomes are always punished, then the decision maker will become more conservative and unwilling to take a chance on creative solutions to problems.

Evaluations often tend to be critical. They become inefficiency audits and do not give as much attention to successes as to failures. This is unfortunate, for it creates a negative and inhibiting influence on an already conservative institution, the civil service.

Evaluation is a potential change agent, and as such runs counter to a dominant value of organization, stability. Thus Aaron Wildavsky questions whether evaluation is compatible with modern organization.[5] An organization that continually evaluates itself will continually develop proposals for change. In a rapid changing world most organizations need to adapt on a regular basis. Yet organizations have a limited tolerance for change, as experience with reorganization makes clear.

Moreover, individuals do not like being evaluated and especially dislike if they get low marks. We know from experience that personnel evaluations frequently are unable to effectuate behavioral changes. Obtaining change from program evaluations may be easier, but experience in the personnel field may still be useful. Personnel evaluation used for punitive purposes increases the anxiety of subordinates and encourages noncooperation. Evaluations that are designed for personnel development may do the reverse. Thus program evaluations which potentially threaten administrators and their programs may be met with non-cooperation. Personnel evaluations that lead to behavioral changes are almost always those that involve the employee in extensive participation in the evaluation. Thus, one might expect to have to involve the manager extensively on program evaluations if one expects him to change.

Most evaluations are undertaken in terms of the achievement of objectives—emphasizing the value, efficiency. Yet public administration is entering an era in which other values are being pressed. Some of these values are incompatible with or irrelevant to efficiency. The growth of collective bargaining has made bargaining a way of decision making. A decision made by compromise through the bargaining process is not one made rationally and scientifically. For example, collective bargaining may lead to a decision to limit class size to 20 students regardless of the efficiency or effectiveness of small classes as opposed to larger ones. What is the role of evaluation in this area? Similarly in some urban programs we have mandated citizen participation in the programs. While some proponents claim that participation leads to better results, even more efficient administration, participation is often proposed as an end in itself regardless of efficiency. What does this mean for evaluation? The political pluralists emphasize political bargaining in the decision process. How do we cope with this in evaluation? Program evaluation is another tool of scientific decision making and shares an emphasis on efficiency. As such it will have an uneasy time in a world that gives high priority to other values than efficiency and effectiveness.

NOTES

1. Yehezkel Dror, *Public Policymaking Reexamined* (San Francisco: Chandler Publishing Co., 1968), pp. 25–69.
2. Peter H. Rossi and Walter Williams (eds.), *Evaluating Social Programs* (New York: Seminar Press, 1972), pp. 31 ff.
3. See *Public Administration Review,* "Symposium on Productivity in Government," Vol. 32, No. 6, (November/December 1972).
4. Dror, *op. cit.*
5. Aaron Wildavsky, "The Self-Evaluating Organization," *Public Administration Review,* Vol. 32, No. 5 (September/October 1972), pp. 509–520.

B. Organization and Reorganization

Reorganization has been a frequent response of American political leaders—legislators and elected executives—to administrative agencies that are not performing to their satisfaction. They have much faith in their ability to substantially alter a wide range of administrative activity through restructuring the bureaucracy. Reorganization has been touted as a means of improving bureaucratic efficiency and democratic responsibility. It is motivated both by the spirit of rationality and the norm of responsibility.

Those characteristics of an administrative system that can be portrayed on an organization chart constitute only a small portion of its total character. Formal structure[1] is the easiest part of any organization to describe and control, however, and its relationship to the total organization does tend (except where the official leadership is exceptionally ineffective) to resemble that of bone structure to the total human body. For these reasons, writers about administration

---

[1] Formal structure may be defined as those patterns of interaction and accountability within an organization that have been officially promulgated as decision rules to guide individual actors in the organizational system.

and chief executives of large organizations have always placed great stress on formal structure as an instrument of organizational control.

Through at least the 1930s, American students of public administration were almost totally preoccupied with formal structural arrangements. In addition, they were normatively oriented. They did little research, but on the basis of reflection upon experience and commonsense logic they elaborated "principles" to guide those responsible for shaping formal organizational patterns. On the whole, their prescriptions were mechanistic. They assumed that the human members of organizational systems would routinely interact as if they had all the properties, and only the properties, attributed to them by the organization chart. Most of those who wrote in this vein acknowledged that they were oversimplifying, but they believed that they had captured the essentials.

As noted elsewhere,[2] the "principles" of administrative management have been devastatingly attacked but not replaced in the last two decades. This is quite a serious matter, because practical men charged with organizing and reorganizing bureaucracies have to rely on *some* general ideas, even if the best available are recognized to be inadequate. Philip Selznick is one the very few writers of the postwar period who has endeavored to go beyond the traditional "principles" on their own terms. That is, he has sought to develop a sociologically plausible general theory of how chief executives can shape their organizations into optimally serviceable instruments of their purposes. In the selection reprinted here, he emphasizes that the shaping of formal structure should be approached as an exercise in estimating the significance and "precariousness" of values, not as one of neatly grouping like activities with one another. In addition, he stresses that formal structure gains meaning only as it is supplemented by education, indoctrination, and practical experiences which give the subunit elites strong senses of collective identity and common purpose. Some of the questions you may wish to consider after reading this selection are the following: Would Herbert Simon consider Selznick's recommendations principles or proverbs?[3] Is Selznick's theory, with its emphasis on elites, applicable to organizational systems in which democracy is a central value? Of what value is Selznick's analysis to students of the politics of administration?

The high regard for reorganization in the nation's capital is the subject of Harold Seidman's selection. A former career official who served in the Bureau of the Budget, Seidman provides a realistic assessment of the significance of organizational structure. He suggests that its main function is as a symbol that is employed for political purposes rather than a device that leads to increased economy and efficiency.

A similar rejection of structural determinism is the major theme in Norman C. Thomas's article. Thomas sharply criticizes the recommendations of a study commission (the Ash Council) for reforming federal regulatory agencies on the grounds that they place excessive reliance on reorganization as the means to the desired end. He argues that although structure establishes the institutional boundaries within which administrative policy making occurs, it cannot determine policies and the values they employ.

---

[2] See Alan Altshuler, "The Study of American Public Administration," in Section I of this text.
[3] Simon's contention that the traditional "principles of administration" are mere proverbs has been outlined and reviewed on pp. 5–7.

Institutional Integrity, Precarious Values, and Elite Autonomy

Philip Selznick

Although every effective policy requires sustaining social conditions, the urgency of this need varies greatly. It is most important when aims are not well defined, when external direction is not easily imposed or early maintained, when fluid situations require constant adaptation, and when goals or values are vulnerable to corruption. This open-endedness, we have argued earlier, generates the key problems of institutional leadership. Among these is the defense of institutional integrity—the persistence of an organization's distinctive values, competence, and role.

The integrity of an institution may be threatened, regardless of its own inner strength, if sufficiently great force is applied to it. But in diagnosis we are mainly concerned with points of special inner weakness. From that standpoint we may say that institutional integrity is characteristically vulnerable *when values are tenuous or insecure.* This variation in the strength of values has received little scientific attention. Yet it commands much energy and concern in practical experience. In the course of building an organization, and establishing its separate units, group responsibility is fixed. But these "custodians of policy" will not be equally capable of sustaining their distinctive aims and standards. We need to know something about the social conditions that affect this competence.

The ability to sustain integrity is dependent on a number of general conditions, including the adequacy with which goals have been defined. Here we shall consider a special problem, the relation between precarious values and professional or elite autonomy. Our primary aim is to illustrate the potential contribution of institutional analysis to administrative theory. Therefore it may be helpful if, before dealing with administration proper, we first consider some other applications of the general idea. To do this, let us examine three ideas and how they are related.

Elite. For present purposes, this term refers to any group that is responsible for the protection of a social value. Often this responsibility is accepted consciously, but that is not essential. There would be no great harm in substituting the term "profession" or "professional group" for "elite," so long as the definition is kept in mind. Both terms have been used to designate men who carry out this basic social function.

Social values are objects of desire that are capable of sustaining group identity. This includes any set of goals or standards that can form the basis of shared perspectives and group feeling.

Autonomy is a condition of independence sufficient to permit a group to work out and maintain a distinctive identity.

These definitions are hardly final or unambiguous, but they will permit us to make some progress. The basic relation to be considered may be formulated as follows: *The maintenance of social values depends on the autonomy of elites.* Let us turn to the bearing of this proposition on (1) the general problem of institutional integrity, as it is familiar to the historian of culture; (2) certain aspects of political organization, as revealed in the history of Communism; and (3) certain technical problems of administrative management.

1. ELITE AUTONOMY AND CULTURAL VIABILITY. . . . It appears that what is critically necessary for the functioning of elites is enough autonomy to allow the maturation and protection of values. The achievement of this autonomy is a central task of professional associations, "little magazines," specialized schools, and a host of other devices for self-insulation used by groups in society that wish to protect and promote a particular set of values. Private universities with large endowments are better insulated from day-to-day pressures than are many public institutions, sustaining the autonomy of their professors and scientists. Literary elites are hard-pressed from the standpoint of autonomy because of the high cost of publishing and the commitment of that industry to the mass market. Hence literary groups may seek the shelter offered by private colleges able to subsidize esoteric journals. In our culture, the legal and medical professions are well insulated, others much less so. Those who are concerned for the protection of political, educational, aesthetic, and religious values, must find ways of providing the conditions needed to sustain the autonomy of culture-bearing elites.

The point summarized here is quite familiar to the historian of culture. But the basic relation between value maintenance and elite autonomy may cast some light on rather different and more unfamiliar situations.

2. POLITICAL ISOLATION AND THE COMBAT PARTY. In an earlier work referred to previously, the author attempted to analyze the organizational aspects of Communist strategy and to understand the inner dynamics of the "combat" party. Here is a characteristic elite phenomenon. The Bolsheviks attempt to build a leadership corps of "professional revolutionaries" that maintains a long-run dedication to the aims of Communism while engaged in the struggle for immediate power objectives. Any elite group, to maintain itself as such, must take special measures to protect its integrity. Among the most common of these measures are: (1) selective recruiting; (2) specialized training, as in the elite school; and (3) withdrawal from the everyday pursuits of mankind, especially from exposed competition in the marketplace. Each of these devices strengthens the isolation of the elite, its capacity to shape its own identity free of external pressures. All of these devices, among others, have played an important part in Bolshevik political and organizational experience. For the purpose of this discussion, a single illustration will suffice.

An important phase of Bolshevik political history took place during a period of "ultra-left isolation" from about 1924 to 1935. During these years the Communist parties throughout the world followed a policy of extreme (but mostly verbal) aggression against democratic and socialist forces. The latter were presented as "social fascists," against whom all means, including violence, were in order. This was a period of "dual" trade-unionism, in which the Communists disdained to work within the legitimate—"yellow"—labor movement but created their own "red" trade-unions. The latter usually included only Communist party members and their periphery, but they did lay the basis for later effective penetration of the mass unions.

The general effect of this ultra-left activity was organizational isolation. At first glance, this seems to have been self-defeating, and the later reversal might be understood as a corrective measure. The Communists did indeed isolate themselves from the main body of the workers, hence from any significant influence in society. Nevertheless, *this long period of isolation served to consolidate the power of the Russian party over the International, to test and train the party cadres, and to intensify reliance on conspiratorial methods.* Out of this period of ultra-left phrases, revolutionary adventures, splits, purges, and intensive indoctrination, there emerged a powerful political movement. This is not to say that the Communist leaders designed it so. But the modern Communist movement is a product of its history; it owes elements of strength, as well as of weakness, to the apparently irrational period of "social fascism" and "uiited front from below."

Specifically, this character-forming period readied the organization for a new period of propagandistic deception and organizational maneuver. After 1935, organizational isolation was definitely—and permanently—rejected. Open Communist propaganda was increasingly retired to the background, and the party turned to slogans of "unity," "peace," and similar generalities that might offer access to wider sections of the population. The "red" unions were abandoned and the party entered the legitimate trade-unions. The old aggression against "bourgeois" politicians was relaxed, and the party could support a Franklin Roosevelt when that was expedient. . . .

. . . In effect the conclusion was drawn that the day for worrying about the Communist integrity of the parties was past; the basic weapon had been forged; the time for wielding it effectively had arrived. Insistence on correct ideological formulae was to be exchanged for acceptance of more flexible slogans, and organizational practices were to be adapted to the conditions of the arena.

The period of ultra-left propaganda and organizational isolation was an *internally oriented* period, dedicated to preparing a weapon that would maintain its integrity when it was thrown into active political combat. It was this period of sharp break with the looser, more relaxed socialist traditions; of heavy emphasis on party discipline, on political orthodoxy, on conspiracy, and on intensive indoctrination that made possible the maintenance of the hard core of the party despite severe shifts in political line (as at the time of the Stalin-Hitler pact), and despite the heavy pressures on party members to become adapted to trade-unionist and reformist perspectives. Communist members could become *deployable agents* in other organizations—always serving the interests of the party—only as they accepted the authority of the party leadership. To create an organization able to exert such authority was a task that could not be accomplished without strenuous effort. Most of the early history of the Communist movement was devoted to that task of building "revolutionary cadres."

The Communist combat party, by assuming an ultra-left propaganda posture, preserved its autonomy as an elite, isolating itself from the pressures of the political arena *until it was ready to resist those pressures.* Put another way, the Bolsheviks wished to maintain an institution embodying a precarious value: a party competent to deploy members as disciplined agents. A period of organizational isolation, fostered by ultra-left propaganda, helped to contribute the sustaining social conditions. This only repeats, in a particular context, the generalization noted above, that the maintenance of values depends on the autonomy of elites. We have drawn here on a general institutional theory to help make sense of a particular historical development. The better developed such a general theory is, the more inferences can be drawn regarding the phenomena under analysis.

3. ADMINISTRATIVE AUTONOMY AND PRECARIOUS VALUES. One of the perennial problems confronting the architect of organizations is administrative autonomy. When should an activity be thought of as distinctive enough to be allowed a relatively independent organizational existence? . . .

Applying the theory of professional or elite autonomy discussed above, we may recast the problem in the following way:

(1) When an organizational unit is set up, especially if it is large enough to have its own administrative staff, an elite is created in the sense that some men now become professionally responsible for the protection of a social value. Probably this elite function is the source of most organizational rivalry.

(2) It follows from our general theory that isolation is necessary during periods of incubation and maturation, but may be modified when this character-forming task has been accomplished. Moreover, the more readily subject to outside pressure a given value is, the more necessary is this isolation. (Roughly, this means that the more technical a function is, the more dispensable is organizational isolation. In highly technical fields, a large degree of *social* isolation is won simply by the use of esoteric techniques and language, and by the evident importance of professional criteria as to appropriate methods of work.)

(3) This provides us with a principle that can help in making decisions about administrative autonomy. We appraise the given value (be it intelligence, health, education, psychological warfare, or customer service) and consider (a) whether the elite function of value-protection is required, and (b) whether special safeguards against outside pressures are needed. This may lead to the conclusion, for example, that a new staff unit ought to be attached directly to a top-command echelon—not permanently, but during a period when its basic perspectives are being laid down, its distinctive mission being evolved. Or such a unit might be attached to one *quite different* in function (but institutionally strong) for the express purpose of offering a haven to an organization charged with defending and developing a precarious value. Strong groups with similar responsibilities, who might feel threatened by the new unit, would thus be restrained from attacking it too directly.

An approach to autonomy in these terms is a radical departure from the attempt to build organizations according to the logical association of functions. That principle—which will of course always be relevant—is often violated in practice, and for good reason. It must be violated whenever values are unequal in strength. Organization planning is unrealistic when it fails to take account of the differential capacity of subordinate units to defend the integrity of their functions. The theory of elite autonomy permits us to deal with this problem systematically and openly. This is important because many decisions that do in fact face up to this issue must now be justified obliquely, and be half-hidden, since there is no accepted administrative principle allowing organizations to be treated differently according to the strength of their respective values.

Let us apply this idea to the classic headquarters-field problem. Given a headquarters organization and a field organization, to whom shall subject-matter specialists (say in recreation, medicine, or personnel selection) be responsible? To the technical staff chief at headquarters or to the head of the local field organization? The dilemma is that the headquarters staff will be concerned over values (whether good accounting procedure or good medical practice), but the field executive will be under pressure to get an immediate job done while perhaps taking insufficient account of the long-run consequences of his decisions. One answer has been "dual supervision," in which certain officers are thought of as "administratively" responsible to one superior while "technically" responsible to another. This recognizes the special role of technical staff personnel in developing and defending values.

But "dual supervision" really presumes an optimum situation, in which a strong value-oriented elite (the technical staff) has had enough autonomy to lay down professional criteria that are accepted by the line officials. When, as in medicine and engineering, values have been effectively matured, dual supervision is relatively easy, for the boundaries within which the technical and administrative personnel may operate are reasonably clear-cut and are tacitly or even formally recognized as part of the code of proper behavior. Even in such fields, however, where the boundaries are unclear, as in the development of criteria for certifying military personnel fit for duty, it is to be expected that the professional group will be vulnerable to external pressure.

When we deal with *precarious* values—say an information and education program, or a political intelligence operation—special attention to the problem of elite autonomy is required. In such cases, we may accept a much closer relation between headquarters staff and field personnel than would otherwise be justified, because we recognize the need for intensive communication during character-forming periods. Such periods also require special measures to resist potentially corrupting external pressures, and this means a more intense professional self-consciousness. Suppose a government agency establishes a new labor relations policy, championed by the headquarters staff, but of necessity using line executives (say on construction jobs) who are not fully in sympathy with this policy. In the early days of the agency, we may expect a centralization of the labor relations program, perhaps manifested in a rule permitting workers to register complaints directly at headquarters and in the establishment of field labor relations specialists who conceive of themselves as self-conscious outposts of headquarters in an alien environment. This centralization permits the autonomous maturation of values; later, when the desired policies have been well established, a greater degree of decentralization will be in order. . . .

The theory of elite autonomy, thus applied, . . . leads us away from rigid rules of administrative organization, yet it helps to identify the key elements that need to be controlled and in terms of which guiding principles can be set forth.

Executive Branch Organization

Harold Seidman

ORTHODOX THEORY: CULT OF EFFICIENCY

Reorganization has become almost a religion in Washington. It has its symbol in the organization chart, old testament in the Hoover Commission reports, high priesthood in the Bureau of the Budget, and society for the propagation of the faith in sundry groups such as the Citizens Committee for the Hoover Report.

Reorganization is deemed synonymous with reform and reform with progress. Periodic reorganizations are prescribed if for no other purpose than to purify the bureaucratic blood and to prevent stagnation. Opposition to reorganization is evil and attributable, according to Mr. Hoover, to the "gang up, log-rolling tactics of the bureaus and their organized pressure groups."

For the true believer, reorganization can produce miracles: eliminate waste and save billions of dollars; restore to health and economic vigor a chronically ill maritime industry; abate noise at airports; control crime in the streets, to name but a few. The myth persists that we can resolve deepseated and intractable issues of substance by reorganization. The report of the Senate Subcommittee on National Policy Machinery to the contrary, the conviction that the weaknesses of one organization can be cured by creating another remains a widely held article of faith.[1] Rare indeed is the Commission or Presidential task force with the self-restraint to forgo proposing an organizational answer to the problems which it cannot solve.

The organizational commandments laid down by the first Hoover Commission constitute the hard core of the fundamentalist dogma.[2] The devils to be exorcised are overlapping and duplication, and confused or broken lines of authority and responsibility. Entry into the Nirvana of Economy and Efficiency can be obtained only by strict adherence to sound principles of executive branch organization. Of these the most essential are the grouping of executive branch agencies as nearly as possible by major purposes so that "by placing related functions cheek-by-jowl the overlaps can be eliminated, and of even greater importance coordinated policies can be developed"; and the establishment of a clear line of command and supervision from the President down through his department heads to every employee with no subordinate possessing authority independent from that of his superior.

The Commission's report on "General Management of the Executive Branch" represents the most categorical formulation of the orthodox or classical organization doctrine derived largely from business administration and identified with the Scientific Management Movement during the early decades of this century and the writings of Gulick, Urwick, Fayol, and Mooney. Government organization is seen primarily as a technological problem calling for "scientific" analysis and the application of fundamental organizational principles: a single rather than a collegiate executive; limited span of control: unity of command (a man cannot serve two

From *Politics, Position, and Power: The Dynamics of Federal Organization* by Harold Seidman, Copyright © 1970 by Oxford University Press, Inc. Reprinted by permission.

masters); a clear distinction between line and staff; and authority commensurate with responsibility.

. . .

Orthodox theory is preoccupied with the anatomy of Government organization and concerned primarily with arrangements to assure that (1) each function is assigned to its appropriate niche within the Government structure; (2) component parts of the executive branch are properly related and articulated; and (3) authorities and responsibilities are clearly assigned.

. . .

. . . While the observations on the discrepancies between the orthodox dogmas and the facts of organizational life and behavior are often pertinent and valid, these do not add up to a rational well-articulated set of working hypotheses for dealing with the present and emerging problems of Federal organization. It is easy to pick the flaws in the concepts of unity of command, straight lines of authority and accountability, and organization by major purpose; it is far more difficult to develop acceptable alternatives.

Warren Bennis is one of the few who has had the courage to make the attempt with his proposal that organizations of the future be "adaptive, rapidly changing temporary systems." These will be organized around problems to be solved. The function of the executive will be to coordinate various project groups. Bennis emphasized that "people will be differentiated not vertically according to rank and role but flexibly according to skill and professional training." But whatever its potential for private institutions or intradepartmental organization, the Bennis approach does not and was not intended to provide a grand design for executive branch structure.

Flawed and imperfect as they may be, the orthodox "principles" remain the only simple, readily understood, and comprehensive set of guidelines available to the President and the Congress for resolving problems of executive branch structure. Individual congressmen can relate them to their own experience within the Congress or in outside organizations. . . .

. . .

Almost every President from Theodore Roosevelt to Lyndon B. Johnson, with the notable exception of Franklin D. Roosevelt, has at one time or another found it necessary to defend reorganization as a means of reducing expenditures. "We have to get over the notion that the purpose of reorganization is economy," F.D.R. told Louis Brownlow and Luther Gulick in 1936, "I had that out with Al Smith in New York. . . . The reason for reorganization is good management."[3] The overwhelming weight of empirical evidence supports the Roosevelt view that reorganizations do not save money.

Of the eighty-six reorganization plans transmitted to the Congress from 1949 through 1969, only three—Reorganization Plan No. 3 of 1952, which would have ended Senate confirmation of Postmasters, Reorganization Plan No. 1 of 1965 reorganizing the Bureau of Customs, and Reorganization Plan No. 5 of 1966 abolishing the National Capital Regional Planning Council—were supported by precise dollar estimates of savings. Plan No. 3 of 1952 was disapproved by the Congress. Granted executive branch reluctance to offer savings estimates which can be taken down and later used in evidence by the Appropriations Committees, the failure to itemize expenditure reductions clearly reflects the reality that economies are produced by curtailing services and abolishing bureaus, not by reorganization.

Emphasis is placed more on form than substance. Frequently studies of executive branch structure degenerate into sterile box-shuffling and another version of the numbers game. This approach is typified by Senator Abraham Ribicoff's citing as indisputable evidence of the need to "streamline and modernize" the Federal Government the fact that "Eight Cabinet departments and twelve agencies are involved in health. Eighteen separate agencies are conducting programs to improve the natural environment. Eight departments and four agencies are operating major credit programs. Ten Cabinet departments and more than fifteen other agencies are involved in education. Ten agencies and three departments are managing manpower programs." One White House task force on Government organization found that if you pushed this approach to its logical conclusion you would end up with a Department of Foreign Affairs, a Department of Domestic Affairs, and a Department of Defense, and even then all overlaps would not be eliminated.

Established organization doctrine, with its emphasis on structural mechanics, manifests incomplete understanding of our constitutional system, institutional behavior, and the tactical and strategic uses of organization structure as an instrument of politics, position, and power. Orthodox theories are not so much wrong when applied to the central issues of executive branch organization as largely irrelevant.

Executive branch structure is in fact a microcosm of our society. Inevitably it reflects the values, conflicts, and competing forces to be found in a pluralistic society. The ideal of a neatly symmetrical, frictionless organization structure is a dangerous illusion. We would do well to heed Dean Acheson's sage advice that "organization—or reorganization in government, can often be a trap for the unwary. The relationships involved in the division of labor and responsibility are far more subtle and complex than the little boxes which the graph drawers put on paper with their perpendicular and horizontal connecting lines."[4]

EXECUTIVE BRANCH ORGANIZATION: THEORY VS. PRACTICE

Organizational arrangements are not neutral. We do not organize in a vacuum. Organization is one way of expressing national commitment, influencing program direction, and ordering priorities. Organizational arrangements tend to give some interests, some perspectives, more effective access to those with decision-making authority, whether they be in the Congress or in the executive branch. As Richard Neustadt has pointed out: "In political government, the means can matter quite as much as the ends; they often matter more."

Institutional location and environment, administrative arrangements and type of organization, can raise significant political questions concerning the distribution and balance of power between the executive branch and the Congress; the Federal Government and State and local governments; States and cities; the Federal Government and organized interest groups, particularly the principal beneficiaries of Federal programs; and finally, among the components of the executive establishment itself, including the President's relationship to the departments and the bureaucracy.

If our democratic system is to be responsive to the needs of *all* our people, organization structure and administrative arrangements need to so balance the competing interests within given program areas that none is immune to public control and capable of excluding less powerful segments of our society from effective participation in the system and an equitable share of its benefits. Failure to maintain this balance has contributed to the present malaise.

President Eisenhower in his farewell address to the nation warned against "the acquisition of unwarranted influence, whether sought or unsought, by the military-industrial complex." Other complexes, notably the science-education and agricultural establishments, wield power equal to or exceeding that of the perhaps overly dramatized military-industrial combine. Scientific research is said to be the only pork barrel for which the pigs determine who gets the pork.

The political implications of organization structure were recognized as early as 1789 when the States endeavored to control the extension of Federal power by limiting the creation of executive departments. In 1849 the bill to establish the Department of the Interior was opposed because "it meant the further extension of Federal authority to the detriment of the states." Opposition to the establishment of the Department of Housing and Urban Development in the 1960's stemmed from much the same concern.

. . .

In their zeal to construct neat and uncluttered organization charts, professional reorganizers and reorganization commissions tend to downgrade, when they do not wholly ignore, environmental influences. Certainly, the poverty program would have been different, whether better or worse depends on one's point of view, if, as many advocated, responsibility at the outset had been given either to the Department of Health, Education, and Welfare or, the choice of the big-city mayors, the Department of Housing and Urban Development. Creation of a new agency is likely to present fewer problems than reform of an old one and enables the President and the Congress to finesse competing jurisdictional claims. Compromise arrangements are possible, and program seedlings under some circumstances can take root and grow within established departments if protected during the developmental period by a self-contained, relatively autonomous status.

Adherence to the principle of organization according to major purposes provides no automatic answers. Herbert Hoover would have resolved the problem by having the Congress define "major purpose" and then leaving it to the President to reorganize executive agencies in accordance with their purposes as set forth in law. Granted that Mr. Hoover made this proposal in 1924, when Federal programs were simple by today's standards, it is incredibly naïve.

Federal programs are likely to have multiple purposes. Disagreements as to priorities among diverse and sometimes conflicting objectives are a major source of current controversies. Is the major purpose of the food stamp program to dispose of surplus agricultural commodities or to feed the poor? Is mass transportation a transportation or an urban development program? Are loans for college housing a housing or education function? Should the Federal water pollution control program have as its principal objective health protection, or should it be concerned more broadly with the development of water resources?

Major purposes cannot be ascertained by scientific or economic analysis. Determination of major purpose represents a value judgment, and a transitory one at that. What is a secondary purpose for one, is a major purpose for another. . . . Major purposes are not constants but variables shifting with the ebb and tide of our national needs and aspirations.

Debates about organizational type also may mask basic differences over strategy and objectives. Orthodox theory postulates that all Federal agencies, with the possible exception of the independent regulatory commissions, be grouped under a limited number of single-headed executive departments and consequently ignores the other possible forms of organization. Except for the regulatory commissions and Government corporations, the Hoover Commissions and President's Committee on Administrative Management took little interest in the typology of organization—a disinterest shared by most students of public administration.

The significance of institutional type has been underrated. In Part II we will endeavor to identify and analyze the rich variety of organizational types which have been developed within our constitutional system. These include executive departments, independent agencies, assorted types of commissions, boards, councils, authorities, wholly-owned corporations, mixed-ownership corporations, "captive" corporations, institutes, foundations, establishments, conferences, intergovernmental bodies, compact agencies, and a wide variety of interagency and advisory committees. The differences among these institutional types are more a matter of convention and tradition than legal prescriptions. Yet some have acquired a "mystique" which can profoundly influence public attitudes and executive and congressional behavior for good or ill. Institutional type can be crucial in determining who controls—the President, the Congress, or the so-called "special interests."

. . .

Up to now we have been discussing mainly the strategic implications of executive branch organization. But power relationships are not always involved in organization decisions. The President, the Congress, and even outside groups may use organizational means to obtain some immediate tactical advantage.

. . .

Presidents have continued to employ committees and commissions to capture and contain the opposition. Committees and commissions can also offer an immediate, visible response in times of national catastrophe, such as the assassinations of President Kennedy and Senator Kennedy or the Watts riot. Study commissions are employed as a kind of tranquillizer to quiet public and congressional agitation about such matters as pesticides, crime, and public scandals. Attention, it is hoped, will be diverted to other issues by the time the commissions report. . . .

Prestigious commissions can also build public support for controversial courses of action. What is wanted is endorsement, not advice, although "run-away" commissions are not unknown. On sensitive issues such as congressional pay, where congressmen are politically vulnerable, a commission report helps to take them off the hook. Both Presidents Kennedy and Johnson used commissions to support legislation to increase executive, congressional, and judicial salaries.

Interagency committees sometimes create an impression of neatness and order within the executive establishment, even when a President cannot or will not resolve the basic differences and jurisdictional conflicts. If differences surface publicly and become embarrassing to the administration, the President's reflex reaction is to appoint another committee or to reorganize existing committees. The pressure is almost overwhelming "to do something" which might do some good and certainly will do no harm. No President can confess that he is stumped by a problem.

Pressure for immediate, tangible answers to highly complex problems may result in reorganizations. President Eisenhower's first response to the national trauma caused by the Soviet Union's successful launching of Sputnik in 1957 was to appoint a special assistant to the President for Science and Technology and to transfer the Science Advisory Committee from the Office of Defense Mobilization to the White House office.

Reorganization may provide a convenient way to dump an unwanted official, particularly one with strong congressional or constituency ties. The maneuver is not always successful, as was seen with Secretary Rusk's abortive plan to abolish the Department's Bureau of Security and Consular Affairs. Mr. Abba Schwartz's version of this incident is highly colored, but there is no question that Secretary Rusk's timing was influenced by his desire to shift Mr. Schwartz from the Bureau directorship to another post. The Bureau of Security and Consular Affairs was the brainchild of Senator Joseph McCarthy, and the Bureau of the Budget had targeted it for reorganization long before Mr. Schwartz arrived on the scene.

Use of reorganization to by-pass a troublesome committee or subcommittee chairman in the Congress can also be hazardous when it does not succeed. Transfer of civil defense activities from the Office of Civil and Defense Mobilization to the Secretary of Defense in 1961 was expected as an incidental benefit to remove the shelter program from the jurisdiction of an unfriendly appropriations subcommittee chairman. Albert Thomas, however, had the power to retain jurisdiction to the great discomfiture of the civil defense officials.

Organization choices may be motivated almost entirely by a desire to exclude billions in expenditures from budget tabulations. The 1969 budget was the first to include trust funds and mixed-ownership Government corporations in the administrative budget. President Eisenhower's 1955 proposal to create a Federal Highway Corporation for financing the construction of the National System of Interstate Highways was deliberately designed to keep the authorized payments of $25 billion out of the budget totals. The proposal was later abandoned when it was found that establishment of a highway trust fund could serve the same purpose. Conversion of the Federal National Mortgage Association from a wholly-owned to a mixed-ownership Government corporation in 1954 also had as its principal appeal the appearance of a multi-billion-dollar budget reduction. When the ground rules were changed with the 1969 budget, legislation was enacted to turn the Federal National Mortgage Association into a "Government sponsored private corporation" so as to keep its expenditures out of the budget.

A new name and a new look may be necessary to save a program with little political appeal, particularly one which congressional supporters find difficult to sell to their constituents. At times reorganization supplies the rationale needed by a congressman to explain his vote. The frequent reorganization and re-naming of the foreign aid agency reflect efforts to bolster congressional support and to demonstrate Presidential interest, rather than to introduce new policies and improve management. There have been no less than eight successive foreign aid agencies—from the Economic Cooperation Administration in 1948 to the Agency for International Development in 1961—until 1961 an average of a new agency oftener than every two years.

For many organization is a symbol. Federal councils on aging, mental retardation, physical fitness, consumers, and the arts, for example, are more important as evidence of national concern than as molders of Federal policies.

Some seek the creation of new Federal agencies or reorganizations to enhance their status in the outside community. The demand for an independent National Archives disassociated from the Government's "housekeeper," the General Services Administration, in part stems from the archivists' desire to improve their standing as a scholarly profession. Several years ago the firemen's association sought Bureau of the Budget support for a Federal Fire Academy. While the academy would not fulfill any identifiable Federal need, it would place firemen on a par with policemen, who had a Federal "sponsor" in the Federal Bureau of Investigation, and thus strengthen their bargaining position in dealing with mayors and city councils.

The Congress is highly skilled in the tactical uses of organization and reorganization. If you come from a district with a jet airport, establishment of an Office of Noise Abatement in the Department of Transportation has tremendous voter appeal. Even though there is doubt that a separate office could do much to reduce noise levels, at least it offers a place where congressmen can send constituent complaints. While the administration was able to defeat an amendment to the Department of Transportation bill to create such an office on the valid grounds that aircraft noise was a research and development and traffic control problem, Secretary Alan Boyd later found it expedient to create an Office of Noise Abatement by administrative action. Congressmen are more susceptible to pressures from sectional, economic, and professional interests than the President, and these often become translated into organizational responses.

Economy and efficiency are demonstrably not the prime purposes of public administration. Mr. Justice Brandeis emphasized that "the doctrine of separation of powers was adopted by the Constitution in 1787, not to promote efficiency but to preclude the exercise of arbitrary power."[5] The basic issues of Federal organization and administration relate to power: who shall control it and to what ends?

The questions that now urgently confront us are as old as the Republic itself. How can we maintain a Government structure and administrative system which reconcile liberty with justice and institutional and personal freedom with the general welfare?

. . .

The struggle for power and position has contributed to fragmentation of the executive branch structure and the proliferation of categorical programs. By narrowing the constituency, agencies are made more susceptible to domination by their clientele groups and congressional committees. Efforts to narrow the constituencies have been accompanied by demands for independent status or autonomy within the departmental structure.

Programs are packaged in such a way as to elicit congressional and clientele support. General programs have far less political appeal than specific programs.

Support can be mobilized more readily for Federal programs to combat heart disease, blindness, cancer and mental illness, than for such fields as microbiology or for general health programs. For this reason in 1955 the National Microbiological Institute was renamed the National Institute of Allergy and Infectious Diseases. As was explained at the time, the Institute had been handicapped in making its case to the Appropriations Committees because "no one ever died of microbiology."

It would be a mistake to assume, however, that dependents always have the wisdom to know what is in their own best interests. The maritime unions have become so obsessed with the idea that an independent maritime agency would solve all of their problems that they have ignored the plain fact that any transportation agency outside the Department of Transportation would be in a very weak competitive position.

We are faced with the strange paradox that the privilege of access to public funds is believed to carry with it the right to exercise public power, where the payment of large amounts in taxes does not. This thesis is expressed in such euphemisms as "decentralization," "grass-roots administration," and "freedom from politics." Thus Yale alumni were reassured that the university's independence has not been compromised by accepting Federal money because "the men who fix the Government's policy in this respect are themselves university and college men. . . ."

The issue of dependence vs. subservience is at the heart of our present dilemma. How can we reconcile a growing Federal involvement in all aspects of our national life with the maintenance of deeply cherished pluralistic values? The typical answer is that offered by Alan Pifer, President of the Carnegie Corporation. He proposed the creation of a Federal center for higher education which would "depend heavily in all its activities on men and women co-opted from the colleges and universities *so that it is as much of higher education itself as it is of government*" (italics supplied).

Few would dispute that Federal domination of science and education would be undesirable. Yet grave risks are run when public power is exercised by agricultural, scientific, and educational elites who are more concerned with advancing their own interests and the interests of the institutions they represent than the public interest. Serious distortions and inequities may occur in the allocation of funds among those eligible for assistance. Vested interests are created which are resistant to change and the reordering of priorities to meet new national needs.

As our one elected official, other than the Vice President, with a national constituency, the President of the United States stands almost alone as a counterweight to these powerful centrifugal forces. Sometimes the executive branch takes on the appearance of an arena in which the chiefs of major and petty bureaucratic fiefdoms, supported by their auxiliaries in the Congress and their mercenaries in the outside community, are arrayed against the President in deadly combat.

Herbert Emmerich, a highly perceptive student of Federal organization, has said: "The Presidency is the focal point of any study of reorganization. . . . The Presidency focuses the general interest as contrasted with the centrifugal forces in the Congress and the departments for the specialized interests of subject matter and of region."[6]

It is significant that the lasting contributions of the first Hoover Commission, the President's Committee on Administrative Management, and the earlier Taft Commission on Economy and Efficiency are to be found in their recommendations to strengthen the office of the Presidency, not in the long-forgotten proposals for reshuffling agencies and providing more efficient and economical administration. Institutional type and organization structure are important because they can help or hinder the President in performing his pivotal role within our constitutional system.

NOTES

1. Senate Committee on Government Operations, Subcommittee on National Policy Machinery, "Organizing for National Security," Vol. 3, 1961, p. 4. The staff report criticized most of the proposals for additions to national policy machinery as based "on the mistaken assumption that the weaknesses of one organization can be cured by creating another."
2. The Commission on Organization of the Executive Branch of the Government, "General Management of the Executive Branch," A Report to the Congress, February 1949.
3. Richard Polenberg, *Reorganizing Roosevelt's Government*, Harvard University Press, 1966, p. 8.
4. Dean Acheson, "Thoughts about Thoughts in High Places," *The New York Times Magazine*, October 11, 1959.
5. Cited in Lewis Meriam and Lawrence F. Schmeckebier, *Reorganization of the National Government*, The Brookings Institution, 1939, p. 132.
6. Herbert Emmerich, *Essays on Federal Reorganization*, University of Alabama Press, 1950, p. 7.

Politics, Structure, and Personnel in Administrative Regulation

Norman C. Thomas

The federal regulatory process as conducted by independent commissions has been a subject of interest and concern to scholars and governmental reformers for much of this century. The recent report of the President's Advisory Council on Executive Organization (Ash Council) and its accompanying proposals have again raised basic questions regarding the nature of government regulation and the efficacy of the independent commission as a regulatory instrument.[1] The Council proposes sweeping changes in the structure of seven independent regulatory agencies, which, it urges, should be implemented prior to any substantive changes in regulatory statutes. In its letter of transmittal to President Nixon the Council states its basic assumption:

> The existing structure, because of its inherent and perhaps unavoidable deficiencies, cannot be expected to accommodate these revised [statutory] mandates which may require that regulation reflect the pace of change in the regulated industries, the interdependence of elements of the economy, and the public interest. A more effective and objective regulatory process, better integrated with other processes of government, requires a new organizational framework for regulation.

Principally the Council proposes the replacement of the collegial or commission form of agency with the single administrator agency. The Council claims that this,

From the *Virginia Law Review*, Vol. 57 (September 1971), pp. 1033, 1054–1068. Reprinted by permission of the publisher.

along with other changes, would correct the major defects in commission regulation and improve the quality of agency heads and staffs.

. . .

THE ASH COUNCIL RECOMMENDATIONS

The principal recommendations of the Ash Council and their supporting rationales can be summarized under four headings:

1. TRANSFORMATION FROM COMMISSION TO SINGLE ADMINISTRATOR FORM OF AGENCY. The functions of the CAB, ICC, FPC, SEC, and the consumer protection functions of the FTC would be performed by agencies headed by single administrators.

The basic concern of the Ash Council Report is with the disadvantages of the collegial form of regulatory agency. A shift to single-headed agencies would "assure coordination of regulatory matters with national policy goals," "improve accountability to the Congress and the executive branch," and "increase the probability of superior leadership for regulatory activities." The single administrator form would help solve the problem of attracting and retaining highly qualified personnel and would improve managerial effectiveness.

2. MODIFIED RETENTION OF THE COLLEGIAL FORM. The FCC would be retained but with a reduction in size from seven to five members. Because of the sensitivity of broadcast regulation, especially in the area of program content, the Ash Council decided that the advantages of the single administrator form had to yield to the "broad-based deliberation" and "non-partisan environment" that a commission provides. A reduction in size would hopefully attenuate some of the problems of collegiality without surrendering protection from partisan control.

The antitrust responsibilities of the FTC would be shifted to a new Federal Antitrust Board consisting of a chairman and two economic administrators. The Board would be a quasi-commission with its chairman having full responsibility for administration and operations, but sharing responsibility for policy-making with the economic administrators, of whom one would be a member of the Council of Economic Advisers and the other director of the Board's economic analysis bureau. Presumably the Board would combine the advantages of the single administrator and collegial forms.

3. REALIGNMENT OF FUNCTIONAL RESPONSIBILITIES. The regulatory functions of the ICC, CAB, and FMC would be combined in a new Transportation Regulatory Agency. The CAB's promotional activities would be moved to the Department of Transportation. The FTC's functions would be divided between the new Federal Trade Practices Agency and the Antitrust Board. The SEC's regulatory functions under the Public Utility Holding Company Act would be transferred to the new Federal Power Agency.

These realignments would be aimed at securing a more rational allocation of power by coordinating governmental responsibility with agency function and industry structure.

4. LIMITATION OF INTERNAL AGENCY REVIEW OF PROCEEDINGS AND TRANSFER OF JUDICIAL REVIEW TO A NEW ADMINISTRATIVE COURT. In order to prevent over-

judicialization of agency procedures and to insure "comprehensive and anticipatory policymaking," the time and scope of an agency administrator's review of examiner's decisions should be limited. This should increase the use of rule-making and informal policy guidelines and reduce adjudicatory proceedings. An Administrative Court with appellate review of decisions from the transportation, power, and securities agencies would "reflect an expertise ideally suited to review of administrative procedures and concerns." It would also ease the case load in other federal appellate courts.

A COMMENTARY ON THE ASH COUNCIL REPORT

The Ash Council report charges that regulatory commissions fail "to respond to current demands" and are unlikely to respond to new ones. This, it is claimed, is "principally attributable to collegial organization, the judicial cast of agency activities, and the misalignment of certain functional responsibilities." The report presents no empirical evidence in substantiation of these rather sweeping allegations and assertions of commission failure, though this writer concedes that it has occurred with some frequency. Furthermore, there are no comparative studies in the Ash Council report or any other analysis, of the degree to which single-headed agencies are devoid of such defects. Therefore, the relationship between agency form and regulatory success or failure must be accepted on faith.

This is not to deny the assertion made in the Ash Council report; it is merely suggested that too much may be claimed for it. As Jaffe has remarked . . . "the critics of the agencies have attributed to the factor of agency independence all sorts of political ills and disappointments for which it bears no responsibility whatever." Likewise, to lay poorly qualified personnel, uncoordinated policy, political irresponsibility, excessively judicialized procedures, insensitivity to economic and technological change, and inefficient management at the doorstep of plural leadershp is to overstate the case for a modest structural reform.

. . . [P]reoccupation with the collegial form and the phenomenon of independence has led many scholars and reformers to ignore or neglect the full ambit of regulation. There is a paucity of studies of the effects of regulatory policies and of regulation as a political process involving a multiplicity of policy areas and a variety of agency forms. The necessary empirical analysis of regulatory forms in terms of the Ash Council's criteria for reforming the commissions—timely policy formulation, effective management, adequate accountability to Congress and the President, and ability to attract and retain able personnel—has not been conducted by the Council or anyone else.

The intuitive and a priori reasoning presented in support of the case for single-headed agencies is especially puzzling in light of the 200 interviews conducted by the Council.[2] It seems appropriate to ask why the interview data were not analyzed systematically to demonstrate the respondents' perceptions of such important phenomena as the relationships between the independent variables of independence and agency form and the dependent variables of personnel quality, political accountability, managerial efficiency, policy coordination, and the effects of regulatory policy. Failure to exploit this potentially rich lode of data with the analytical methodology of social science is one of the most disappointing characteristics of the report.

Three of the most serious problems that the Council attributes to the structure of regulatory commissions are over-utilization of adjudicatory procedures, inadequate funding of the commissions, and a lower than desirable quality of commission personnel. Each of these asserted relationships deserves further attention.

Is the collegial form the cause of case-by-case policy-making and extensive use of adjudication in the conduct of regulation? It may well contribute somewhat to that mode of decisional activity, but the record suggests that more important determinants are the organized efforts of the American Bar Association and its supporters in Congress along with the traditional American preference for using adversary proceedings to resolve conflicts between the government and private parties. The Ash Council Report presents no data regarding the frequency of adjudicatory proceedings in single-headed agencies, nor does it offer convincing evidence that a shift to single administrators will result in a sharp decline in adversary proceedings or the substitution of rule-making for case-by-case policy determination. The single-headed agency form may produce a modest tendency in this direction, but it is questionable whether the sweeping results envisaged in the Ash Council Report will be accomplished.

Is inadequate budgetary support of commission regulation a function of the collegial form and of independence? The assumption that an end to independence and the abandonment of plural executives will automatically increase presidential and congressional support for funding has no basis in fact. Fenno's study of the appropriations process reveals great variability in funding for operating agencies. He explains this differential success in terms of the strategies agencies employ, the popularity of their programs, and other non-structural factors. It may also be true that the level of budgetary support for regulatory agencies is directly related to public support for regulation and the agency leaders' ability to convert those public attitudes into larger appropriations. Changing regulatory structure is unlikely to affect this relationship. How well are single-headed departmental regulatory agencies such as the FDA and the FAA funded? While the report provides no data on that matter, it seems quite likely that there is substantial variability in the appropriations of departmental regulatory bodies and the differences probably can be explained by the same factors that affect the funding of operating agencies.

Several questions need to be raised with respect to the supposed relationship between the structure of regulatory agencies and the quality of their personnel. Most fundamental among these concerns the criteria for determining the quality of appointed regulatory administrators and their staffs. The Ash Council Report and most other scholars and study groups leave the observer in a position similar to Justice Stewart's assertion that, while he cannot precisely define hard core pornography, he knows it when he sees it. If the objective is to obtain high quality people for public office, how is quality measured or determined? What standards are especially relevant for regulatory officials and their staffs? How can conflicting standards be reconciled? Even if it is conceded that many standards are elusive and defy operationalization, more is required than to lecture the President on the need for talented, strong, well-qualified, men of administrative excellence. Failure to define the components of such qualities is not limited to the Ash Council Report. Other reformers who have studied the characteristics of federal executives and regulatory commissioners have also failed to formulate criteria for appointment.

An attempt to develop criteria that will produce qualified personnel quickly leads to confusion and potential conflict, revealing why the subject remains so pristine. Some of the more obvious criteria and the questions they engender include:

AGE: Youth seems to be increasingly desired, but how much?

RACE: To what extent should blacks be sought?

SEX: How important a consideration will it become in regulation as consumerism and women's liberation increase?

POLITICS: Within statutory restrictions, this is an obvious presidential prerogative. But, how much should patronage enter into the picture?

EDUCATION: How much is minimally necessary? What professional training, other than law, is appropriate? Is the reputation of the educational institution of any consequence?

EXPERIENCE: What kinds are most desirable? How much is needed?

ATTITUDES: What perceptions of regulation and regulatory goals are most helpful? To what extent is an explicit consumer or industry orientation desired and permitted?

Obviously these are not immutable criteria. They will vary widely with regulatory areas, external economic and industrial conditions, and political factors such as presidential and congressional goals and expectations. They are not equally susceptible to measurement, nor is there likely to be agreement on what is specifically desired. Their relationship to agency structure is unknown but by a reasonable estimate it is no more than modest; it may even be indirect or tangential.

Current evaluations of regulatory personnel tend to be based on imprecise and conflicting criteria. Education is recognized as essential, but there is a tendency to accord higher merit to graduates of Ivy League universities and national law schools than of other institutions. Prior public service is regarded as relevant experience, but it is often taken as evidence of patronage. Relevant private experience is also considered useful, but raises the spectre of capture by the regulated interests.

Beyond the problem of developing reliable criteria for appointment lies the difficulty in evaluating the performance of regulatory administrators and their staffs. Logic would seem to dictate that the prime consideration should be the success of the agency in meeting regulatory goals. Except on an impressionistic basis, however, this type of analysis has not been done. Even with the recent advances made by economists, the methodological obstacles are formidable. In addition, regulation has been almost universally accepted as necessary and viable, while specific regulatory objectives have not been questioned. The possibility that some regulatory agencies may be asked to perform exceedingly difficult if not impossible tasks has not been taken into consideration. As Cary commented, "[s]omehow the public and writers [have] seemed to expect too much of regulatory agencies." Condemnations of at least some regulatory personnel and their agencies may be unfair in light of the unreasonable and unrealistic demands that are made of them. Also, some heavily castigated agencies may be effectively regulating according to statutory goals but their critics overlook the viability of those objectives. Caves suggests that the major fault with air transport regulation lies not with the CAB as an institution or with its personnel, but with the traditional regulatory objectives of maximum incentive to develop new aircraft, sustained promotion, and extension of service.

The Ash Council Report does not delve into the complexities involved in the recruitment and retention of personnel or in the evaluation of performance. It speaks confidently, however, of a clear causal relationship between agency form and the quality of personnel. This relationship is asserted but never demonstrated. A reading of the reports prepared by "Nader's Raiders" on the FTC and the ICC, however, bolsters the conclusion that the quality of regulatory personnel, both appointive and staff, on those agencies is not high, even when assessed in purely impressionistic terms of propensity to enhance the public interest. But the same conclusion is reached in their report on the FDA. Taking the manifest consumer protection bias of Nader and his associates into account, it seems at least tenable that the problem of personnel quality, however imprecise the criteria for measurement, is endemic to the regulatory process. Industry capture of the regulatory agency is by no means a phenomenon peculiar to the commission form. Indeed, Lowi argues persuasively that it is the dominant feature of agency-public relationships in non-regulatory policy areas as well.[3] It is hardly a condition that can be corrected by structural changes alone. The most that might be hoped for is that a shift to the single administrator form will accomplish a marginal reduction in the number of opportunities for establishing agency-clientele relationships that are inimical to the public interest. The problems of personnel and industry control are not structural, they are functional in that they inhere in regulation as a governmental activity.

Nevertheless, the Ash Council report states that "the inability of commissions to perform satisfactorily results more from their organizational structure than defects in the recruitment process. *Even if the best qualified person filled each position, the collegial structure would impede effective performance.*" Assuming that commissions do perform unsatisfactorily, the report never shows, beyond the level of a priori assertions, that other regulatory forms perform more effectively. Nor is there any analysis of the recruitment process for other forms of regulatory agencies. Even more sweeping, however, is the final assertion. Not only is it unsupported, in spite of the claim to have been "found," it is intemperate. If such a claim is valid then why does the Council propose to retain the FCC and to create a hybridized Antitrust Board that is neither fish nor fowl? Surely if the collegial form is so incapable of effective performance that even the "best personnel" cannot overcome it, there is no justification for its retention in any agency. Alternatively, if structure is so much more important than the quality of personnel and the recruitment process, why does the Council argue that single-headed agencies will greatly improve personnel quality?[4]

Some of the Ash Council's recommendations for specific regulatory agencies bear upon the relationships between form and various problems. The argument supporting the proposal to replace the SEC with a single administrator ignores the widely held belief that the agency has attracted competent people since its inception and that it has been the most effective and successful of the federal regulatory commissions. There is no evidence that the recent increase in delays in SEC proceedings can be attributed to collegial decision making. In fact data supplied in the Report suggest that the failure of appropriations and personnel to keep pace with the growth in workload is the primary cause of the increase.

Similarly, the FPC's backlog of cases is not demonstrated to be the result of its structure. The claim that a single administrator would be more apt to resolve issues through rule-making than the FPC has been is more a promise than a fact. Much will depend on the administrator's background, his perception of regulation, and the agency's statutory directives. The Council's exaggerated claims of expedited procedure overstate the case for a single administrator.

The Ash Council makes a good case for the collegial form in its proposal to retain the FCC. The Council distinguishes the FCC from the other agencies by the kinds of issues involved in communications, but this is a debatable point. Despite the alleged uniqueness of communications, the Council cannot avoid attenuating the case that it makes elsewhere against the collegial form. Furthermore, the case for the Antitrust Board takes back much of the earlier condemnation of the commission form. The operational effectiveness of the Antitrust Board's hybrid structure will depend largely on the personal compatability of the chairman and the two economic administrators. It could prove highly efficacious or become hopelessly immobilized.

CONCLUSION: REGULATION AS A POLITICAL PROCESS

The basic contention of this article is that until scholars and reformers conceive of regulation as a political process and approach it in that frame of reference, they will lack the understanding necessary to develop realistic proposals for improvement that have a reasonable prospect of adoption and some probability of success. The existing literature on regulation, while substantial in volume, does not provide the requisite knowledge. It is heavily subjective in approach, it has not sufficiently utilized the systematic methods of social science, and it contains a critical lacuna in studies of the single administrator form.

In developing a conception of regulation as a political process, several elements are essential: general goals and expectations, statutory objectives, organizational structure, procedures, policy control, personnel, and the effects of regulatory policies. It is quite possible to reformulate these elements, but they have all in various ways attracted the attention of those who study the regulatory process, and they seem to encompass its essential features. Unfortunately, the full ambit of the process is seldom taken into consideration, even in studies of its component elements. The predominant tendency has been to consider only a single factor such as procedure, or a few manifestly related factors such as structure and policy control. It is imperative that the interrelationship of all the various elements be kept in mind if understanding is to be advanced. The fable of the blind men describing an elephant in a variety of ways, each according to his own perception of its single most distinguishing characteristic, is worth keeping in mind.

The purposes of regulation also provide an obvious and crucial starting point for most inquiries. Two questions must be asked: what do we expect the regulation under study to accomplish; and, how have these expectations been expressed in the regulatory statutes? Generally, regulation is justified on the grounds that abuses of monopoly position by firms in non-competitive industries must be prevented, markets must be protected against unfair, fraudulent, and deceptive practices, and public safety must be insured. Seldom are questions raised as to whether regulation is the proper means to implement these general goals in specific situations, nor is the question raised once the initial decision to regulate has been made. It is also widely assumed that effective regulation is necessarily aggressive, vigorous, and public-oriented. The concept of regulation as a negative, combative process is so predominant that the possibilities for achieving regulatory goals through positive and conciliatory strategies, such as selective incentives, is largely unexplored. This suggests that periodic reviews focusing on the need for regulation and the appropriateness of current regulatory strategies vis-à-vis alternative strategies would contribute to the development of more realistic expectations for the process.

The implementation of specific regulatory objectives in statutes also requires more attention than it now receives. A familiar theory of regulatory administration holds that the initial goals are only broadly defined and dimly perceived when the legislation is enacted. Consequently, statutory standards that accompany the delegation of legislative power use necessarily ambiguous language such as "just and reasonable" or "public interest, convenience, and necessity." This ambivalence is removed as the agency acquires experience and expertise and a growing body of clarifying decisional precedent is formed and supplemented by rules and regulations. Empirically, this theory has often proved defective for both descriptive and predictive purposes. Jaffe observes that a vague, broad delegation may be highly functional at the outset of regulation, but when the initial objectives are realized ambiguity ceases to function in "a sense of mandate," and "[e]xternal forces rush in to fill the vacuum." Lowi argues that the phenomenon of capture by regulated interests is attributable primarily to vague and abstract standards of delegation. He dates the ICC's decline . . . from the 1920 grant of the power over minimum rates with no accompanying guidelines other than that they be "just and reasonable." This led to case-by-case bargaining between the commission, the railroads, and motor carriers which placed it "on all sides of its own rules and rationalizations." Friendly regards the clarification of general initial standards as imperative for several reasons including the maintenance of agency independence and intraagency policy consistency.

If scholars such as Jaffe, Lowi, and Friendly are correct, and their case is so well stated that it seems imprudent to deny the possibilty that they may be, then statutory standards deserve more attention as a focus for regulatory reform. Moreover, if evaluation of regulation is to be conducted, at least in part, in terms of achieving regulatory goals, then statutory formulation of objectives is an obvious subject for investigation.

The political, economic, and social forces that contribute to the formulation of regulatory goals also need to be identified and analyzed. Regulation is created in response to demands made on government. The interests that originate those demands continue to influence regulatory policy formulation and implementation through the articulation of additional demands and by granting or withholding support for the regulatory agency. Identification of those interests and a knowledge of their objectives and patterns of operation is essential to an understanding of the entire regulatory process.

Regulatory procedures have long been a concern of lawyers. Students of administrative procedure have tended to stress its relationship to structure and to policy control. Extensively judicialized procedures are claimed to be associated with the collegial form. Case-by-case decision-making is said to reduce control by political officials and facilitate control by clientele groups. But what most research on administrative procedure overlooks is the relationship of procedure to the implementation of regulatory goals and its impact on the effects of regulatory policy. Does adjudication hamper the achievement of regulatory goals? What types of procedure are associated with desirable regulatory outcomes? Procedure deserves most of the attention it receives, but it needs to be examined in the broader context of the full regulatory process.

The matter of policy control is central to any discussion of regulation. It is generally posed as a problem in democratic responsibility involving the threat of industry-mindedness. The preferability of public, politically responsible control by the President and Congress over private, politically non-responsible control by regulated interests is regarded as axiomatic. The conditions that facilitate or impede responsible political control over regulatory agencies need to be determined and explored. They certainly extend beyond structural factors. Jaffe's statement that industry orientation is endemic in any regulatory agency stands in sharp contrast to the Ash Council's assertion that it is primarily a defect of the commission form. The charge of irresponsibility has been leveled at commissions for years, but it has not been ascertained to what degree single-headed agencies are susceptible to this defect. The Nader study of the FDA suggests that Jaffe is probably right. The entire problem of how patterns of policy control affect the determination of regulatory objectives and the effectiveness with which they are implemented has not been thoroughly examined.

Enough has already been said about the effect of regulatory policy on regulated industries to indicate its importance in any assessment of regulation. The evaluation of policy outcomes on the basis of objectives is a difficult but essential task. The relationship of such intervening factors as procedure, structure, personnel, and policy control, to the outcomes is also critical in developing proposals for reforming the process.

The problem of personnel is always present in American administrative agencies given the greater rewards available in the private sector, especially at top levels, and the general preference for private over public enterprise. The most familiar dilemma encountered is the conflict-of-interest situation. Most qualified people are likely to come from industry or the supportive professions, and many are likely to return to them following their governmental service. If their past loyalties and future aspirations are oriented toward the private sector, and especially to regulated industries, how is the public interest to be maintained and advanced? Yet if such persons are excluded, the task of securing competent men is further complicated. The challenge is to find ways to make service in regulatory agencies attractive to a wide range of qualified people. What are the factors peculiar to regulatory administration that make it attractive? How important is the prospect of a lucrative subsequent position with one of the regulated industries or a law firm that represents them? How much does the visibility of the agency and the popularity of its regulatory program matter? (Indications are that the current popularity of consumer protection has increased the attractiveness of staff positions with the FTC.) Is the clarity of the regulatory statute of any significance? Are structural characteristics of the agency any consideration? These questions can only be answered through a systematic survey of past, present, and prospective regulatory agency personnel.

It should be noted that although the same questions apply to the recruitment of appointive administrators and professional agency staff members, each involves a different recruitment process; therefore, the answers may be quite different. The selection of a few score regulatory administrators is a politically sensitive operation even though it usually does not involve direct or intense presidential participation. The recruitment of several thousand staff members is a sizeable enterprise, and it is almost exclusively a function of the agencies and the Civil Service Commission. Systematic analysis of the criteria for appointment and the recruitment process for appointees and agency staff is lacking. If obtaining and retaining well qualified personnel is a necessary condition for effective regulation, then these matters must be examined. Existing information is either too general, being based on government-wide studies, or too subjective to provide satisfactory answers.

Finally, structure must be acknowledged as an important element in the regulatory process, but its major function is to establish the institutional boundaries within which regulation occurs. It does not warrant the central role accorded it in the literature. The relationships between structure and the other elements of the process undoubtedly exist, but their strength has never been assayed through careful empirical analysis. The significance attributed to structure is based upon unsubstantiated assertions and impressionistic assumptions. To suggest, as the Ash Council Report does, that the principal defects that afflict the regulatory process can be overcome through "a fundamental restructuring" is to ignore the complex political character of the process and to promise results that probably cannot be delivered. At best restructuring by itself can offer a marginal promise of improvement, at worst it may generate substantial expectations that cannot be met. Failure to meet such expectations can lead to consequences—erosion of support for government generally, and increased alienation from the political system among important segments of the public such as the young, the poor, and the blacks—that are potentially far more serious than the conditions for which correctives are sought.

This is not to suggest that structural changes cannot, in appropriate circumstances, have highly efficacious results. Rather it is to urge that the limitations of reorganization be clearly recognized. In many fundamental respects, governments will perform basic political and social functions regardless of structural arrangements.[5] The importance of structure for power relations is clear, however. Structure facilitates or impedes access to decision-makers, it can be used tactically by some groups and individuals to great advantage as they pursue their goals, and it can be made to reflect certain societal values at the expense of others.[6] But structure cannot determine policies and the values they embody, it cannot set fully the terms and conditions of political conflict and choice, and it cannot affect the outcomes in society and the economy of public policies once they are promulgated.

The Ash Council Report also neglects to show that commission regulation is largely a failure, even though many may intuitively agree that this is true. Furthermore, the Council neglected to examine problems and factors in the regulatory process that are antecedent and subsequent to the agency itself. The report simply assumes that structural reorganization can correct the defects of the regulatory process without understanding or analyzing the full dimensions of the process.

NOTES

1. The President's Advisory Council on Executive Organization, A New Regulatory Framework: Report on Selected Independent Regulatory Agencies (1971) [hereinafter cited as Ash Council Report].
2. These interviews constituted a source of hard data which could have been used in the conduct of systematic supportive analyses, but the Council chose not to present any of that evidence, either in quotations or in tabular form. A skeptic might suggest that perhaps the net import of the interviews is not as convincing as the council would like us to believe.
3. T. Lowi, *The End of Liberalism: Ideology, Policy, and the Crisis of Public Authority* (1969).
4. In fairness, it should be noted that the report later mitigates the claim of structural omnipotence when it acknowledges that "[t]here can be no assurance that a single administrator may not be short-sighted. . . . The form itself will not automatically produce an effective leader." *Ash Council Report, supra* note 1, at 44.
5. D. Easton, *A Framework for Political Analysis* (1965).
6. The reflection of core values in the structure of public bureaucracy is an important theme in the work of Herbert Kaufman, *See, e.g.,* Kaufman, *Administrative Decentralization and Political Power,* 29 Pub. Ad. Rev. 3 (1969); Kaufman, *Emerging Conflicts in the Doctrines of Public Administration,* 50 Am. Pol. Sci. Rev. 1057 (1956).

C. The New Federalism: Government by Grant-in-Aid

Throughout American history a high premium has been placed on avoiding unnecessary concentrations of power. Within the governmental system, the major expressions of this priority have been federalism, checks and balances, the Bill of Rights, and the lack of hierarchical discipline in both Congress and the national party organizations. In the social system as a whole, however, the most significant manifestation of this priority has been the national emphasis on minimizing the scope of governmental (and particularly federal) responsibility. During the nineteenth and early twentieth centuries, this objective was substantially achieved. The size of the public sector increased, but its rate of growth was scarcely more rapid than that of the total labor force and national income. More recently, the trend line of governmental growth has veered sharply upward. From 1927 through 1962, total public expenditures in the United States (federal, state, and local combined) rose from 10.0 percent of gross national product to 31.5 percent. Public employment levels rose a bit more slowly, from 8.9 percent of the labor force to 19.4 percent.[1]

The federal government has accounted for only about half this growth,[2] but it is the half that has involved armed force, esoteric technologies, extraordinary

[1] Tax Foundation, *Facts and Figures on Government Finance, 18th Biennial Edition, 1975.* (Washington, D.C.: Tax Foundation, Inc., 1975), Section I, pp. 24, 33.
[2] Federal spending rose from 2.5 percent of gross national product in 1929 to 20.4 percent in 1973. Federal employment, including the armed forces, rose from 2.5 percent of the labor force in 1929 to 8.3 percent in 1973.

degrees of secrecy, and the capacity to make all society's other great institutions appear as pygmies beside it. Quite naturally, therefore, its half is the one that has preoccupied those concerned about the long-term threat of "big government" to American liberty and democracy. The primary way in which federal policy makers have sought to allay such fears has been to rely increasingly on state, local, corporate, academic, and other private nonprofit institutions to administer its programs.[3] In view of the wide distribution of political influence in the system, moreover, and the frequent mixing of the federal government's funds with those of its administrative "instruments," it has not always been clear just who was serving whom, and in what degrees. Some have argued that it could hardly matter less, so long as all parties find it beneficial to continue cooperating. In the free market, after all, one does not worry about whether buyer or seller is dominant so long as each is happy with their transactions.

To optimists about the future of American liberty and democracy, then, the picture has been one of the American genius for pragmatic improvisation in action. The cobwebs of dogma have been brushed away. New techniques of government have been devised to fit contemporary circumstances. The public and private sectors—and within the former, the federal, state, and local sectors—have been blending, but the distribution of power in the social system has remained more than adequately pluralistic to preserve liberty and democracy unimpaired. Some have argued, in fact, that as a result of increasing specialization, the very strong market position of highly trained men, and these new administrative devices, the trend is in the direction of more pluralism rather than less.

To pessimists, on the other hand, the picture has been one of the federal government extending its tentacles ever outward, subverting with a complex array of new financial lures the autonomy of the only institutions in the society that remained potential centers of resistance to its policies—and to its growth. The increases in public spending and employment, in this view, do not begin to measure the growth of federal power that has taken place over the past forty years. Power cannot be measured literally, but quite obviously the American system has been transformed. From one in which free enterprise, states rights, isolationism, antimilitarism, and legislative supremacy were the dominant themes, another has emerged in which the economy is "managed," state and local tax revenues so largely to match federal grants, presidentially defined national security requirements override all other political considerations, and Congress becomes perceptibly more passive with every decade.

The first selection is from a report by a Senate subcommittee on the attitudes of federal grant-in-aid officials toward the "new federalism" they administer. Although written rather colorlessly, it deals in concise and informative fashion with many of the most fundamental issues of contemporary intergovernmental relations, among them the following: Should the state and local recipients of grants-in-aid be left a wide area of discretion in determining how to spend them? To what extent, if any, do federal aid officials and their local counterparts have

---

[3] Allaying such fears is by no means the only advantage that an agency secures by contracting out. Several others of importance are the following: (1) contractors can frequently lobby with fewer inhibitions and greater effect on behalf of the agency's programs than mere divisions of the agency itself could; (2) private institutions, being able to offer higher salaries and better working conditions than the government, can employ many possessors of scarce skills who would otherwise be unavailable to the agency; and (3) contracting enhances the agency's flexibility, by permitting it to avoid long-term staff obligations and to choose among competitive bids whenever it has work that it wishes to assign.

divergent objectives and perspectives? To what extent are those administering the "new federalism" concerned with the impact of their endeavors on the overall intergovernmental relations system? In other words, is the objective of nationalizing the revenue base of our attacks on national problems without concentrating power at the national level a living part of the intergovernmental relations system, or is it simply an academic rationale based on an idealized vision of reality? If you judge the latter to be true to a significant degree, you might consider what would be involved in changing the system to approximate the former.

The basic instrumentality of the administrative aspects of the federal system is the grant-in-aid. Michael D. Reagan evaluates the grant-in-aid system and finds that it has served the nation rather well, although not without creating certain problems. The alternatives to cooperation between the national, state, and local governments with the first as the senior partner have not been fully explored. President Nixon wished to decentralize policy control while retaining the superior revenue-generating capabilities of the federal government. The method he developed to achieve this objective, revenue sharing, was only partially implemented before he left office. The general revenue-sharing legislation of 1972 appears to be well established, but the special revenue-sharing programs in broad areas such as education which were to replace categorical grants-in-aid were not adopted. Experiences under general revenue sharing leave unanswered the question of how much the determination of spending priorities should be retained in Washington so long as the federal government provides a substantial proportion of the funding. The New Federalism developed under the Nixon administration, which would replace grants-in-aid with general and special revenue sharing, would presumably transfer significant amounts of policy control to state capitals and city halls. However, it has yet to be fully implemented. If it should ever exist in approximately the form in which it was proposed, it is likely that new problems of administrative federalism will accompany it.

The Federal System
as Seen by Federal Aid Officials

INTRODUCTION

The resolution creating this subcommittee charges it with the responsibility "to examine, investigate, and make a complete study of intergovernmental relationship-ships between the United States and the States and municipalities. . . ."

At its first meeting, Senator Muskie discussed the subcommittee's objectives:

> . . . What we hope to do in the work of this subcommittee is to give this . . . hidden dimension of government (intergovernmental relations) definition and identity—to understand what it is and what its potential is, and in what direction it is moving. . . .

From *The Federal System as Seen by Federal Aid Officials,* a study prepared by the U.S. Senate, Committee on Governmental Operations, Subcommittee on Intergovernmental Relations (committee print, December 15, 1965), pp. 1–2, 5–8, 21–22, 93–101.

It is clear that many Americans hold drastically conflicting views on the relative roles of the different levels of government, and it is our intention to give careful attention to every point of view to determine which pattern of interrelationships best serves the needs of the United States during this period of our history. . . .

More and more, the emphasis is on cooperation rather than competition among levels of government. We hear less talk about States' rights and more talk about States' responsibilities. . . .

There is no sense denying that the 20th century has seen the rise of revolutionary demands on the part of the people for the provision of services by the Government. What we are striving to achieve is a new balance of governmental activity which unshackles all levels of government to perform these tasks adequately. . . .

To this end the subcommittee has held hearings, considered legislation, issued reports and conducted research. The hearings have covered a wide range of topics exploring intergovernmental relationships in general, as well as specific problem areas. The subcommittee has also considered a number of bills to implement findings based on its hearings and on the reports of the Advisory Commission on Intergovernmental Relations and to carry out recommendations that emerged from subcommittee research studies.

One such research effort assayed the views of State and local officials on Federal-State-local relations. Through the distribution of a 97-item questionnaire a pattern of attitudes was identified, and valuable background information on various legislative proposals was amassed.

The subcommittee now turns to Federal aid officials for their views on intergovernmental relations. These officials are responsible for the operation of some 125 programs of assistance to State and local governments, including grants-in-aid, shared revenues, technical assistance, and loans. Excluding loan payments and technical assistance, they disbursed close to $13 billion in fiscal 1964. Their views on the federal system clearly are of more than minor significance. . . .

FEDERAL AIDS

"The use of Federal grants-in-aid has been increasing both in variety and magnitude since the initiation of the device in 1862, and especially since the end of World War II." This was probably the least controversial statement in the 1961 report by the Advisory Commission on Intergovernmental Relations on grants-in-aid, and subsequent developments have only underlined the accuracy of their assessment. From the inauguration of President Kennedy to the close of the 88th Congress, 29 new grant programs were added to the ACIR's original list of 45. Federal expenditures for such assistance soared more than 41 percent during this same brief period. This remarkable increase provides additional evidence of the importance of grants-in-aid in the maintenance of our federal system during a period of significant domestic change. The use of grants strengthens federalism by promoting national goals within a cooperative framework. The grant device has, in effect, prevented the nationalization of functions by strengthening and preserving State and local government.

The grant-in-aid has been responsive to the changing needs of this country throughout its development. Land grants assisted the States and local governments as our Nation emerged. Money is now the measure of Federal support.

As grant programs and the administrative machinery have matured, the pattern has become more complex. The earlier subcommittee report, "The Federal System As Seen by State and Local Officials," stressed that this proliferation of grants and the continual amending of older grants have created confusion and a somewhat critical view of such Federal aids at the State and local levels.

In hearings held before this subcommittee, William G. Colman, Executive Director of the ACIR, cited one of the basic reasons for this attitude.

> Grants-in-aid are increasing, in numbers and magnitude, at a rapid rate and we may come to a situation where grants-in-aid are an impenetrable jungle of legal, financial, and political and professional interlacings which will sorely try the minds of officials at all levels—Congressmen, Cabinet members, Governors, mayors, and county officials—in trying to maintain any kind of rational legislative and administrative direction of the areas of Government affairs in which grants play so large a part.[1]

This "impenetrable jungle" has been the subject of increasing examination since the first Hoover Commission dealt this topic a glancing blow in its 14-page report on Federal-State relations over 16 years ago. The Commission recommended that greater Federal attention be paid to the use of grants-in-aid and to revisions of the tax system.

Another early but more comprehensive report was prepared by the Council of State Governments for the Hoover Commission. This included a discussion of grants-in-aid. In addition to treating this topic generally the Council described the actual operation of 18 federally supported programs. Two sets of recommendations emerged from their analysis. Defects in the structure of State government formed the basis of the Council's suggestions for State consideration, while the use of grants-in-aid was the focal point of the recommendations for the Federal level. Several of the still unresolved questions raised in the Council's findings were covered in this survey of Federal executives.

The Council proposed that national grants be made for broad categories of public services. The subcommittee asked Federal administrators whether multipurpose grants, or permitting transfers of funds between grants, is desirable. The previous survey of State and local officials requested similar information. The Council also recommended that

> Grant-in-aid programs should be based, in all cases, on close cooperation between the National and State Governments. In no event should the National Government attempt to deal directly in grant programs with the political subdivisions of the States or with individuals.[2]

This recommendation parallels questionnaire items 1 and 2 which deal with the channeling of aid requests and aid disbursements.

The Council urged the restriction of national supervision of the administration of grant programs to initial approval of overall plans, post-audit of expenditures, and technical assistance and guidance during operation. The implications of this broad statement apply to various questions asked in both subcommittee surveys, including a whole section of this study dealing exclusively with intergovernmental fiscal relations.

Finally, the Council recommended that "the present patchwork of grant-in-aid programs should be systematized, with provision for cooperating planning, appraisal, and administration on a continuing basis." This perennial problem received extensive coverage in both subcommittee questionnaires, including items 1, 2, and 5 in this survey.

These reports and recommendations lay dormant until the creation in 1953 of the Commission on Intergovernmental Relations, better known by the name of its second chairman, Meyer Kestnbaum. Unlike the Hoover Commission, this group confined its efforts specifically to intergovernmental relationships. The Kestnbaum Commission traced the use of grants-in-aid, weighed their advantages and disadvantages, examined the operation of many particular grant programs, and measured the impact of this assistance on the functioning of State and local government.

This "blue ribbon" panel then discussed improvements in the operation of grant programs and the means of determining where such aid is needed. Three basic conclusions were reached:

> (1) A grant should be made or continued only for a clearly indicated and presently important national objective. This calls for a searching and selecting test of the justification for national participation. The point has been made . . . that existence of a national interest in an activity is not in itself enough to warrant national participation. Related questions are the relative importance of the national interest and the extent to which it may be served by State and local action. Consequently, where the activity is one normally considered the primary responsibility of State and local governments, substantial evidence should be required that national participation is necessary in order to protect or to promote the national interest.
> (2) Where national participation in an activity is determined to be desirable, the grant-in-aid should be employed only when it is found to be the most suitable form of national participation. It is important to compare the strong and weak points of the grant-in-aid device with those of other forms of national-State cooperation as well as with those of direct national action. It is likewise important to consider the types of objectives and situations for which the grant is best adapted. The probable effect on State or local governments is an important consideration.
> (3) Once it is decided that a grant-in-aid should be made, the grant should be carefully designed to achieve its specified objective. This requires careful attention to the shaping of apportionment formulas and matching requirements, the prescription of standards and conditions, and the provision for administrative machinery and procedures. Objectives as varied as cancer control, old-age assistance, highway construction, and forest fire prevention call for imaginative use of varied types of standards, controls, and fiscal formulas. It is more important to shape these elements of the grant to a particular purpose to achieve complete uniformity among the programs. At the same time, in order to ease the impact of grants-in-aid on State and local government, as much uniformity should be striven for as is compatible with the achievement of specific objectives.[3]

Much of the present debate over grants-in-aid is still based on the work of this Commission. Consequently, many of the questions posed in the subcommittee's questionnaire find their roots in its final 1955 report to the President.

The Commission report had an impact on Washington. First, Meyer Kestnbaum was asked to stay on to work for the adoption of the proposals put forth by the first Hoover Commission and the Commission on Intergovernmental Relations. Later, President Eisenhower addressed the Governors' Conference on June 21, 1957. In this speech, he called for the creation of a task force to draw up an action program for congressional consideration. This Joint Federal-State Action Committee was assigned three tasks:

(1) to designate functions that might be shifted from the Federal Government to the States;

(2) to recommend Federal revenue sources that might be turned over to the States to finance these functions; and

(3) to identify emerging problems that might require governmental action and recommend the appropriate division of Government responsibility for them.[4]

The recommendations adopted by this committee asked the States to assume responsibility for the vocational education program and construction of local waste treatment works. In return, the Federal Government was to give up a portion of the Federal telephone tax and to end its participation in the two aid programs.

The report was transmitted by the President to Congress, but the recommendations were not adopted. The two principal reasons for their rejection were highlighted during hearings held by the House Intergovernmental Relations Subcommittee. The subcommittee found that:

(1) Such an exchange would adversely affect the lower income States, which would lose far more in grants than they would gain in tax revenue. Many of the higher income States, on the other hand, would obtain substantially more revenue than needed to carry on the activities concerned.

(2) While grants purport to assist the States in supporting specific activities of national concern, it appears that many States would be unable or unwilling to carry on these functions alone. The result would likely be very uneven, with some States discontinuing or impairing programs because of their inability or unwillingness to impose the necessary taxes.[5]

This question of equalizing the differences between high and low income States is a perennial one. The return of taxes to the States in exchange for their assumption of a grant-aided program is also a longstanding issue. Question 3a of this study asks Federal administrators if their particular programs should reflect the variations in fiscal capacity among States and local governments. The earlier questionnaire also explored the desirability of recognizing disparities among the States in income or resources. State and local officials were asked if they favored the return of tax sources in exchange for the full responsibility of carrying out a program currently underwritten with grant funds.

Congressional interest in Federal-State-local relations (and the use of grants-in-aid in particular) increased when the House Intergovernmental Relations Subcommittee began its 3-year study of grants-in-aid in 1956. A comprehensive questionnaire to Federal agencies and State and local officials served as the basis for a series of public hearings. These proceedings were held both in Washington and in the field. The subcommittee wound up the investigation with a consideration of the two recommendations of the Joint Federal-State Action Committee. Other broad findings and recommendations concerning Federal grants, as well as some valuable appendixes, are also included in this report by the House Committee on Government Operations. The subcommittee found general satisfaction with the use of grants-in-aid in its nationwide survey and concluded that the grant-in-aid has been an important device in promoting cooperation among levels of government.

The creation of an advisory commission on intergovernmental relations was one of the major suggestions of this House report. Joint hearings were held on bills introduced by Senator Muskie and Representative Fountain to implement the proposal. On September 4, 1959, President Eisenhower signed an act creating a permanent, bipartisan Advisory Commission on Intergovernmental Relations.

The outstanding work of the Commission has brought the issue of Federal grants into sharper focus. The subcommittee has worked closely with it on this and other questions. The provisions of title III of S. 561, the proposed Intergovernmental Cooperation Act of 1965, for example, find their origin in the 1961 Commission report "Periodic Congressional Reassessment of Federal Grants-in-Aid to State and Local Governments." Specifically, this title requires that any new grant-aided program authorized for 3 or more years shall be reviewed with the following considerations in mind: (1) the extent to which the purposes for which the grants-in-aid are authorized have been met; (2) the extent to which such programs can be carried on without further financial assistance from the United States; and (3) whether or not there should be any changes in purpose, direction, or administration of the original program, or in the procedures and requirements.

The subcommittee has conducted its own probe of this subject. The first survey of State and local officials contained one section dealing specifically with grants-in-aid. The observations of these officials have assisted the subcommittee in its legislative efforts as well as in its research undertakings. In the present study Federal officials were asked for their opinion on the use of Federal aids. . . .

OVERALL QUESTIONNAIRE RESULTS

National domestic goals continue to be achieved through Federal programs of assistance to State and local governments and other public and private agencies, as well as through direct government activity. The expansion of the range and variety of these shared activities has reached the point now that it is difficult to find an area of public concern that does not involve government and, in turn, some form of Federal-State-local collaboration. The grant device, then, has become the foremost, symbol of the partnership between and among the levels of government.

The historical pattern of this development has been irregular, however. From the beginning of the century to the great depression it was gradual and fairly uniform, with totals reaching approximately $200 million by 1932. By 1940 Federal grants reached more than $2.3 billion, but by 1946 they had slipped back to below $1 billion. From 1948 until the present, grant payments began to increase again at a fairly constant rate, as old programs were expanded and new ones were added. At the latest count, 10 executive departments of the National Government and 11 of its independent agencies are involved in administering some 143 general programs of Federal aid to State and local governments.

This development has produced a wealth of background material and a continuing debate on the role of grants-in-aid in our federal system. Yet it apparently has exerted little impact on many Federal program administrators. This section deals with four of the topics that have figured in this debate—channeling procedures, equalization provisions, suspension of payments, and the use of incentive grants. Several Federal officials provided hasty and superficial responses to these questions; some did not even bother to reply; and most of those who did respond seemed quite content with the present operation of their programs. Suggestions for change were few.

Whether the responding official administered a Federal-State, Federal-local, or Federal-State-local aid program, replies to the question on channeling and disbursement exuded satisfaction with present practices and provisions. These officials were equally sanguine when asked to comment on present equalization provisions (if any) found in their programs. Only 15 percent of the aid administrators and 21 percent of the grant officials who responded saw a need for greater recognition of differences in State and local fiscal capacity. Some of those answering "no change needed," of course, administer programs which permit the transfer of funds or sliding matching scales to reflect differences between wealthy and poorer States.

The question of incentive payments encountered general indifference from most of the survey's respondents. Sixty-three percent of those grant respondents answering saw little need for a provision of this type and only half of those conceding that it might be desirable felt that such a provision would improve the administration of their individual programs. In light of the personnel and planning problems cited by many in response to other questions, it is somewhat surprising that more of these officials did not see the use of incentive grants as a possible method of correcting some of these difficulties.

In general, only a few of the responding officials considered the four issues raised here in terms of the extraordinary growth in the number, cost, and significance of Federal grants-in-aid. Only a few considered the dynamic changes which State and local governments now are experiencing. Only a few analyzed the future of their individual programs in light of these developments. Most confined the scope of their answers to the administration of their own programs. Only a few, then, dealt with the questions posed in terms of a broader intergovernmental context. Indifference, standpattism, and a narrowly defined functionalism—these were the themes that dominated the majority of responses to these grant-in-aid questions.

This functional orientation has deep roots. The legislation establishing grants is usually initiated by a particular coalition of legislators, administrators, and special-interest groups who are deeply concerned with expanding existing programs or establishing new substantive ones. Concurrence of a substantial number of legislators is required in order to achieve congressional enactment. These factors insure that the program will be a matter of national concern.

But the approach followed throughout this legislative process is basically a functional one. It is geared to meeting specific, often urgent, problems. Relatively little consideration is given generally to the impact on other programs or on the State and local units which will administer it. Comparatively little thought is spent on such intergovernmental niceties as cooperative planning, appraisal, and administration. Program administrators, then, tend to have little awareness of questions of an intergovernmental nature because little in their mandate requires or promotes it.

Further, there is not much likelihood that interlevel problems will be explored at any length after a program's enactment. The aid administrator is called upon to carry out successfully the specific goals of his program. Many deviations from this course would place him in a precarious position. And the professional expertise that characterizes Federal administrators at this "upper-middle management level" also guarantees a preoccupation with the purposes of the program. The functional bias once again reveals itself as aid administrators and satellite interest groups fight to protect "the integrity of the program." They may view as intruders those legislative committees, top administrators, and commissions concerned with the broader problems of policy consistency, interlevel administrative procedures, interagency coordination, and structural reorganization.

Thus, program goals, professionalism, and clientele pressures, as well as the legislative process itself, combine to explain why Federal executives in general have neither the mandate nor the desire to assess their grant-in-aid programs in terms of their intergovernmental significance.

BUREAUCRACY AND FEDERALISM: SOME OBSERVATIONS AND PROPOSALS

This study began as a survey of the views of Federal aid administrators on some of the more troublesome issues confronting our federal system. As the study progressed, it also involved an analysis of some of the problems in contemporary public administration. As such, it became a study of middle management, since practically all of the survey's respondents are bureau chiefs or division heads.

The conventional wisdom of public administration holds that middle management is the principal home of the specialists—not the generalists—in the bureaucratic structure. This is not surprising, since the civil service classification system is still largely based on specialized principles and since appointment to this level usually comes to in-grade bureau personnel, not to outsiders. Further, the administrative unit which middle management executives head is the bureau or division. And this relatively homogeneous structure is built to perform one task or a series of closely related tasks. As such, it is a highly stable organizational unit that reorganization plans may shift around, but rarely abolish. Finally, most bureau chiefs and nearly all division heads have permanent tenure and thus are able to exert a continuing influence toward achieving unity and consistency in administering the programs falling under their jurisdiction. Stability based on tenure; professionalism based on technical training, experience, and program goals; and a narrow functionalism based on the relatively homogeneous program mandates of the bureau and division—these are the usual traits of middle management found in the lexicon of public administration experts.[6]

Four behavioral themes recur throughout the questionnaire responses of nearly all of the 109 administrators participating in this survey. These themes both correspond to and expand on the foregoing traits of middle management.

Functionalism, or the respondents' preoccupation with protecting and promoting the purposes of their individual programs, was the most important single conditioner of their comments regarding the items examined in all five parts of the questionnaire. This is in keeping with the normal role of an executive assigned to this administrative level and with the specific character of their program mandates. It is this norm that accounts for their intense desire to maintain clear channels of communication and to promote the closest possible relationship with their functional counterparts at the State and local levels. It is this norm that helps explain the aggressive defense of their programs' objectives. It is this norm that generates the special brand of politics—program politics—which successful middle management administrators so adroitly practice. And it is this norm that produces their general insensitivity to many of the diplomatic niceties required for more successful intergovernmental relations.

Professionalism, or the deep commitment to the merit system principle and to the technical and ethical standards of the specialized group to which they belong, dictated their answers to nearly all of the questions in the preceding chapters on State Organization and Intergovernmental Personnel. It is this norm that explains their keen interest in upgrading the expertise, tenure, and administrative capabilities of their counterparts at the State and local levels. It is this norm that explains their attempts to reduce to a minimum the meddling of "dilettante generalists" at any point in their administrative operations. It is this norm that explains their distrust of partisan intrusions into the administration of these programs. And it is this norm that explains their difficulty in arriving at a balanced definition of the public interest as it applies to the State or metropolitan level.

Standpattism, or the rigid defense of traditional practices, procedures, and principles, is a theme found in the great majority of their answers to the items covered in the chapters on Federal aids, financial administration, and metropolitan area problems. As the conservative defenders of administrative continuity and stability against innovating pressures from above, from below, and from outside, these middle management officials could hardly be expected to indicate that present channeling and disbursement practices, accounting and auditing procedures, and program activities in metropolitan areas are something less than sensible and sound. This norm, of course, is necessary to balance the impetus for change and to provide the proper administrative milieu for the implementation of any program. Yet, this norm and its adherents must also be recognized as the major obstacle to any reform in the problem areas reviewed in this survey.

The fourth behavioral norm—indifference, or the cavalier dismissal of serious questions and topics as being irrelevant or unimportant—was reflected in responses to every section of this questionnaire. Nearly every item produced a large percentage of "no opinion" replies, and several items produced "not relevant" comments from agency heads whose programs clearly were covered by the issue under examination. And even the clear-cut answers of many respondents indicated a complete indifference to the critical significance of the topic in question. This attitude, of course, is partly an extension of the three traits previously discussed. Middle management executives, with a strong functional, professional, and status-quo orientation, are not likely to approach broad questions of a multifunctional, interlevel, interagency, or coordinating nature with any great enthusiasm or concern. But this attitude also relates to other factors. It stems in part from the ignorance that only the narrow specialist can display toward broader questions of management, policy, and governmental operations. It stems in part from an acute awareness that their expertise is needed and that their administrative positions are fairly secure. It stems in part from their recognition that many of the larger intergovernmental questions can only be resolved by others more directly involved in the decision-making processes at the Federal, State, and local levels.

If the behavioral traits of this select middle management group conform fairly closely to the descriptions of authorities on public administration, their theory of federalism bears little resemblance to more familiar interpretations found in political addresses or in works dealing with intergovernmental relations.

The orthodox or conventional theory, now enunciated primarily by States righters, views the federal system as one in which competition is principally between or among the levels of government. The powers of the Federal Government and those of the State, so the interpretation runs, are and should be kept distinct from and independent of each other, and the activities at these levels should be confined to different spheres, with only incidental administrative collaboration. The ideal model, premised by this traditional theory, is one where "the functions of government are almost entirely assigned to a single one of the levels of government and the competitive friction is designed to preserve the insulation." In the familiar analogy from the pantry, the federal system ideally is like a layer cake, but the great contemporary problem is that the Federal layer now is not only on top, but is getting too thick. This clearly is not the view of the Federal aid officials.

The "marble cake" theory, developed by the late Morton Grodzins and further developed by Daniel J. Elazar and others, views the system as involving both competition and cooperation, but with an emphasis on the latter. The American federal system, then, is not and has never been a system of separated governmental activities. Whether cooperative federalism was intended by the Founding Fathers is difficult to prove, say these authorities. Events quickly demonstrated its necessity, however. "Governments operating in the same territory, serving the same people, generally sharing the same goals, and faced with the same demands, could not maintain a posture of 'dual federalism' (the separation of functions by levels of government)," Prof. Elazar contends.[7] By the 1960's, the principles and mechanisms of cooperative federalism have become an accepted part of the American governmental process and most of these came into being in the 19th century. The principles include "national supremacy, broad national legislative and appropriation powers, noncentralized government, and maximum local control." The mechanisms include "a nondisciplined, noncentralized party system; routinized legislative 'interference' in administration; regular intergovernmental consultation; and a system of grants-in-aid from higher to lower levels of government." This cooperative federal theory is not that of the survey's respondents, although it resembles their view more closely than the States righters' interpretation or the theory that follows.

A composite theory of federalism, which blends features of both the competitive and the cooperative concepts, emerged from the subcommittee's earlier survey of State and local officials. Four basic attitudinal positions were identified in this analysis: the Orthodox States Righters (ultraconservatives), who comprised 11 percent of the sample; the Neo-Traditionalists (moderate conservatives), who accounted for 43 percent; the Pragmatic Cooperative Federalists (realistic liberals), who represented 33 percent; and the New Nationalists (ultraliberals), who made up 13 percent of the total. The two middle groups differed in ideological emphasis, but shared a common viewpoint of many of the specific and practical problems confronting elected officials at the State and local levels. This fairly wide area of agreement permitted the piecing together of an operating or practicing theory of intergovernmental relations to which more than three-quarters of that survey's respondents adhered in the day-to-day carrying out of their official duties. The basic principles of that composite theory, which included both ideal and real features, were identified as follows:

1. As a practical matter, Federal, State, and local governments are viewed as loosely related parts of one overall system. Each level, however, vigorously maintains its separate institutional identity and freedom of action in policymaking.

2. The domestic functions of government are not neatly parceled out among the three levels; instead, several governmental activities are assumed jointly by each governmental level with significant and continuing responsibilities being assumed by all.

3. Decision making in the intergovernmental process is shared fairly equally among various public bodies on the three planes, thus preserving a cardinal principle of traditional federalism.

4. The administration of programs of joint concern is a mutual undertaking. Such devices as joint boards, joint inspection, the sharing of specialized information, and use of another level's technical personnel reveal the benefits of this collaboration among equals; competition rather than collaboration, however, is produced when administrative regulations are unilaterally imposed without full consultation with another level's officials and without recognition of the merit of some administrative practices of other jurisdictions.

5. The Federal grant-in-aid is and will continue to be an inescapable and important feature of contemporary intergovernmental relations. It provides a necessary means whereby the three levels of government can collaborate to fulfill common purposes. If not encumbered with excessive administrative redtape, it can also serve to strengthen State and local governments, since it utilizes the existing institutional framework for administering these activities of common concern.

6. Representative, responsive, and responsible State governments are vital for the proper operation of American federalism. They have a vital role in collecting a sizable proportion of total revenues, directly administering several important governmental services, providing vital assistance to their local units of government, and serving as political laboratories for testing new policies.

7. When properly empowered, financed, and aided, county and municipal governments singly and in voluntary association with one another can meet many of the challenges that ubiquitous urbanization has created.

8. Intergovernmental relations should be viewed primarily as a network of functional, financial, and administrative arrangements which seek to advance the commonweal. Parity with respect to the power positions of the various levels is an indispensable ingredient for successful collaboration in this area. Inequality, after all, undermines the voluntarism that is so essential for any full-fledged cooperative endeavor.

9. Every level has a fundamental duty to preserve the interlevel balance, but a primary responsibility for implementing this ideal rests with Congress. Its past enactments constitute the greatest single force shaping the federal system under which we live, and its future actions will exert no less an impact.

This composite, or hybrid, theory, which resembles a marble cake cut into layers, clearly is not that of the Federal aid administrators who participated in this questionnaire survey. But they would take fewer exceptions to this theory than to that of the States' righters.

What, then, *is* the theory of these Federal executives?

At no point did any of the respondents develop one. Nor was it expected, since middle management executives are supposed to be pragmatic administrators, not political theorists. Yet careful assessment of the answers to certain key questions indicates that the respondents do have a general idea of what intergovernmental relations are and how they should operate. In short, they have a theory of federalism, and more than three out of four adhere to the same interpretation of the system.

Few among the majority would recognize the elements of this theory as being the logical corollaries of their responses to one or more of the survey's questions. None probably would accept all of its provisions. Yet the following hypotheses are, in fact, the basic features of the theory of federalism which emerged from the majority's responses.[8]

(1) The Federal, State, and local governments are interrelated parts of a single governmental system; each level, however, must effectively discharge its mandated responsibilities if all of its rights as a member of this partnership are to be preserved.

(2) Most domestic functions of government are shared, but the Federal Government, as the senior, most progressive, and most affluent member of this partnership, has been forced to assume a disproportionate share of this responsibility.

(3) Policymaking in intergovernmental relations is a multilevel process, but obstruction—not collaboration—is as likely to be encountered from elected policymakers at the State and local levels.

(4) The administration of joint action programs is a mutual—and, ideally, a professional—undertaking. Their authorizing legislation establishes them on a functional basis, and the vertical lines of communication and collaboration between and among the functional specialists in Washington and their counterparts in the field must be kept clear and unbroken if the bases of genuine cooperation are to be maintained.

(5) The Federal grant and other aid devices are, and will continue to be, the most prominent and positive feature of contemporary federalism. They—not block grants, tax credits, or similar devices—provide the only time-tested techniques whereby the levels of government can collaborate effectively to fulfill common purposes and to meet certain national standards. Moreover, if not burdened with partisan or nonprofessional interference, they can also serve to strengthen the States and local units of government, since they rely primarily on these jurisdictions for administrative purposes and tend to upgrade the caliber of the civil servants employed by these levels. Efforts to achieve greater consistency and uniformity in the operation of aid programs ignore the basic fact that each program is designed to accomplish a specific public purpose; hence, administrative and financial practices and procedures must be geared to the needs of the individual program and not to any abstract standardized principles.

(6) Responsive and responsible State governments are vital for an effective

federal system; yet most States do not possess these characteristics and are not likely to acquire them in the near future. Most States have failed to exert a maximum tax effort, to eliminate outdated limitations on the taxing authority of local units of government, to adopt statewide merit systems, to improve the salaries and professional opportunities of their civil employees, to establish greater order in their own metropolitan areas, and to revamp their political systems. In short, they have failed to achieve the minimum requirements of a democratic government in the mid-20th century. It is necessary, therefore, to continue those provisions in grant and other aid programs which minimize threats to effective collaboration among program administrators at the various levels.

(7) General units of local government, when properly empowered and financially aided by the States, can act as effective partners in Federal-State-local and Federal-local joint action programs. Special-purpose districts and authorities grow out of particular local and areawide needs and of the States' failure to strengthen the fiscal base of general units of local government; as such, they serve a useful purpose in helping to implement certain Federal aid programs.

(8) Rapid urbanization challenges traditional intergovernmental functional relationships; yet it is largely through strengthening these individual relationships, along with some increase in informal interagency contacts, that this challenge will be surmounted. Excessive preoccupation with regional or areawide principles and mechanisms can slow up the implementation of much-needed urban development and, in some cases, subject program administrators to additional political pressures.

(9) Intergovernmental relations are primarily a vertical and diagonal system of financial, functional, and administrative arrangements; the primary purpose of each and all of these relationships is to meet the demands of the American people for better or new public services. Intergovernmental relations, then, function as the essential means to this great end, not as an end in themselves.

(10) Successful intergovernmental relations are chiefly successful bureaucratic relations. Authorizing legislation, funds, and oversight come from legislative bodies. Policy directives, budgetary review and control, and administrative rules and regulations come from top management. And advice, assistance, and support, as well as complaints, criticism, and censure, come from officeholders at all levels, individual citizens, and interest groups. These basic forces of our pluralistic political system shape and sustain the broad, complex pattern of intergovernmental relations. The day-to-day conduct of these relations, however, fall to Federal middle management administrators, their field personnel, and their functional counterparts at the State and local levels. Well-intentioned but misguided reforms that ignore or undermine the team effort of these wheelhorses of federalism threaten the dynamism of the system itself.

These, in brief outline, are the features of the majority's rather unusual theory of American federalism. To revert to the kitchen, the ideal dessert of these respondents is not a layer or marble cake, and certainly not a marble cake cut into layers, but a large brick of harlequin ice cream containing 143 (depending on your aid count) flavors. And they want their end-of-the-dinner delight straight from the freezer with no melting at the bottom or top and no special syrup over it. With this theory of federalism, we leave the pantry and go to the refrigerator.

These contrasting analogies, of course, are based on contrasting emphases and principles. This theory's cooperative, functional, and anti-State-and-local-elected-official bias makes it completely unacceptable to the States' righters. Its nearly equal recognition of the role of competitive forces and its basic stress on the professional administrators as the real architects of cooperative federalism do not conform to the Grodzins-Elazar thesis. Its unsympathetic treatment of such topics as the power position of the States and general units of local government and their elected policymakers; more flexible regulations for aid programs; and Congress' role as strengthener of the federal system—to mention only three of the foremost differences—is in marked contrast to the positive positions taken on these issues by the majority participating in the previous survey. This, then, is an atypical interpretation of our federal system.

Like others, this "harlequin" theory both identifies points of tension within the system and creates tension points by the mere fact that its adherents occupy a critical position in contemporary intergovernmental relations. The basic problem areas highlighted in the theory are threefold.

First, there is tension horizontally between administrators at the various levels, created by the failure of the governments at the lesser levels to upgrade the professional capability of their civil employees.

Second, there is the tension vertically between the professional goals of administrators of intergovernmental programs and the political goals of the policymakers at the various levels of government.

Third, there is tension, both vertically and horizontally, between individual program administrators at every level and public administration authorities, some intergovernmental relations experts, and some sectors of top management. The latter, in their search for greater manageability, coordination, and simplicity and for less fragmentation, program insulation, and administrative pluralism, lose sight of the fact that these programs, and the larger system of which they are a part, are geared to serving the people's public needs, not the private or public needs of politicians, top administrators, or levels of government.

This theory of federalism also generates friction, since its proponents are major participants in the intergovernmental process and since its normative features—to a greater degree than its descriptive features—actually condition the official behavior of these respondents.

First, its unifunctional and professional bias, along with the normal motives for bureaucratic survival, tends to create tension among the Federal administrators of the various aid programs. This is especially true of the relations between the administrators of newer and those of older, more traditional programs.

Second, the theory's specialized program and bureau emphasis creates severe problems for departmental officials and various units in the Executive Office of the President. This occurs because top management and staff are charged with the duty of integrating the functions of individual bureaus and divisions with the national function of developing a coherent, timely presidential program based on scaled priorities; with the ultimate executive task of balancing the bias of particular administrative units with the general role of government as the "impartial instrument of a symmetrical national development," as Woodrow Wilson once phrased it.

Third, this theory's antipolitical and anti-innovation bias conflicts with, and even threatens, the efforts of policymakers and others at all levels who are seeking to bridge the communications and authority gaps at the Federal, State, and metropolitan levels, especially where the gaps impede the proper formulation and administration of urban development programs.

To sum up, the theory adhered to by three out of four of these Federal aid officials identifies three major sources of conflict in contemporary Federal-State-local relations:

(1) Professionalism at the higher level versus a lesser degree of professionalism at the other levels;

(2) Professional program administrators versus elected policymakers at all levels; and

(3) Administrators of individual aid programs versus intergovernmental reformers.

And because this "harlequin" theory of federalism is an operating precept as well as a descriptive interpretation, it produces its own areas of conflict:

(1) Professional administrators of one aid program versus the professional administrators of others;

(2) Specialized middle management versus generalized top management; and

(3) Conservative bureau heads versus innovators seeking to strengthen other components of the federal system—the States, our metropolitan communities, and the decision-making process at all levels.

NOTES

1. U.S. Senate, Subcommittee on Intergovernmental Relations, Committee on Government Operations, *Problems of Federal-State-Local Relations*, 88th Cong., 2d sess. (U.S. Government Printing Office, September 18, 1962), p. 13.
2. Council of State Governments, "Federal-State Relations," report of the Commission on Organization of the Executive Branch of the Government (Senate Doc. 81, 81st Cong., 1st Sess., Washington: Government Printing Office, March 25, 1949).
3. The Commission on Intergovernmental Relations, *A Report to the President for Transmittal to Congress*, House Doc. No. 198, 84th Cong., 1st Sess. (Washington: Government Printing Office, June 28, 1955), pp. 123–124.
4. Joint Federal-State Action Committee, Final Report to the President of the United States and to the Chairman of the Governors' Conference (Washington: Government Printing Office, February 1960), p. 2.
5. U.S. Congress, House of Representatives, Subcommittee on Intergovernmental Relations, Committee on Government Operations, 30th Report, *Federal-State-Local Relations, Federal Grants-in-Aid*, House Report No. 2533 (Washington: Government Printing Office, 1958), pp. 28–29.
6. Leonard D. White, *Introduction to the Study of Public Administration*, Fourth Edition (New York, Macmillan Co.), pp. 88, 99; and Mary C. H. Niles, *Middle Management* (New York, Harper, 1949), *passim*.
7. Daniel J. Elazar, "The Shaping of Intergovernmental Relations in the Twentieth Century," *The Annals*, Vol. 359, May 1965, p. 11.
8. The minority differed primarily with the majority only with respect to the principles developed in items 6, 7, and 8.

Grants-in-Aid: The Cutting Edge of Intergovernmental Relations

Michael D. Reagan

Grants-in-aid may be defined as money payments furnished by a higher to a lower level of government to be used for specified purposes and subject to conditions spelled out in law or administrative regulation. Grants are thus distinguished from, although first cousins to, the concept of general revenue sharing, which means money given by one level of government to another *without* advance specification of purpose and without specified conditions—that is, "no strings attached" aid. The range of functions in which federal-state-local cooperation takes place by means of grants-in-aid includes cooperative state agricultural experiment stations (the granddaddy of the system, started in 1887), vocational education, aid to the blind and to families with dependent children, airport construction, urban renewal, water-treatment works construction, defense-related educational activities, mass transportation, air pollution control, highway beautification, waste-disposal facilities, model cities, adult work training, and even educational television. Health, highways, welfare, education, and community development are the major categories of aided functions, with public assistance programs (more commonly known as "welfare") accounting for by far the largest single block of funds, $7.5 billion in fiscal 1970. The precise number of grant programs currently in operation depends a bit upon one's definition. Using the criterion of separate authorizations, the Advisory Commission on Intergovernmental Relations estimates a total of 530 grant-in-aid programs in 1970. Four-fifths of these were enacted after 1960; indeed 143 were instituted in the first two years of the Nixon Administration. This astonishing rate of proliferation of grant-in-aid programs is more than matched by the exploding rate of increase in the dollar volume of appropriations accounted for by the grants. The 1971 estimate was of $30.297 billion, compared with an actual 1970 figure, just one year earlier, of $23.955 billion, and a 1961 figure of a mere $7 billion. In fiscal 1947, right after the Second World War, grants-in-aid amounted to $1.668 billion, and in 1951 the figure was $2.287 billion. Making all due allowance for the impact of inflation upon these actual dollar figures, it is clear that the Congress has recently become very fond of the grant-in-aid idea. This is, as we have seen, partly in response to the state-local fiscal crisis and the consequent simple need for revenue; but it is also (and perhaps in larger part) a response to pressures from federal agencies, functional specialists in and out of government, and specific interest groups, all of whom have become well aware of the potentials of the strategy under which one obtains action in all states by using the leverage one has at one pressure point—that is, the national Congress.

. . .

Grants-in-aid constitute a major social innovation of our time, and are the proto-typical, although not the statistically dominant (they now constitute over 25 percent of domestic federal outlays), form of federal domestic involvement.

Although grants serve a number of different purposes, and although there are several aspects of the political and economic rationale underlying them, I suspect that the most important single reason for their popularity among both politicians and professionals of the functional areas aided is that the grant device bypasses all the difficult questions of governmental structure in a federal division of authority. In this respect, grants constitute a halfway house very similar to the post-Keynesian system of economic stabilization and business regulation in which the public sector has a decisive influence upon private economic activity but does so through indirect means that avoid the structural question of capitalism versus socialism. By using grants, one doesn't have to face the question: At which level of government does this function belong? If the activity is traditionally a local one, its direct operation can remain there, while its financial problems are solved with federal aid. If the federal government wants to inject its sense of values and priorities into the shaping of a program, the grant provides a vehicle for programmatic leverage without its being necessary to take over the whole function and remove it from local hands.

. . .

TYPES OF GRANTS

There are several different ways that we can characterize the subdivisions of the grant-in-aid system. One important division is between categorical grants and block grants. While there is—as always with such analytic distinctions—a gray area of overlap, categorical grants are by and large those for specifically and narrowly defined purposes, leaving very little discretionary room on the part of a recipient government as to how it uses the grant, while block grants are broader in scope and although tied to a clearly stated area (such as health, or elementary education, or community facilities development) they do not specify the exact objects of permitted expenditure and hence create much larger zones of discretion on the part of the receiving government or agency. Another way of putting this is that categorical grants have a much greater potential impact on federalism—changing the locus of policy-making more sharply from the state-local to the national level—than do block grants. In terms of federalism, state-local discretion in the use of federally provided funds is the functional equivalent of fiscal autonomy.

Beyond block grants, there is a further step in the direction of state-local autonomy in the form of revenue sharing, which is generally defined as a kind of fiscal federalism that constitutes an alternative to grants-in-aid rather than a sub-type of grant. President Nixon's 1971 plans for special revenue sharing . . . come very close to what is usually meant by the phrase "block grants"; the phrase "revenue sharing," in that context, constitutes nothing but a rhetorical device to make state-local discretion *appear* to be larger than it is in fact. His plans for general revenue sharing do constitute a real alternative, as that kind of revenue sharing (at least as presented to the Congress originally) would be without any programmatic strings.

An example of the specificity of categorical grants is provided by the different programs for sewage-treatment facilities. Under one program administered by the

Farmers' Home Administration, cities of less than 5500 population can apply for grants to finance sewage-collection systems. For cities with a larger population, collection systems are financed by the Department of Housing and Urban Development. In the case of interceptor sewers, which transmit the sewage from the collection systems to the treatment plants, financing is available from the Environmental Protection Agency (EPA). EPA will also finance sewage-treatment plants and sewer outfalls under the same grant programs as the interceptors, but these need not be financed under the same grant. The Economic Development Agency also plays a role in financing sewage systems; for economically depressed areas, it will guarantee loans or make grants for any segment of a sewage system from collection to out-fall sewer. Normally these grants or loans will finance the local contribution required by EPA, HUD, or FHA grants. Another good example is provided in the area of recreation. A city that wants to buy open land for park purposes, build a swimming pool on it and operate an activity center for senior citizens, put in trees and shrubberies and purchase sports equipment must make as many different grant applications as there are items mentioned in this sentence. In the process of accommodating to the burgeoning demands for federal aid in the 1960s, some things got a bit out of hand. The ACIR reports, for example, that the Office of Education in HEW at one point listed eight separate programs under six different laws authorizing grants to libraries.

As we shall see, what has come to be called (perhaps too cutely) "hardening of the categories" constitutes one major reason for widespread interest in the revenue sharing alternative. A more likely response to over-categorization is a probable expansion of block grants. These are not now widely used, although politicians as diverse as Senator Edmund Muskie and President Richard M. Nixon are both pushing for grant consolidation which would move in this direction. The leading example of a block grant at the present time is the Partnership in Health Act of 1966, which pulled together a number of grants previously administered separately to aid states in the treatment of several diseases. On the premise that effective administration of cooperative federal-state health programs required "strengthening the leadership and capacities of state health agencies," Congress gave them more room for maneuvering—more responsibility to set their own priorities—by consolidating into a single program previously quite separate grants in the areas of tuberculosis control, heart disease research and control, cancer, radiological facilities, venereal disease abatement, neurology and sensory disease abatements, community health services, home health care, dental disease, chronic disease, general public health, and mental disease.

In lesser degree, the Model Cities program (under which a city can get a grant for a comprehensive attack on all the problems of a single neighborhood, as a demonstration—it is hoped—of what integrated massive efforts could accomplish) could be said to partake of the characteristics of a block program. At least, it has encouraged communities to think through a "package" of grant proposals that will all mesh together into an integrated community development program. The carrot to encourage this integrated planning is a promise that, although the grant proposals must still be acted upon individually, those which are tied to an integrated plan will receive higher priority than those which are simply *ad hoc*.

However, Model Cities programs, since they must still be approved in all their components by the federal officials, do not really possess the discretion characteristic of a block grant.

President Nixon's "special revenue sharing" plans vary considerably in the degree of discretion that they would provide to the recipient agencies, although the Administration distinguishes them from block grants by eliminating matching fund requirements and maintenance of effort requirements. (This means that federal funds will do *less* than previously to increase aggregate effort, becoming more a way to enable the receiving governments to avoid raising their own money while maintaining current levels of service.) Like block grants, special revenue sharing would be allocated to identified functions in particular amounts fixed by formula. The receiving units therefore do not have discretion over use of the funds as regards the proportion spent on each of the six specified areas: law enforcement, manpower training, urban development, transportation, rural development, and education. The formulas themselves contain rather clear federal value choices, e.g. the urban development shares would be weighted toward degree of overcrowding, condition of a city's housing units, and proportion of poverty-level families. For example, the education grants are weighted toward low-income areas. Further, the states are not trusted to pass on a reasonable share to their constituent communities: urban development funds would go directly to cities; a partial "pass through" is required of transportation and education funds. What these demonstrate on the whole is that, despite the President's expressed desire to turn power back to state and local governments, political reality argues against his doing so without retaining a definite rein in Washington's hands.

Just as the grant system as a whole stands somewhere between total state-local autonomy and total federal takeover of specific functions, so also does the block grant constitute (at least potentially) a reasonable compromise between the values of categorical grants and shared revenues. Federal *policy* is very clearly stated in the laws authorizing the block grant programs, and if there is adequate means for ensuring programmatic accountability of the recipient governments, then such grants may be a useful way of centralizing policy while decentralizing administration and permitting considerable local choice and decision-making on particular programs.

A second basis for distinguishing among types of grants is found in the criteria for distribution. Formula grants are to be distinguished from project grants by this means. As the name implies, the formula grant is one whose funds are divided among all eligible recipients on the basis of some announced criterion that is applied proportionately across the board and without any discretion in the hands of the grant-giving officials. An example is provided by public-assistance grants for aid to the blind. Under this program, the national government promises to match state payments of benefits to blind persons in accord with a statutory ratio. The needy blind in every state are eligible and the national government is committed to supplying its share of the benefits for as many persons as the state welfare departments certify as eligible. Formula grants are distributed to all eligible jurisdictions as a matter of "right." The discretion, if there is any, lies in the hands of the recipient governments that decide how much matching money they want to use to obtain a particular federal grant. Federal influence under formula grants lie in the administrative requirements that accompany the grant, rather than in the substance of the grant.

In project grants, on the other hand, which require specific approval by federal agency officials of the proposal made by a potential recipient government or agency, the potential for federal influence and control is decidedly greater. Project grants are made to meet specific problems and are not spread among all potential recipients according to any fixed proportions. Although every community in the country may be eligible for a waste-treatment plant grant, for example, the funds available for the program will sharply limit the number of communities that can be aided. In such a situation, the community whose proposal most nearly satisfies the definitions of appropriate action in the minds of the federal officials administering the grant program will be the successful one. . . .

. . .

PURPOSES OF GRANTS

Decisions regarding when to use formula grants and when to use project grants, and evaluation of the merits of each type, depend partly on the purposes for which one has a grant at all. We sometimes assume off-hand that the purpose of all federal grants-in-aid is financial in nature: to supplement inadequate state-local resources. This is too simple. At least as important as the purely financial objective are the following:

1. To establish minimum national standards in some program that exists in all states, but at widely differing levels. . . .

2. Equalization of resources. Closely related to the first objective, the emphasis here is upon the use of the federal tax system to apply the Robin Hood principle: to take more money from the states with higher per capita incomes and transfer it to those with lower per capita incomes, enabling the latter to upgrade their public services. Many federal formula grant programs have sliding scales that vary federal contributions from one-third to two-thirds, inversely related to the capacity of receiving states to raise their own funds.

3. To improve the substantive adequacy of state programs. Under project programs particularly, in the process of inviting, aiding in the design of, reviewing, and approving proposals from state-local agencies, officials of the grant-giving agency have an opportunity to provide technical assistance in accord with the highest professional standards. Inasmuch as only a few states are able to compete with the national government in attracting outstanding professional talent, such technical assistance can be an important vehicle for upgrading the quality of public services at the state level. . . .

4. A related way in which the federal government may improve state programs, concentrate a "critical mass" of attention in a given area, and avoid useless state duplication and the frittering away of energies in many efforts no one of which can be adequate, is exemplified in air pollution research grants from the National Air Pollution Control Administration. . . .

5. The stimulation of experimentation, and the demonstration of new approaches, are major objectives of a high proportion of the project grant programs

in the areas of health care, education, human resources development, and community development. . . .

6. Improvement of state-local administrative structure and operation. At least since the adoption of the public-assistance grant programs in the mid-'thirties and the 1939 amendment to the Social Security Act that established a merit system requirement for participating state agencies, the general administrative require- ments attached to a great number of federal grants in a variety of substantive areas have been extremely important in inducing grant-receiving governments to profes- sionalize their organizational structures and their personnel and financial practices. Merit system and auditing requirements have had double effects. Directly, they have established new standards of competence and accountability in the agencies handling federal funds. Indirectly, these standards have constituted, if only by contrast, bench marks against which to measure the quality of operation of state agencies not subject to federal supervision. While a few states have always been the equal (even occasionally the superior) of the national government with regard to administrative quality, the great majority has been extremely laggard in adopt- ing modern management knowledge. The national government has therefore played an indispensable role in relaying to the states the management knowledge it has itself developed and assimilated from the most advanced private business practice. From the standpoint of maintaining a healthy federalism, the adminis- trative improvement impact of the federal grant system upon the states may have been at least as important (i.e. by improving state-local government capacity to govern) as the provision of funds.

7. Encouragement of general social objectives. The "boiler-plate" provisions of federal programs (i.e. the provisions that are automatically included in every grant agreement between the grantor agency and the grantee government) have also been used as inducements to attain unrelated social objectives. The most notable among these is, of course, the non-discrimination clause that has made grants-in-aid a potent lever in the struggle to persuade the more recalcitrant state governments to provide public services equitably to their minority populations.

8. Minimize the apparent federal role. Perhaps the most important political achievement of the grant system is to have solved the apparent dilemma arising from the American electorate's contradictory desires (a) to attack problems that the state and local governments lacked the resources to handle while (b) not enlarging the federal government. The solution to the dilemma is that the federal role is in fact enlarged, always in financial terms and often in programmatic terms, without that enlargement being apparent either in the size of the federal civil service or in the number of occasions upon which the individual citizen deals with a national functionary. It is a nice way of having one's cake while eating it. . . . Not all of these purposes apply to all grants, or even to any individual grant. Yet each of these purposes is significant for a number of grants.

RATIONALIZING THE GRANT SYSTEM

Closely related to, yet conceptually distinguishable from the functions served by a particular grant program are the economic and political rationales underlying the entire grant system. If one sees grants-in-aid as occurring largely in areas once thought to be the more or less exclusive provinces of state-local governments under a federalized "division of labor," then the question becomes, What justification is there for the national government to enter the picture, even through grants-in-aid, let alone through direct action programs? From an economic standpoint, there are two parts to the answer. First, the simple fact elaborated earlier, that it is much easier to raise the needed revenue for public service operations at the national level than at the local level, although the problems for which the revenue is needed still have to be handled at the local level. Second, and this is an argument much developed in recent years, there stands the doctrine of external or "spill-over" benefits. This says that when an expenditure produces benefits that are felt beyond (i.e. spillover) the jurisdiction of the governmental unit making the expenditure, it is proper that all benefiting jurisdictions share in the cost. Otherwise, some of them are engaged in free-loading.

. . .

According to a leading authority on intergovernmental fiscal relations, George F. Break, categorical grants-in-aid are economically justifiable only on the basis of and to the extent of their externalities or spillover benefits. He suggests that in evaluating grant-in-aid programs we ask of each program whether it generates external benefits, the exact nature of those benefits, and how important they are. By applying our scale of values regarding the importance of the projected benefits, and assuming that we can measure in some way the extent of the benefits, then we have a basis for determining the appropriate federal share of expenditure in that area. The conceptualization here is somewhat in advance of our empirical knowledge (that is, while we know what to measure, we do not yet know how to measure it in many instances), yet the reasoning is generally persuasive. . . .

Even in the absence of spillover benefits, however, there is a strong political rationale for federal grants. One of the more thoughtful analyses has been provided by political scientist Phillip Monypenny. In a 1960 article he argued that federal grant programs were a response to a

> . . . coalition which resorts to a mixed federal-state program because it is not strong enough in individual states to secure its program, and because it is not united enough to be able to achieve a wholly federal program against the opposition which a specific program would engender.

. . .

Further, an important impetus toward grant-in-aid programs arises from the most fundamental feature of American federalism—that to achieve action at the state level means to mount a campaign in fifty different locations, while to mount at the national level requires and encourages centralized, unified action in one place, which is generally easier to achieve. Once the national government has been persuaded to enact a program, the leverage of "free money" can be counted upon to encourage many of the states to join in. Granting that ancillary political campaigns will sometimes be needed at the state level, the effort becomes a good deal more effective when preceded by national authorizing legislation. The reasons, incidentally, for not seeking a directly national program are not only the lack of sufficient political power to achieve that possible goal, but also the fact that wholly national action runs into more ideological obstacles than does federal aid, so one simply may have no desire to substitute national for state action, but simply want to beef up state action.

A final over-all reason for bringing the federal government into previously state-local problem solving through the grant-in-aid device is that the definition of what is national and what is local has changed, as well as our conception of federalism, which has gone from a competitive to a cooperative image. In terms of *Realpolitik* it has been well said that "any objective is manifestly and significantly national in character which survives the arduous, lengthy 'testing process' that Congress provides with its polycentric power structure and limited majority norms." That may sound too simple or even too cynical, yet when one tries to grapple with the question of what is a national problem, or what situations warrant national action, it is difficult to find any other single criterion that will fit every instance. Only two generalizations seem to be quite certain. One is that many more problems today than in the past are national in the sense of being affected by developments elsewhere in the nation or having their own impact upon other parts of the nation. Our society has become thoroughly interdependent in its economy, its transportation and communication patterns, etc. Second, what can safely be left to local discretion is not answerable across the board; it depends on particular functions. This is true not only of relations between the national and state governments, but even of relationships between a city as a whole and its neighborhoods. . . .

In an important book on the problems of administering grant-in-aid programs, James L. Sundquist argues that in about 1960 the grant-in-aid system underwent a fundamental change. Prior to that date, he writes, "the typical federal assistance program did not involve an expressly stated *national* purpose. It was instituted, rather, as a means of helping state or local governments accomplish *their* objectives." Legislation passed since 1960 is characterized by "forthright declarations of national purpose, experimental and flexible approaches to the achievement of those purposes, and close federal supervision and control to ensure that the national purposes are served." He suggests that aid for highways, hospitals, sewage-treatment plants, and the building of airports all constituted instances in which the federal grants really are *in aid* of state-local functions. On the other hand, in the cases of urban renewal, area redevelopment, manpower development, the poverty program, and model cities he contends that the grants are for the purpose of getting the state and local governments to participate in the administration of programs designed to achieve objectives chosen by the national government initially. Urban renewal, dating from 1949, he includes in the latter group as an early exception, incidentally.

Whether the original impetus for a grant program in a particular area came from state-local officials, or from federal officials or national legislators may be important in terms of legislative history, but does not, I think, matter much in the operation of programs once enacted. Even if it was the states that originally set the goal of "getting the farmers out of the mud," when the federal government enters the highway picture by supplementing state financing isn't it making that goal a national goal also? Since the federal government does not aid every single state and local purpose, in the process of selecting those purposes that it will aid it is making a determination of the state-local functions in which there is the greatest national interest. As Sundquist himself later suggests, as major domestic problems develop, public attitudes pass through different phases. First, a problem is seen as local. Secondly, federal aid is proposed to help the states solve *their* problem. Finally, the problem is redefined as being national and requiring a national solution which the states merely help to bring about.

So we come back to the beginning. Those things are national and justify grant programs which the Congress *says* are national. The concepts of local and national interest are squishy at best. What matters for present purposes is that both constitutionally and politically we have as a nation accepted the notion that it is appropriate for the national community to imbed its scale of values (i.e. those values that a majority of national legislators can agree upon) in programs that offer state and local governments financial inducements to be persuaded that the national scale of values should also be the local priorities. In assessing the long-range trend line of federalism, this is to say that the balance is shifting toward the dominance of national majorities over state and local majorities, with cooperative action toward national objectives replacing the futile deadlock of the old competitive dual federalism.

PRELIMINARY BALANCE SHEET

Although complete evaluation of the grant-in-aid system we have been describing must await further analysis and elucidation of revenue sharing as a widely heralded alternative, it is possible and desirable at this time to draw up a preliminary balance sheet of the system's accomplishments and its problems. The most obvious accomplishment of federal grants is to enable state and local governments to do much more for their citizens than they could afford to do with their own resources. To say that grant-in-aid funds account for over 20 percent of state-local revenues is to say that those governments would do one-fifth less for their citizens without federal aid.

The political corollary of this financial advantage is, of course, to keep the states alive (if not well), forestalling what might otherwise be the total collapse of federalism through the political and financial bankruptcy of state government. Whether most state governments deserve the confidence placed in them may be a matter for debate, but that confidence has been so placed is undeniable. . . .

. . . .

If, as the late Morton Grodzins and his disciples have argued, modern federalism is and must be cooperative rather than competitive, then one has to say that the grant-in-aid device constitutes a major social invention. It is what makes cooperative federalism a functioning reality instead of just a constitutional lawyer's phrase. Intergovernmental cooperation does exist in forms other than grant-in-aid, also. (An example would be local, state, and national police forces sharing information and techniques.) But the grant relationship is far and away the most decisive means of intergovernmental cooperation today. Because it solves (or at least ameliorates) the fiscal problem of modern federalism while permitting widely varying degrees of federal influence along with the funds, it makes the continuation of formal federalism possible.

A by-product advantage of the grant system that is not always given sufficient attention is the way in which it enables the national government to provide technical assistance to state and local governments. Since, by and large, the national government can better tap top-drawer professional talent, whether of highway engineering, social insurance, housing-market analysis, or education, than can a multitude of state and local governmental bodies, it is in a position to bring such talent to bear on local problems in a way that the jurisdiction having the problem could never afford to do autonomously. Further, even when the professional innovation takes place initially in an individual state, the existence of a national grant-in-aid program provides a means for information transfer from the initiating state to all others which would not otherwise be available. From this standpoint, one could even say that it is a good thing that the state and local governments are in a financial bind! If they could afford to act entirely on their own and the federal grant system had never been started, they would often be acting at a much lower level of professional quality than is now the case when the federal government sets the standards.

We have mentioned earlier that there is a varying structure of interest group power at different levels of government. Because of this, the grant-in-aid system also serves as a way by which the national government can respond to societal needs not politically strong in many states, stimulating states to act in areas that would otherwise be neglected because of the short-sighted, status quo views of local elites. The poverty program, aid to education, community mental health, and environmental protection are all areas that fit this description in a number of states. The most general point to be made in this connection is that the grant-in-aid system accomplishes an in-between answer to what would otherwise be a stalemate: the state-local level can't or won't solve all its problems with its own resources, yet the electorate appears not to want the entire responsibility transferred to the national level. Therefore, through grant-in-aid we find a way to put the resources where the problems are: to get the jobs done. . . .

THE SYSTEM'S PROBLEMS

Like every other human invention, the grant-in-aid system lacks perfection. Four types of problems that the system either fails to solve or self-creates need to be mentioned. First, the strong trend toward project grants, which are very useful for targeting the aid and for stimulating innovation, also has less desirable consequences. Project grants, for one thing, tend to run counter to the need for equalization of resources among jurisdictions. . . .

A related set of charges that are sometimes made against the entire grant-in-aid system rather than just specifically of project grants is that they tend to skew state-local budgets. The argument is that, to the extent that formula or project grants require matching funds from the receiving government, state legislatures and city councils will be coerced into putting their money where the grants are, even if those are not the areas of greatest local need. It is hard to resist a program that enables one dollar to become two or three, when the same dollar has no "multiplier" effect of this kind when used for some other area. Since grants are fairly tightly defined and do not cover all possible areas of state-local need, the inflexibility of the grants perhaps requires that receiving governments be overly flexible in accommodating to Washington's priorities.

This problem may be somewhat lessened today, as compared with ten years ago, because of the proliferation of grant authorizations. That is, there are now so many grant programs for so many different purposes that, although each is very narrow, the local government can get what it wants by picking and choosing among the programs it decides to enter.

The other side of the coin, however, is that the proliferation of programs has created a very substantial coordination problem at both the giving and receiving levels of the grant system. As the Advisory Commission on Intergovernmental Relations has said,

> . . . excessive categorization and overlapping of grants create administrative problems at all levels and handicap the development of a coordinated attack on community problems . . . state and local governments may be bewildered as to the differences between seemingly like programs or uncertain as to whether they are using the more appropriate program . . . confusion is aggravated by the existence of varying requirements under similar programs, which may cause applicants to seek the program which seems most attractive from the standpoint, say, of non-Federal matching required although overall considerations, such as the specific uses as to which the money can be put, may make it less attractive.

When communities are whole beings, but programs for their development are separately categorized and separately administered by separate agencies, some classic confusions result. One such instance concerned conflict between an urban renewal development that had been approved by one agency for a location through which another planned a freeway.

Finally, the grant-in-aid system can, of course, do nothing to help the states and cities directly as regards their lack of funds for services that lie outside the aided categories. Moreover, to the extent that aid programs call for matching grants, the city or state may be simply more hard-pressed to finance its unaided services.

VII

Securing a Responsible Bureaucracy

Is democratic control of the federal government in jeopardy? One's answer will depend largely upon the trends he or she emphasizes. Quite clearly, numerous strands of recent American history lend themselves to the view that democracy is ascendant. Malapportionment, suffrage restrictions, and election frauds have all been attacked with a high degree of success; free speech guarantees have progressively been extended; cultural barriers between regions, ethnic groups, and classes have been declining; and the educational level of the electorate has been rising.

On the other hand, those who actually govern the nation are probably less constrained by public opinion with every passing decade. The diversity and complexity of modern governmental activities overwhelm the electorate's capacity to develop strong opinions. To a lesser but profound and increasing degree, congressmen are similarly disarmed. The pace of change is such that even specialists who spend their lives working in a single policy area frequently lose their capacity to "keep up" well before retirement age. The possessors of valued skills typically organize themselves into professions, and then bend their efforts to securing insulation from public scrutiny and control. Public agencies are increasingly bold in their endeavors to build favorable public images by controlling the flow of information about their activities. The litany might be extended, and the individual propositions refined, almost indefinitely.

Even more ominous are the developments that reached their climax in the mid-1970s with the disclosures that emerged from the Watergate affair. The establishment of a domestic political intelligence unit within the presidency, the "plumbers," whose function it was to stop leaks, the extensive use of wiretapping to monitor the telephone conversations of political adversaries, journalists, and presidential staff members whose loyalty was suspect, the involvement of White House personnel and close political associates of President Nixon in the bungled burglary of the Democratic national headquarters in the Watergate Hotel, and the subsequent efforts of the president and his top staff to cover up their involvement led to the first presidential resignation in American history. The questionable role of official intelligence agencies in the Watergate affair resulted in both presidential and congressional inquiries into the activities of the Central Intelligence Agency. Those investigations revealed further illicit and questionable operations, including CIA plots to assassinate unfriendly foreign leaders in the 1950s and 1960s. It is little wonder that various opinion surveys revealed extensive and growing public distrust of government in the 1970s as compared with only a decade 'earlier.

This section is concerned with trends of the latter type: those which contribute to the apparently widening gulf between the public's independent opinions and the political system's policy outputs.[1] Its purpose is to stimulate your thought, first, about how fundamentally these trends are altering the political system, and second, about how the system is compensating for them. Among the more optimistic lines of interpretation that you may wish to explore— selected on the premise that pessimistic examples will readily occur to you—are the following: (1) Perhaps the chain of command from the public to its governors has become longer, more indirect, and more difficult to trace precisely, without becoming substantially less effective. (2) Perhaps what should be emphasized is that even as the democratic influence has been declining within the government, the government has been increasing its influence on the rest of society. The net result may well be a gain in terms of democracy's impact on the social system as a whole. (3) Perhaps theory should focus on the ever-increasing significance of professionalism as a supplement to democracy in the checking of bureaucratic arbitrariness. (4) In the same vein, perhaps the taking-off point for analysis should be that Americans have never considered responsiveness to be the sole criterion of a good governmental system. On the contrary, their most characteristic position has been that an excess of democracy leads to mischievous results, and that it is best conceived as a process for imposing broad constraints upon government—not for controlling its activities in detail. (This approach should lead to a consideration of the precise kinds of constraints that the electorate *can* now impose upon the government, and whether their effectiveness is dangerously on the wane.)

The challenge of reconciling bureaucracy with democracy by making it responsible has been a persistent theme in the intellectual development of American public administration. It was early recognized that the roots of the problem were to be found in the necessary exercise of discretion by administrative officials. The solution was disarmingly simple; recognize that policy making involved deciding and could be kept quite separate from administration, which involved doing. Those officials who made policy could be made politically accountable. Those whose tasks were merely ministerial could be chosen and evaluated on the basis of competence and performance by their political superiors.

The politics-administration dichotomy, by suggesting that goals and means were clearly divisible, discouraged serious thought about the political significance of bureaucratic discretion. In a well-ordered governmental system, students of administration assumed, bureaucratic discretion would involve little more than experimentation and techniques of cost reduction. However, as the politics-administration dichotomy came under scholarly fire in the thirties and forties, attention suddenly focused on the vast degree of bureaucratic freedom that the

---

[1] For simplicity's sake, the term "independent" is here employed to include all opinions but those which policy makers can treat as manipulable over the short run.

effective conduct of public business required, and on the enormous value implications of the decisions that many administrators made.

As the profession took a careful look, it became apparent (1) that all realistic goal choices were based heavily on assumptions about their feasibility, and about the acceptability of the means that their implementation would require; (2) that means invariably affected many values other than those they were designed to serve, with the result that few but the lowest level means choices were purely technical; and (3) that consequently the distinction between means and ends normally dissolved the more closely one examined specific choice situations.

Among the practical effects of these abstract propositions were the following: (1) that a high proportion of all statutes originated in the bureaucracy; (2) that politicians charged with evaluating legislative proposals typically relied heavily on bureaucratic advice; (3) that bureaucrats were extremely active "sellers" of ideas to both elective policy makers and the general public; (4) that most laws left room for a wide range of interpretations (frequently not less than the Constitution's "due process" clauses), and that the courts typically treated administrative interpretations that were remotely plausible as authoritative; and (5) that the vast multiude of statutes allowed many public agencies substantial discretion about which to emphasize and which to treat as dead letters.

How were these findings to be reconciled with the ideal of democratic control? Some of the most interesting normative writings ever produced by the American political science profession have been addressed to this problem over the past thirty-odd years. A few of the more provocative lines of attack that have been suggested are highlighted in the selections which follow.

Carl Friedrich proposed, in several essays published between 1935 and 1940, that the path to control of the bureaucracy in those realms where full answerability to political superiors was unfeasible lay in the development of professionalism. Professions, he maintained, might encourage the progress of knowledge, develop criteria for judging the work of individual practitioners, and cultivate the consciences of their members. To the extent that they performed these functions well, the threat of arbitrary government would be erased. The public will, normally vague and highly general in content, would be elaborated faithfully and implemented effectively. Government would be "responsible" in the fullest possible sense. Herman Finer vehemently criticized nearly every aspect of Friedrich's argument in two articles which appeared respectively in 1936 and 1941. Their debate is probably the most famous single episode in the whole history of the "administrative responsibility" controversy. The selections reprinted here are from the final summations of each.

Norton Long's concern is the power potential conferred on the bureaucracy by its knowledge. Among the questions with which he grapples are the following: How can the bureaucracy's capacity to shape public, and even congressional, opinion through its command and interpretation of the "facts" be disciplined? Can its expertise be employed in salutary fashion to constrain the demagogic instincts of politicians? During the gestation period of policy proposals originated by the bureaucracy—at which stage most are eliminated, and the rest are decisively shaped—how can consideration of the widest possible range of values most effectively be encouraged? Long's recommended answers are highly controversial, but they are worthy of the most serious consideration.

Emmette S. Redford, a longtime student of the administrative process, views the achievement of responsibility as a moral problem. The bureaucracy should be made to conform fully "with the tenets of democratic morality." Redford sees the key to this task in the concept of workable democracy, which he defines as "the inclusive representation of interests" in the organs of the administrative state. The achievement of this condition requires a "humane" and "open" society. In sum, administrative responsibility depends ultimately on the social and political climate of the nation.

The "new public administration" places even greater reliance on morality as the basis of administrative responsibility. Eugene P. Dvorin and Robert H. Simmons reject traditional approaches that focus on the power of an agency vis-à-vis its external environment. They argue that primary attention to the moral ends of administrative activity rather than to agency survival or efficiency is the only way in which democracy can be served by bureaucracy. This means, however, that public administration must concern itself with moral values and cannot take refuge in the value-free postures of social science, business efficiency, the authority of bureaucratic hierarchy, or unswerving loyalty to political superiors.

The consequences of a public administration that had become insufficiently attentive to morality and served other values are most recently manifest in Watergate. James L. Sundquist, a former federal official, examines the implications of Watergate for public administration. He believes that the most fundamental cause of the scandal was the placing of excessive reliance on the president, a long term secular development. The solution that he suggests is a form of plural decision making for major national policies coupled with a new constitutional procedure that would empower Congress to remove the president and call new elections.

You will want to consider carefully the solutions to the problem of securing administrative responsibility proposed in this section. Clearly, moral values, normative constraints grounded in public service professionalism, and formal institutional checks are all needed. None is sufficient by itself. What moral values, then, should be emphasized? Who is to decide between conflicting value claims? How can professional education for the public service prepare prospective bureaucrats to make such choices? What kinds of normative standards are and should be imparted through that educational process? If formal institutional checks are inadequate, how can they be improved?

Each generation confronts these and related questions. Answers framed under one set of circumstances often prove unsatisfactory later on. Yet there are some responses that do not lose their validity over time. Fundamental standards of public and private morality exist independently of temporal factors. Much of the quest for administrative responsibility involves distinguishing between solutions and values that require modification and those that do not. It is a never-ending task that must be assumed as long as Americans persist in their desire to enjoy the benefits of democracy and bureaucracy.

Public Policy and the Nature of Administrative Responsibility

Carl J. Friedrich

RESPONSIBILITY AND POLICY FORMATION

The starting point of any study of responsibility must be that even under the best arrangements a considerable margin of irresponsible conduct of administrative activities is inevitable. For if a responsible person is one who is answerable for his acts to some other person or body, who has to give an account of his doings (Oxford English Dictionary), it should be clear without further argument that there must be some agreement between such a responsible agent and his principal concerning the action in hand or at least the end to be achieved. When one considers the complexity of modern governmental activities, it is at once evident that such agreement can only be partial and incomplete, no matter who is involved. Once the electorate and legislative assemblies are seen, not through the smoke screen of traditional prejudice, but as they are, it is evident that such principals cannot effectively bring about the responsible conduct of public affairs, unless elaborate techniques make explicit what purposes and activities are involved in all the many different phases of public policy. It is at this point that the decisive importance of policy determination becomes apparent. Too often it is taken for granted that as long as we can keep the government from doing wrong we have made it responsible. What is more important is to insure effective action of any sort. To stimulate initiative, even at the risk of mistakes, must nowadays never be lost sight of as a task in making the government's services responsible. An official should be as responsible for inaction as for wrong action; certainly the average voter will criticize the government as severely for one as for the other.

Without a well-defined and well-worked-out policy, responsibility becomes very difficult to bring about. Yet such policies are the exception rather than the rule. Many of the most severe breakdowns in contemporary administration, accompanied by violent public reactions against irresponsible bureaucracy, will be found to trace back to contradictory and ill-defined policy, as embodied in faulty legislation. There are numerous familiar illustrations. . . .

. . . In the light of the large amount of legislative work performed by administrative agencies, the task of clear and consistent policy formation has passed . . . into the hands of administrators, and is bound to continue to do so. Hence, administrative responsibility can no longer be looked upon as merely a responsibility for executing policies already formulated. We have to face the fact that this responsibility is much more comprehensive in scope.

From Carl J. Friedrich and Edward S. Mason, eds., *Public Policy: 1940* (Cambridge: Harvard University Press, 1940), pp. 3–14, 19–24. Copyright 1940, by the President and Fellows of Harvard College. Reprinted by permission.

POLICY-MAKING AND POLICY EXECUTION

It has long been customary to distinguish between policy-making and policy execution. Frank J. Goodnow, in his well-known work, *Politics and Administration*, undertook to build an almost absolute distinction upon this functional difference.

> There are, then, in all governmental systems two primary or ultimate functions of government, viz. the expression of the will of the state and the execution of that will. There are also in all states separate organs, each of which is mainly busied with the discharge of one of these functions. These functions are, respectively, Politics and Administration.[1]

But while the distinction has a great deal of value as a relative matter of emphasis, it cannot any longer be accepted in this absolute form. Admittedly, this misleading distinction has become a fetish, a stereotype in the minds of theorists and practitioners alike. The result has been a great deal of confusion and argument. The reason for making this distinction an absolute antithesis is probably to be found in building it upon the metaphysical, if not abstruse, idea of a will of the state. This neo-Hegelian (and Fascist) notion is purely speculative. Even if the concept "state" is retained—and I personally see no good ground for it—the idea that this state has a will immediately entangles one in all the difficulties of assuming a group personality or something akin to it.[2] In other words, a problem which is already complicated enough by itself—that is, how a public policy is adopted and carried out—is bogged down by a vast ideological superstructure which contributes little or nothing to its solution. Take a case like the AAA. In simple terms, AAA was a policy adopted with a view to helping the farmer to weather the storm of the depression. This admittedly was AAA's broad purpose. To accomplish this purpose, crop reduction, price-fixing, and a number of lesser devices were adopted. Crop reduction in turn led to processing taxes. Processing taxes required reports by the processors, inspection of their plants. Crop reduction itself necessitated reports by the farmers, so-called work sheets, and agreements between them and the government as to what was to be done, and so forth and so on. What here is politics, and what administration? Will anyone understand better the complex processes involved in the articulation of this important public policy if we talk about the expression and the execution of the state will? The concrete patterns of public policy formation and execution reveal that politics and administration are not two mutually exclusive boxes, or absolute distinctions, but that they are two closely linked aspects of the same process. Public policy, to put it flatly, is a continuous process, the formation of which is inseparable from its execution. Public policy is being formed as it is being executed, and it is likewise being executed as it is being formed. Politics and administration play a continuous role in both formation and execution, though there is probably more politics in the formation of policy, more administration in the execution of it. In so far as particular individuals or groups are gaining or losing power or control in a given area, there is politics; in so far as officials act or propose action in the name of public interest, there is administration.

The same problem may be considered from another angle. Policies in the common meaning of the term are decisions about what to do or not to do in given situations. It is characteristic of our age that most legislation is looked upon as policy-deciding. Hence policy-making in the broad sense is not supposed to be part of administration. While these propositions are true in a general way, they tend to obscure two important facts, namely, (1) that many policies are not ordained with a stroke of the legislative or dictatorial pen but evolve slowly over long periods of time, and (2) that administrative officials participate continuously and significantly in this process of evolving policy. To commence with the latter fact, it is evident that in the process of doing something the administrator may discover another and better way of accomplishing the same result, or he discovers that the thing cannot be done at all, or that something else has to be done first, before the desired step can be taken. In our recent agricultural policy, examples of all these "administrative" policy determinations can be cited, as likewise in our social security policy. The discussions now taking place in both fields amply illustrate these points. What is more, such administrative participation alone renders policy-making a continuous process, so much in a state of flux that it is difficult, if not impossible, to state with precision what the policy in any given field is at any particular time. But, if this is true, it follows as a corollary that public policy will often be contradictory and conflicting in its effects upon society. Our myth-makers, of course, remain adamant in proclaiming that this should not be so, and let it go at that. It is hard to disagree with them, but we still have to face the question of responsibility, seeing that policies are in fact contradictory and conflicting. Who is responsible for what, and to whom? To what extent does such responsibility affect the actual conduct of affairs? A complex pattern appears when we attempt to answer such questions.

Some time ago I pointed out that administrative responsibility had not kept pace with our administrative tasks. In relying upon the political responsibility of policy-making persons and bodies, we had lost sight of the deeper issues involved. At that time I wrote:

> . . . autocratic and arbitrary abuse of power has characterized the officialdom of a government service bound only by the dictates of conscience. Nor has the political responsibility based upon the election of legislatures and chief executives succeeded in permeating a highly technical, differentiated government service any more than the religious responsibility of well-intentioned kings. Even a good and pious king would be discredited by arbitrary "bureaucrats"; even a high-minded legislature or an aspiring chief executive pursuing the public interest would be thwarted by a restive officialdom.

An offended commentator from the British Isles exclaimed loudly that if I imagined that to be true of England I was "simply wrong." But I think it would be easy to show that the officials of a seventeenth-century prince were more responsible, i.e., answerable, to him, their sovereign, than the officials of any modern democracy are as yet to the people, their supposed sovereign. In the comparison there was no judgment as to the positive amount of responsibility found in either. Admittedly, many commentators have dwelt at length upon the frequently irresponsible conduct of public affairs in Great Britain and elsewhere.

THE NEW IMPERATIVE: FUNCTIONAL RESPONSIBILITY

It is interesting that the administrators themselves attach so little weight to the influence of parliamentary or legislative bodies. Leading Swiss officials—and

Switzerland has as responsible a government service as any country in the world—told the author that "responsibility of the public service in Switzerland results from a sense of duty, a desire to be approved by his fellow officials, and a tendency to subordinate one's own judgment as a matter of course. Still, in a case like the arrival of Social Democrats into the Federal Council, it might happen that official conduct would be slow to respond to the new situation." They also felt that officials are not unwilling to allow a measure to lapse, although actually provided for in legislation, if considerable opposition is felt which the public might be expected to share. Thus a wine tax was quietly allowed to drop out of sight, just as the potato control act remained a dead letter in the United States.[3] There are, of course, ways by which the legislature secure a measure of control that enables it to enforce responsibility, usually of the negative kind which prevents abuses. Legislative committees act as watchdogs over all expenditure.[4]

What is true of Switzerland and the United States without "parliamentary responsibility" seems to be equally true of England and France. In both countries complaints against the increasing independence of officials are constantly being voiced. In a very important discourse, Sir Josiah Stamp called attention to the creative role the civil servant is called upon to play in Great Britain. "I am quite clear that the official must be the mainspring of the new society, suggesting, promoting, advising at every stage." Sir Josiah insisted that this trend was inevitable, irresistible, and therefore called for a new type of administrator. An editorial writer of *The Times*, though critical of this development, agreed "that the practice, as opposed to the theory, of administration has long been moving in this direction." He added, "In practice, they (the officials) possess that influence which cannot be denied to exhaustive knowledge; and this influence, owing to the congestion of parliamentary business and other causes, manifests itself more and more effectively as an initiative in public affairs." Testimony of this sort could be indefinitely multiplied; and as we are interested in practice, not in ideology, we must consider the question of responsibility in terms of the actualities. Such cases throw a disquieting light upon the idea that the mere dependence of a cabinet upon the "confidence" of an elected assembly insures responsible conduct on the part of the officials in charge of the initiation and execution of public policy, when those officials hold permanent positions. It is no accident that the Goodnow school should fully share such illusions. After pointing out that the British Cabinet unites in its hands power of legislation and administration, and thus both formulates and executes policies, Goodnow remarks:

> So long as their action meets with the approval of Parliament . . . there is none to gainsay them. If, however, they fail to gain such approval . . . they must resign their powers to others whose policy is approved by Parliament. . . . In this way the entire English government is made responsible to Parliament, which in turn is responsible to the people.[5]

This is no longer very true. It is objectionable to consider administrative responsibility secure by this simple device, not merely because of interstitial violations but because there is a fundamental flaw in the view of politics and policy here assumed. The range of public policy is nowadays so far-flung that the largely inoperative "right" of the parliamentary majority to oust a Cabinet from power belongs in that rather numerous group of rights for which there is no remedy. The majority supporting the Cabinet may violently disagree with this, that, and the other policy advocated and adopted by the Cabinet, but considerations of party politics, in the broadest sense, will throttle their objections because the particular issue is "not worth a general election" and the chance of the M.P.'s losing his seat.[6] As contrasted with the detailed and continuous criticism and control of administrative activity afforded by Congressional committees, this parliamentary responsibility is largely inoperative and certainly ineffectual. When one considers the extent of public disapproval directed against Franklin D. Roosevelt's Congressional supporters who were commonly dubbed "rubber stamps," it is astonishing that anyone extolling the virtues of British parliamentarism should get a hearing at all. For what has the parliamentary majority in Britain been in the last few years but a rubber stamp of an automatic docility undreamt of in the United States?

THE MODERN PHASE: ADMINISTRATIVE DISCRETION

British observers are not unaware of this development. Indeed, the Committee on Ministers' Powers, whose able report has already been cited, was created in response to widespread criticism of the irresponsible bureaucracy which was supposed to be developing. While Lord Hewart's *The New Despotism* undoubtedly exaggerated, his critical attack upon the growth of discretion allowed administrative agencies corresponded to a widespread sentiment. Unfortunately, his views were expressive of an unrealistic nostalgia for legal traditions which the forward march of social development has irrevocably assigned to limbo. Like Beck's *Our Wonderland of Bureaucracy*, Lord Hewart's denunciation of policy-determining officials failed to take into account that this "bureaucracy" had arisen in response to undeniable needs, and that therefore the real problem is how to render these functionaries responsible, not how to take all power away from them. The Committee on Ministers' Powers addressed itself to the real task. They set out to reduce the extent of the rule-making power of administrative agencies and to subject the making of such rules and regulations to a measure of parliamentary control. A standing committee of each house was to scrutinize bills with a view to whether they contained any such delegated legislative power, and, if so, to report upon the provisions in the light of given standards. Without going into the details of these recommendations—for they have not been put into effect—it must be said that they fail to cope with the decisive issue, the responsibility of officials for the policy adopted. No doubt technical improvements would result here and there, errors would be corrected, and mistakes avoided. But wherever the acquisition of discretionary rule-making power would be considered desirable by the government in power, of its exercise in a particular instance justifiable in terms of its policies, it is scarcely probable that under the British parliamentary system a committee composed of a majority of the government's party would cause any real difficulties. Either in getting such discretionary power on the statute books, or in exercising it as the permanent officials see fit, the government's view is more than likely to prevail.

The Report itself is illuminating on this score, though it soft-pedals the real trouble. The Report states that tactical considerations of party politics will play a role, and that, as realists, the committee members recognize it. An interesting illustration is afforded by their discussion of the so-called "Henry VIII Clause." This clause bears its nickname reminiscent of Tudor absolutism because it empowers the appropriate minister to modify the provisions of an act he is called upon to administer so far as may appear to him necessary for the purpose of bringing the act into operation. A number of important statutes in the last few decades contain such a clause. By way of illustrating the inevitability of such a clause, the Report remarks that the Committee had been assured that the National Insurance Act, 1911, could never have been brought into operation without the powers conferred by the Henry VIII Clause. Furthermore, it says:

> We have been told, rightly or wrongly, that if that Bill had not passed into law in 1911, the chance of it passing the Parliamentary ordeal with success in 1912 or 1913 would have been small; with the result that a social measure . . . of far-reaching importance would never have passed at all. In other words, the practical politician has to seize the tide when it serves or may lose his venture. We admit this truth: and because we admit it, we consider that the Henry VIII clause is a political instrument which must (sic) occasionally be used.[7]

The Committee recommended, of course, its sparing use and all that, but the only sanction they could think of was a parliamentary standing committee dominated by the government's majority. Evidently, a monarch could count on his officials' acting more nearly responsibly and in accordance with his will than the people can under such arrangements.

A DUAL STANDARD OF ADMINISTRATIVE RESPONSIBILITY

But are there any possible arrangements under which the exercise of such discretionary power can be made more responsible? The difficulties are evidently very great. Before we go any further in suggesting institutional safeguards, it becomes necessary to elucidate a bit more the actual psychic conditions which might predispose any agent toward responsible conduct. Palpably, a modern administrator is in many cases dealing with problems so novel and complex that they call for the highest creative ability. This need for creative solutions effectively focuses attention upon the need for action. The pious formulas about the will of the people are all very well, but when it comes to these issues of social maladjustment the popular will has little content, except the desire to see such maladjustments removed. A solution which fails in this regard, or which causes new and perhaps greater maladjustments, is bad; we have a right to call such a policy irresponsible if it can be shown that it was adopted without proper regard to the existing sum of human knowledge concerning the technical issues involved; we also have a right to call it irresponsible if it can be shown that it was adopted without proper regard for existing preferences in the community, and more particularly its prevailing majority. Consequently, the responsible administrator is one who is responsive to these two dominant factors: technical knowledge and popular sentiment. Any policy which violates either standard, or which fails to crystallize in spite of their urgent imperatives, renders the official responsible for it liable to the charge of irresponsible conduct.

In writing of the first of these factors, technical knowledge, I said some years ago:

Administrative officials seeking to apply scientific "standards" have to account for their action in terms of a somewhat rationalized and previously established set of hypotheses. Any deviation from these hypotheses will be subjected to thorough scrutiny by their colleagues in what is known as the "fellowship of science." . . . If a specific designation were desirable, it might be well to call this type of responsibility "functional" and "objective," as contrasted with the general and "subjective" types, such as religious, moral and political responsibility. For in the former case, action is tested in terms of relatively objective problems which, if their presence is not evident, can be demonstrated to exist, since they refer to specific functions. Subjective elements appear wherever the possibility of relatively voluntary choice enters in, and here political responsibility is the only method which will insure action in accordance with popular preference.[8]

Similarly, John M. Gaus writes:

The responsibility of the civil servant to the standards of his profession, in so far as those standards make for the public interest, may be given official recognition. . . . Certainly, in the system of government which is now emerging, one important kind of responsibility will be that which the individual civil servant recognizes as due to the standards and ideals of his profession. This is "his inner check."[9]

Yet this view has been objected to as inconceivable by one who claimed that he could not see how the term "responsibility" could be applied except where the governed have the power to dismiss or at least seriously damage the officeholder.[10] Thus, with one stroke of the pen, all the permanent officials of the British government, as well as our own and other supposedly popular governments, are once and for all rendered irresponsible. According to this commentator, political responsibility alone is "objective," because it involves a control by a body external to the one who is responsible. He also claims that its standards may be stated with finality and exactitude and its rewards and punishments made peremptory. For all of which British foreign policy leading up to Munich no doubt provides a particularly illuminating illustration.

It seems like an argument over words. The words, as a matter of fact, do not matter particularly. If you happen to feel that the word "objective" spells praise, and the word "subjective" blame, it may be better to speak of "technical" as contrasted with "political" responsibility, or perhaps "functional" and "political" will appeal. Whether we call it "objective" or "functional" or "technical," the fact remains that throughout the length and breadth of our technical civilization there is arising a type of responsibility on the part of the permanent administrator, the man who is called upon to seek and find the creative solutions for our crying technical needs, which cannot be effectively enforced except by fellow-technicians who are capable of judging his policy in terms of the scientific knowledge bearing upon it. "Nature's laws are always enforced," and a public policy which neglects them is bound to come to grief, no matter how eloquently it may be advocated by popular orators, eager partisans, or smart careerists.

POLITICAL RESPONSIBILITY

The foregoing reflections must not deceive us, however, into believing that a public policy may be pursued just because the technicians are agreed on its desirability. Responsible public policy has to follow a double standard, as we stated before. We are entirely agreed that technical responsibility is not sufficient to keep a civil service wholesome and zealous, and that political responsibility is needed to produce truly responsible policy in a popular government. Discarding the wishful thinking of those who would tell us that Great Britain has solved this difficult problem, it is first necessary to repeat that such truly responsible policy is a noble goal rather than an actual achievement at the present time, and may forever remain so. All institutional safeguards designed to make public policy thus truly responsible represent approximations, and not very near approximations at that. One reason is the intrusion of party politics, already discussed; another is the tremendous difficulty which the public encounters in trying to grasp the broader implications of policy issues, such as foreign affairs, agriculture, and labor today. Concerning unemployment, all the general public really is sure about is that it should disappear. . . .

SHALL WE ENFORCE OR ELICIT RESPONSIBLE CONDUCT?

. . . Responsible conduct of administrative functions is not so much enforced as it is elicited. But it has been the contention all along that responsible conduct is never strictly enforceable, that even under the most tyrannical despot administrative officials will escape effective control—in short, that the problem of how to bring about responsible conduct of the administrative staff of a large organization is, particularly in a democratic society, very largely a question of sound work rules and effective morale. As an able student of great practical experience has put it:

> This matter of administrative power commensurate with administrative responsibility, or the administrator's freedom from control, is not, under our system of government, anything absolute or complete: it is a question of degree. . . . Nothing which has been said should be construed to mean that preservation of administrative freedom, initiative and resourcefulness is not an important factor to be considered in organization: quite the contrary, it is one of the major factors.[11]

The whole range of activities involving constant direct contact of the administrator with the public and its problems shows that our conception of administrative responsibility is undergoing profound change. The emphasis is shifting; instead of subserviency to arbitrary will we require responsiveness to commonly felt needs and wants. The trend of the creative evolution of American democracy from a negative conception to a positive ideal of social service posits such a transformation. As the range of government services expands, we are all becoming each other's servants in the common endeavor of operating our complex industrial society.

It seems desirable to consider one further problem of especial significance in this area, and that is the role and the importance of satisfactory relations of the government to its employees of all ranks and classes. Private employers are becoming increasingly aware of the decisive role which all their employees must play in the public relations of business concerns. Competition through service is becoming an ever more important factor, and the contact of the general public with particular businesses is through their employees. It is evident that the government through its expanding services is placed in a similar position. The Postal Service has long recognized this and has evolved careful regulations concerning the dealings of its employees with the public. As a result, the letter carrier has become a symbol of cheerful service. By contrast, the arbitrary official of authoritarian regimes abroad has always been acknowledged as the antithesis of democracy.

Although such conduct was often condoned as part of administrative efficiency, we know today that this view is mistaken. Just as morale within the service is of decisive importance in bringing about responsible administration, so likewise morale should extend beyond the confines of the service itself.

The most serious issue revolves around the problem of the employees' right to organize, to bargain collectively, and to strike if their demands are rejected. . . . It is obvious that in lieu of the possibility of bringing their complaints and grievances forcibly to the attention of their employer, the government, government employees must be provided with exceptionally well-ordered institutional safeguards for mediation and arbitration. Such mechanisms have a fairly long tradition in some countries; they are rapidly developing in this country. . . . [Democracy] cannot possibly hope to develop and maintain responsible conduct unless it accords its employees a status at least equal in dignity and self-respect to the status its labor laws impove upon and demand from private employers. In short, even though the government did not feel justified in conceding the right to strike, it should not discriminate against employees who join an organization which advances this claim. For merely to demand this right is not a crime, since reasonable men may differ as to the right answer. Employees who are denied the rights of ordinary citizens cannot possibly be expected to remain loyal and responsible public servants.

The right policy is to be sure that all necessary disciplinary rules are loyally accepted by the entire staff, irrespective of what organization they belong to. This formula works well as long as those responsible for the rules respect the rights of the persons working under them. It must be kept in mind, however, that there are quite a few difficult border-line cases, where the infraction of a given rule has been due to faulty behavior or hostile attitudes on the part of the higher-ups. . . . The possible frictions of this type are endless; it is evident that adequate representative organization of the employees is the only possible way of coping with the situations as they arise.

Another important problem which is closely related to the foregoing, and equally controversial, is the right of officials to talk and write about issues of general public policy, more particularly those on which they themselves possess exceptional information and understanding because of their official position. There was a time when officials were supposed never to speak their mind in public. But the American and other democratic governments have gradually relaxed these restrictions. It must seriously be doubted whether technical responsibility, which, as we have shown, is coming to play an ever more important role in our time, can be effectively secured without granting responsible officials considerable leeway and making it possible for them to submit their views to outside criticism. The issue is a very complex one. Opinions vary widely. People try to escape facing these difficulties by drawing facile distinctions, such as that officials might discuss facts but not policy. It might cogently be objected that facts and policies cannot be separated. Any presentation of facts requires a selection, and this selection is affected by views, opinions, and hence bears upon policy. What is worse, in many of the most important matters intelligent and well-informed students disagree frequently on what are the facts.

The simplest solution, and one to which the authority-loving politician has recourse without much hesitancy, is to forbid such public utterances altogether. It is undeniable that great inconveniences might and often do result from technical authorities' bringing out "facts" which make the official policy appear in a questionable light. Hence instances of "gag rules" are quite frequent. At one time a federal department head ruled that no official in his organization was to give any more interviews, because one of them had annoyed him. Thereupon six reporters proceeded to that department and got six different stories, all of which were printed and sent to the administrative head to show him that his rule had been foolish and could not really be enforced. In this case the power of the press forced the abandonment of an unsound policy which would seriously interfere with making the administration responsible in the formulation and execution of policy. While many cautious administrators will aver that an official should not discuss policy, it seems wiser, in a democracy, to avoid such a gag rule. Many officials will hesitate to express themselves, anyway, for obvious reasons. A great deal depends upon the nature of the case. In matters of vital importance the general public is entitled to the views of its permanent servants. Such views may often provide a salutary check on partisan extravagances. Such views should be available not only to the executive but to the legislature and the public as well. Gag rules seek to insulate the specialist so that he is no longer heard. A large benefit is thus lost. Irrespective of what one thinks of the particular policies involved, a presidential order not to talk against administration bills to Congress is particularly doubtful, for Congress certainly is entitled to the advice and expert opinion of permanent officials of the government, who may be presumed to have a less partisan viewpoint on particular policy proposals. In fact, the rule can easily be circumvented by an official determined to make his views known: he can prime Congressional questioners to ask the right questions, and, as the officials must answer, their views become available to whole committees. This is true, but while it is alleged that no president would dare punish a man for what he says in answer to a Congressional query, it may often seem to the official undesirable to incur the presidential wrath. Hence no such rule should be allowed at all.

What applies to enlightening Congress really applies likewise to a wider field. It seems inexcusable that highly trained professional economists, for example, should be handicapped in addressing themselves to their colleagues in a frank and scientifically candid manner. Even when they are permitted to do so, they will be only too prone to be overcautious. The only sound standard in a vast and technically complex government such as ours is to insist that the public statements of officials be in keeping with the highest requirements of scientific work. If a man's superiors disagree with him, let them mount the same rostrum and prove that he is wrong; before the goddess of science all men are equal.

CONCLUSION

The ways, then, by which a measure of genuine responsibility can be secured under modern conditions appear to be manifold, and they must all be utilized for achieving the best effect. No mere reliance upon some one traditional device, like the dependence of the Cabinet upon majority support in Parliament, or popular election of the chief executive (neither of which exists in Switzerland), can be accepted as satisfactory evidence. At best, responsibility in a democracy will remain fragmentary because of the indistinct voice of the principal whose agents the officials are supposed to be—the vast heterogeneous masses composing the people. Even the greatest faith in the common man (and I am prepared to carry this very far) cannot any longer justify a simple acceptance of the mythology of "the will of the people." Still, if all the different devices are kept operative and new ones developed as opportunity offers, democratic government by pooling many different interests and points of view continues to provide the nearest approximation to a policy-making process which will give the "right" results. Right policies are policies which seem right to the community at large and at the same time do not violate "objective" scientific standards. Only thus can public policy contribute to what the people consider their happiness.

NOTES

1. Frank J. Goodnow, *Politics and Administration* (New York: Macmillan, 1900), p. 22.
2. See Carl J. Friedrich, *Constitutional Government and Politics* (New York: Harpers, 1936), pp. 29ff. and elsewhere.
3. See Schuyler C. Wallace, "Nullification: A Process of Government," *Political Science Quarterly*, vol. XLV, no. 3 (September 1930), p. 347.
4. See George C. S. Benson, *Financial Control and Integration* (New York: Harpers, 1934).
5. Goodnow, *op. cit.*, p. 154.
6. See Ramsay Muir, *How Britain is Governed* (New York: Richard R. Smith, Inc., 1930), pp. 81–91, 120–132.
7. Committee on Ministers' Powers, *Report* (London, 1936; Cmd. 4060), p. 61.
8. Carl J. Friedrich, "Responsible Government Service under the American Constitution," *Problems of the American Public Service* (New York: McGraw-Hill, 1935), p. 38.
9. John M. Gaus, "The Responsibility of Public Administration," *The Frontiers of Public Administration* (University of Chicago Press, 1936), pp. 39–40.
10. Herman Finer, "Better Government Personnel," *Political Science Quarterly*, vol. LI, no. 4 (December 1936), pp. 569ff. esp. pp. 580ff.
11. Lewis Meriam, *Public Personnel Problems* (Washington: Brookings Institution, 1938), p. 340.

Administrative Responsibility in Democratic Government

Herman Finer

My chief difference with Professor Friedrich . . . is my insistence upon distinguishing responsibility as an arrangement of correction and punishment even up to dismissal both of politicians and officials, while he . . . believes in reliance upon responsibility as a sense of responsibility, largely unsanctioned, except by deference or loyalty to professional standards. . . .

I

. . . Professor Friedrich begins his article in *Public Policy* with some remarks on the Munich Pact, with the intention presumably of showing that administrative

From the *Public Administration Review*, the journal of the American Society for Public Administration, Vol. 1 (1941), pp. 335, 344–350. Reprinted by permission of the publisher.

responsibility to Parliament is ineffective. He offers it as evidence that "pious myth-makers" have no right to accept the claim that the formal dependence of the Cabinet upon the confidence of the House of Commons effectively insures responsible conduct of public affairs by officials, high and low. (He reverts to this example later also.) As a matter of fact, this example proves the exact converse of Professor Friedrich's intention. The Munich Pact only too well carried out the will of Parliament. Mr. Harold Nicolson, M.P., now Under Secretary to the Ministry of Information, even jeopardized his career by denouncing the hysteria with which the invitation to Munich and peace was received by Parliament. It is true that thereafter, as the consequences came to light, Parliament and people felt that the Government had been wrong—but they too were completely implicated. The revulsion of feeling caused the Government, under parliamentary pressure, to give up its appeasement policy and push on with civil defense preparations and rearmament. . . .

Professor Friedrich has somehow come to believe that "parliamentary responsibility is largely inoperative and certainly ineffectual." Is he referring to the policy-making powers of administrators, or the acts of the Cabinet? His criticism seems to apply to the Cabinet, and not to the subject of his essay, viz., the responsibility of *officials*, for, citing the case of Munich and "the last few years," he seems to be concerned mainly with a foreign policy of which he did not approve but of which a large majority of his "ineffectual" Parliament emphatically did. And then he claims the benefit of this demonstration, I suppose, for the thesis that in England the civil service is out of hand?

On this point there are two records which might be summed up as follows. On questions of foreign policy, the Government, misguided as it may have been (in my view as well as Professor Friedrich's), was steadily supported by a large majority in Parliament, and I should guess a large one in the country. As for control over the administration, has Professor Friedrich head of Parliament's actions on the Unemployment Regulations of 1934, the reform of the Post Office, the reform of the constitution of the B.B.C., the special areas, the preparation of the scheme of civil defense, the partial success in getting a Minister for the Coordination of Defense, the overthrow of Sir Samuel Hoare, the speeding up of arms production? And, during the war, the successful pressure of Parliament for the removal of certain ministers, e.g., from the Ministry of Information, for more reasonable use of the powers of interning refugees, its control over government contract methods, over appointments in the civil service, over the Defence Regulations proposed by the Home Secretary, over economic and fiscal policies and administration, and, finally, over the very existence of the Chamberlain Government itself? I have listed only a few of the outstanding successes of Parliament in controlling (a) the government in general, and (b) the proposals of administrators and their parliamentary chiefs before they were "made" into policy by Parliament.

The conclusion of this section of the essay reads: "Admittedly, many commentators have dwelt at length upon the frequently irresponsible conduct of public affairs in Great Britain and elsewhere." This is of course true; they have; and they have been right. But that does not mean that the examples are many, important, or long continuing. Nor would any person claim perfection for any system. You do not prove the value of your enthusiasm by showing that there are some flaws in existing political arrangements. Rather is political science a comparative weighing of the imperfections of alternative consequences. Even so, this should hardly lead the author to the conclusion that runs like a scarlet thread throughout the entire treatment, that if political responsibility is imperfect it is to be cast out in favor of a sense of responsibility in the bosom of the official: "a sense of duty, a desire to be approved by his fellow officials, and a tendency to subordinate one's own judgment as a matter of course," a point that Friedrich cites with evident approval from shaky evidence given to him orally by a Swiss official. Without the existence of the Federal Assembly, for how long does Professor Friedrich think the Swiss civil service would remain in tune with the humor of the people and responsive to its wants?

Professor Friedrich then turns to that agitation against the civil service which was summed up in Lord Hewart's book, *The New Despotism.* Alas, for the thesis of the author! *The Report of the Committee on Ministers' Powers,* while showing that, certainly, our civil service was very useful, showed that only in a few respects, and those not very important or deep-seated, were its members escaping control. He seems to harbor an objection to the power which the parliamentary majority would have over the rule-making authority of the administrator though submitted to a committee of the House for sanction. What is wrong with this? Even if a special scrutinizing committee is organized, why should not the majority views of the whole House prevail? What is wrong with the majority? . . .

In the effort not to let reconsideration correct his first misconception of "responsibility," Professor Friedrich finds himself compelled to adopt quite an undemocratic view of government, and to throw scorn upon the popular will. I do not think for a moment that he really is antidemocratic, but his line of argument presses him to enunciate views which might lead to this suspicion. The error in his conception leads to an error in the consequence; and the error in the consequence is precisely what officials (not constrained by principle and institutions to the dictates of political responsibility) would begin to use as an argument to justify their irresponsibility: conceit of themselves and scorn of the popular will. Thus

> The pious formulas about the will of the people are all very well, but when it comes to these issues of social maladjustment the popular will has little context, except the desire to see such maladjustments removed. A solution which fails in this regard, or which causes new and perhaps great maladjustments, is bad; we have a right to call such a policy irresponsible if it can be shown that it was adopted without proper regard to the existing sum of human knowledge concerning the technical issues involved; we also have a right to call it irresponsible if it can be shown that it was adopted without proper regard for existing preferences in the community, and more particularly its prevailing majority.

The answer to this argument is this. It is demonstrable that the will of the people *has* content, not only about what it desires, but how maladjustments can be remedied, and some of its ideas are quite wise. The popular will may not be learned, but nevertheless the public's own experience teaches it something, the press of all kinds teaches it more, and political parties and the more instructed members of the community play quite a part. "The people" consists of many kinds of minds and degrees of talent, not of undifferentiated ignorance and empty-mindedness. Legislative assemblies created by election, in which political parties play a vital part, also exist; and they are not so dumb. Their sagacity is not to be ignored or derided. Second, a policy which is based upon an incomplete or faulty grasp of technical knowledge is *not* an irresponsible policy, for to use the word "irresponsible" here is to pervert it by substituting it for the words "incomplete" or "faulty" or "unwise." It is surely wisest to say that the full grasp of knowledge is to be used by the official within the terms of the obligation and policy established for him by the legislature or his departmental superior; otherwise it looks as though an independent position were being claimed for the official. Nor is it wise to make responsibility to "the community" an addendum to a "proper regard to the existing sum of human knowledge, etc., etc." And, by the way, the state seems to have cropped up again in the word community!

"Consequently," continues Professor Friedrich, "the responsible administrator is one who is responsible to these two dominant factors: technical knowledge and popular sentiment. Any policy which violates either standard, or which fails to crystallize in spite of their urgent imperatives, renders the official responsible for it liable to the charge of irresponsible conduct." But just as surely there is no responsibility unless there is an obligation to someone else; no one is interested in a question of responsibility as a relationship between a man and a science, but as it involves a problem of duty—and the problem of duty is an interpersonal, not a personal, matter. Responsibility in the sense of an interpersonal, external sanctioned duty is, then, the dominant consideration for public administration; and it includes and does not merely stand by the side of responsibility to the standards of one's craft in the dubious position of a Cinderella. If the community does not command, there is no call for the technical knowledge whatever; and, however magnificent the grasp of technical knowledge and the desire to use it, it must be declared irresponsible whenever it becomes operative except under a direct or implied obligation. Many a burglar has been positively hated for his technical skill.

There is another consequence of his thesis which Professor Friedrich would not like, I feel certain, if he had developed its implications. He declares: "Administrative officials seeking to apply scientific 'standards' have to account for their action in terms of a somewhat rationalized and previously established set of hypotheses. Any deviation from these hypotheses will be subjected to thorough scrutiny by their colleagues in what is known as the 'fellowship of science.'" What is the force of the phrase "have to account for their action?" Exactly to whom? By what compulsion? Does this phrase mean only that there is left to the official the vague, tenuous reaching out of his qualms in view of the known or possible public opinions of the men with whom he studied or those who are the present leaders of the profession? Suppose he despises their grasp of knowledge and scorns their judgment—is he therefore irresponsible? Suppose that they are conservative, while he is one of a minority of progressive practitioners? When is he responsible and when irresponsible? When he follows the ancients or marches with, perhaps even leads, the pioneers?

This question takes us directly into the history of these professional organizations of colleagues, "the fellowship of science," the associations, the guilds, of medical men, engineers, accountants, lawyers, and others. Even if such fellowship were fully organized to implement Professor Friedrich's wish, whom could the ordinary man trust for a better deal, the great osteopath, Mr. (later Sir as a mark of popular gratitude) Herbert Barker, or the elders of the British Medical Association, the organization which banned him; Whistler, Charles Ricketts, or the Royal Academy; an Epstein or the stone chippers favored by the Society of Sculptors? I do not err, I believe, in thinking that there are analogous instances in American experience, which Professor Friedrich could supply better than I can. But there is before us the judgment of the District Court of the District of Columbia regarding the American Medical Association's action against medical practitioners—their expulsion because they participated in a group medicine clinic. Which criterion: groupist or antigroupist?

I do not deny all value to such guild organization; I affirm and applaud some of these organizations. Yet, appraised from the very angle of the theory which I am here opposing, they must be seen as broken reeds in a long-run view of governmental devices to keep men in the van of social progress, technically defined, and still less to satisfy progress as the populace, the consumer, asks for it. Professor J. M. Gaus, who is quoted in support of the claim that responsibility is professional, is by no means so zealous in the service of the notion as Professor Friedrich who quotes him, for he says: "The responsibility of the civil servant to the standards of his profession, *in so far as those standards make for the public interest,* may be given official recognition." I have italicized the proviso, and it is essential, I am sure, to Professor Gaus's view. Who would define the public interest—who could define it? Only the public, I believe, or its deputies.

Professor Friedrich seems to be so obsessed by modern technology, and the important part which the knowledge of it must play in the establishment of policy, that he seems to forget how old this problem is, and what the answer of the ages has been to the very problem he poses. Does he think there was no question of "technical needs" three hundred years or three thousand years ago, or of the relationship of those who provided the knowledge and service to those members of the public who were its consumers? Governments owned warships, weapons, sewers, baths, roads, and irrigation works, and even had mines and forests to administer, and domestic and foreign trade to regulate. The relationship of the public to the mysteries of religion and ecclesiastical procedures—a very important technique in the context of good living—was for centuries one of the most critical problems in the history of political responsibility. "The creative solutions for our crying technical needs," as Professor Friedrich calls them, have for centuries been offered by the experts of various kinds, and the verdict of mankind has been that they need the expert on top and not on top. All important questions are begged by throwing in the word "creative." It is no news to tell us, as we are told here, that nature will have her revenge if her laws are not understood and followed in any particular piece of administration. Of course that is so. But there is a wider concept of nature than that which relates to interest in the "technical"; there is also the nature of man as a political animal. We are entitled to believe, from the reading of his millennial administrative history, that *his* nature, as well as physical nature, is thwarted where the primacy of public responsibility is challenged by blurred interpretations, theoretical and practical, of the term responsibility.

Nor is there any novelty in the fact that political responsibility (the importance of which Professor Friedrich admits in a scanty oasis of one paragraph in twenty-four pages) acts by its power on the official mind in anticipation of action by the sanctioning organs of popular control. In pursuance of his denigration of the British system of political responsibility he rather misinterprets the function of questions in the House of Commons. Their principal function is not to inform ministers of public reaction to policy, but to discipline administration. Ministers know already through other procedures. Questions are a *force*. Only ask the officials who prepare the information for the ministers whether they are not in an anxious sweat until the House is appeased!

Why, this is almost the ideal instrument for exercising that power of antici- pation over the officials' mind, and therefore upon his sense of obligation to the community, which indirectly implies an obligation to the expertness he commands. I say this with diffidence, since the article seems a little severe on British experi- ence. Nor am I an idolator of every item of parliamentary technique as it now operates. It should certainly be improved; but it ought not to be scouted.

There are occasions when Professor Friedrich seems to admit the fundamen- tality of political responsibility, but the relapse certainly and fatally follows. Thus he says: "The whole range of activities involving constant direct contact of the administrator with the public and its problems shows that our conception of administrative responsibility is undergoing profound change. The emphasis is shifting; instead of subserviency to arbitrary will we require responsiveness to commonly felt needs and wants." Whose is the arbitrary will? The parliamentary assembly's emanating from popular election? . . .

I come now to the last matter in which I care to take issue with Professor Friedrich, the relationship between administrative responsibility and the doctrine of official anonymity.

Professor Friedrich believes:

> It must seriously be doubted whether technical responsibility, which, as we have shown, is coming to play an ever more important role in our time, can be effectively secured without granting responsible officials considerable leeway and making it possible for them to submit their views to outside criticism. The issue is a very complex one. Opinions vary widely. People try to escape facing these difficulties by drawing facile distinctions, such as that officials might discuss facts but not policy. It might cogently be objected that facts and policies cannot be separated.

The rejoinder to this statement in the first place is that it is possible in some cases at any rate to distinguish facts and policy quite clearly. For example, the government or the representative assembly in seeking a policy to deal with rural water supplies might properly expect to receive from an official a description of the existing situation, in terms of the total water resources of the country, the supplies and the sources of supply in various rural vicinities, what those supplies cost per thousand gallons, whether the nearest supplies beyond the jurisdiction of each unit need pumping stations or whether the water will come down by being piped, what are the costs of pumping and distribution in various other areas, and so on. What the assembly shall do about it, once these facts are before it, is a matter of policy. A wise civil servant, careful to preserve his own usefulness and that of his col- leagues, and not reckless in the face of the always imminent cry of bureaucracy and despotism, would not urge a policy upon it. Still less would he use public advocacy to spur on his political chief or connive with reformist groups having a purposeful policy. He would rather confine himself to frank private demonstration of the alternatives and their advantages and disadvantages, to his political chief, or where the political system requires, to the committee of the assembly at their request.

That, however, is not all. If Professor Friedrich really believes that the severance of fact and policy is impossible, then a fortiori the civil servant should preserve his anonymity, on pain of bringing himself and his colleagues into partisan contempt. And Professor Friedrich does really seem to contemplate a war of all against all. He seems to approve of the fact that six reporters proceeded to a federal department whose head had ruled that his subordinates were not to give interviews and violated the chief's rule by getting six different stories. Is this the way to promote official responsibility to the chief? To the technical standards? To the "fellowship of science"? Does Professor Friedrich approve of this piece of press impudence? Has he ever investigated what such impudence cost the T.V.A. in prestige, morale, and administrative efficiency in the old days? Nor can I view with equanimity the grave consequences of such proposals as this: "In matters of vital importance the general public is entitled to the views of its permanent servants. Such views may often provide a salutary check on partisan extravagances. Such views should be available not only to the executive but to the legislature and the public as well."

This doctrine surely is to set up the official against the political parties, to make the official the instrument of conflict between the "general public" (which I thought had already been thrown out of court earlier in Friedrich's article) and the legislature. He would set the official, I suppose, against the chief executive also, for he has been elected by the general public, and may utter as many "partisan extravagances" as he pleases in the course of a four-year term. It is not clear whether Professor Friedrich thinks that the civil servant shall pursue moral responsibility as far as a crown of thorns, whether once he has embroiled parties and public and legislature he must resign. As matters are, he would certainly be kicked out by the legislature or chief executive, and it would serve him right. For democracy is ill served by and justifiably abhors those who, appointed to be its servants, assume the status and demeanor of masters.

II

. . . Never was the political responsibility of officials so momentous a necessity as in our own era. Moral responsibility is likely to operate in direct proportion to the strictness and efficiency of political responsibility, and to fall away into all sorts of perversions when the latter is weakly enforced. While professional standards, duty to the public, and pursuit of technological efficiency are factors in sound administrative operation, they are but ingredients, and not continuously motivating factors, of sound policy, and they require public and political control and direction.

The public and the political assemblies are adequately sagacious to direct policy—they know not only where the shoe pinches, but have a shrewd idea as to the last and leather of their footwear: and where they lack technical knowledge their officials are appointed to offer it to them for their guidance, and not to secure official domination; and within these limits the practice of giving administrative latitude to officials is sound.

Contemporary devices to secure closer cooperation of officials with public and legislatures are properly auxiliaries to and not substitutes for political control of public officials through exertion of the sovereign authority of the public. Thus, political responsibility is the major concern of those who work for healthy relationships between the officials and the public, and moral responsibility, although a valuable conception and institutional form, is minor and subsidiary.

Public Policy and Administration: The Goals of Rationality and Responsibility

Norton E. Long

I

No problem is more momentous for the modern democratic state than its capacity to develop rational, responsible, goal-oriented policy. In many fields, including the most crucial ones, foreign policy and defense, the staff work on which well conceived public policy must depend can scarcely be supplied elsewhere than in the great government departments. To only a somewhat lesser degree this is true of agriculture, finance, commerce, and labor. Accordingly, a major task of administration is the formulation of policy proposals for consideration by the political executive and the legislature. The capacity of our administrative organizations to perform rationally and responsibly the task of formulating the policy alternatives for politically responsible superiors is the major criterion of organization efficiency. The beginning of wisdom in administrative analysis consists in a realistic assessment of the capacity of the organization to think.

The conception, now formally abjured, of the separation of policy and administration has obscured the vital "thinking" role of organized bureaucracy in government. The doctrine of the political supremacy of the elected over the nonelected branch of the government has inspired the delusion that to be politically supreme the legislature must not only make final decisions on policy but must also have primacy in the whole process of policy formulation—that the bureaucracy should be an instrument rather than a brain. The necessities of the case have forced the abandonment of this view save as folklore and political metaphysics. In practice it must be recognized that the bureaucracy is a part, and a highly important part, of the collective brain that somehow thinks or emotes a government policy.

The attempt of some writers, influenced by logical positivism, to construct a value-free science of administration may well have the unintended and logically unwarranted result of reviving the policy-administration dichotomy in new verbiage. Policy would become a matter of determining values, a legislative-political matter; administration would consist in the application of the values set by the political branch to sets of facts ascertained by the administrative. In this reasoning, administration could arrive at determinate answers without being sicklied o'er by the pale cast of policy thought. . . .

But, alas, we know this institutional divorce, however requisite for a value-free

From the *Public Administration Review*, the journal of the American Society for Public Administration, Vol. 15 (1954), pp. 22–24, 27–31. Reprinted by permission of the publisher.